weightwatchers
Cook it Fast

Four-Vegetable Stir-Fry with Tofu, page 244

250 Recipes in **15, 20, 30** Minutes

weightwatchers

Cook it Fast

ST. MARTIN'S GRIFFIN NEW YORK

Note: Many recipes in this book were previously released in the *Momentum Cookbook* and *Pantry to Plate,* both Weight Watchers meeting room cookbooks.

WEIGHT WATCHERS COOK IT FAST. Copyright © 2014 by Weight Watchers International, Inc. All rights reserved. Printed in the United States of America. For information, address St. Martin's Press, 175 Fifth Avenue, New York, N.Y. 10010.

On the front cover: Pasta Salad with Apple and Chicken, 202; and Grilled Flank Steak with Tomato-Fennel Salad, 211
On the back cover, from top: Bacon, Cheddar, and Egg–Topped English Muffins, 11; Breakfast Bruschetta, 94; Four-Vegetable Stir-Fry with Tofu, 244; and Lemon Soufflés, 329

www.stmartins.com

Editorial and art produced by W/W Twentyfirst Corp., 675 Avenue of the Americas, New York, NY 10010.

WEIGHT WATCHERS is a trademark of Weight Watchers International, Inc. Printed in the USA

The Library of Congress Cataloging-in-Publication Data is available upon request.

ISBN 978-1-250-05295-7 (trade paperback)
ISBN 978-1-4668-5481-9 (e-book)

St. Martin's Griffin books may be purchased for educational, business, or promotional use. For information on bulk purchases, please contact Macmillan Corporate and Premium Sales Department at 1-800-221-7945, extension 5442, or write specialmarkets@macmillan.com.

First Edition: August 2014

10 9 8 7 6 5 4 3 2

About Weight Watchers International, Inc.

Weight Watchers International, Inc. is the world's leading provider of weight-management services, operating globally through a network of company-owned and franchise operations. Weight Watchers holds over 40,000 meetings each week where members receive group support and learn about healthful eating patterns, behavior modification, and physical activity. **WeightWatchers.com** provides innovative subscription weight-management products over the Internet and is the leading Internet-based provider of these products in the world. In addition, Weight Watchers offers a wide range of products, publications (including ***Weight Watchers Magazine,*** which is available on newsstands and in Weight Watchers meeting rooms), and programs for those interested in weight loss and weight control. For the Weight Watchers meeting nearest you, call **1-800-651-6000.** For information about bringing Weight Watchers to your workplace, call **1-800-8AT-WORK.**

Weight Watchers Publishing Group

VP, Editorial Director
Theresa DiMasi
Creative Director
Ed Melnitsky
Photo Director
Deborah Hardt
Managing Editor
Diane Pavia
Assistant Editor
Katerina Gkionis
Food Editor
Eileen Runyan
Editor
Jackie Mills, R.D.N.
Nutrition Consultant
U. Beate Krinke
Photographers
Rita Maas
Alan Richardson
Food Stylists
Anne Disrude
Michael Pederson
Prop Stylists
Cathy Cook
Bette Blau

Chicken and Napa Cabbage Salad, page 107

Contents

A Quick Note

Admit it. There's something thrilling about serving up a delicious, home-cooked meal in 15, 20, or 30 minutes flat. Lucky then that, in this book, you'll find dozens of dishes and lots of clever tricks and shortcuts that will help you do just that.

Because we want you to cook. It's healthier, it's usually less expensive, and you'll feel a sense of accomplishment and delight in knowing you created something delectable in a snap. There's nothing more enjoyable than gathering your family and friends around a table and serving a fresh-from-the-oven roast, a nourishing soup, or a scrumptious pie. Why deny yourself these pleasures?

The difficulty is we lead busy lives, so it's easier to order in or go out to restaurants rather than make ourselves something wonderful and comforting to eat. Those options are okay once in a while; we're not saying you have to cook every single meal. But we do think that when you see how easy it is to do you'll find it a viable and healthier alternative to dining out.

To make cooking fast and fuss-free, we've carefully written each recipe so it's easy to follow, with few ingredients and short, precise steps—no previous cooking knowledge needed. Turn the page and you'll discover meals that will satisfy a variety of tastes from many cultures and countries. We've included Weight Watchers member favorites, recipes we know are crowd-pleasers, and meals we've made time and time again for our own families and friends. In short, we've assembled our greatest hits and hope these recipes will become your greatest hits, too.

For the weekends when you opt for leisure over pace, we've included a chapter devoted to dishes that take a little longer to prepare—restorative, comforting, toothsome concoctions—but are still uncomplicated, including slow-cooker meals that let you relax while dinner cooks itself. Many of these dishes serve six or eight, so you can use them when you entertain or have enough leftovers for an effortless meal later in the week.

In addition to great recipes, you'll find tips for decluttering and organizing your kitchen, menu planning, and buying the best time-saving tools. We talk about shopping for quality ingredients because starting with fresh, seasonal produce means you get maximum flavor minus the fuss. We tell you which kitchen tasks are worth the time (like maintaining your quick-meal pantry) and which are not (who has time to make homemade pasta?). We also give you our take on which convenience products to invest in and absolutely essential canned goods to keep on hand.

Weight Watchers wants to make it easy for you to enjoy delicious, satisfying meals that don't sacrifice flavor—or use too many ***PointsPlus*** values. With this indispensible cookbook, you'll gain cownfidence in the kitchen, and the pleasure of knowing your family will be eating nourishing, healthy food. Meanwhile, you still get "me" time at the end of the day and extra hours to spend with the people you love. So go ahead—throw away those takeout menus and start cooking fresh food, fast!

—Theresa DiMasi
Editor in Chief / VP, Content

Grilled Salmon with Quick Tomato Tapenade, page 61

Sliced Steak with Crispy Polenta, page 208

Weight Watchers and the Simply Filling Technique

Weight Watchers is with you—and for you—all the way to your weight goal. Our meetings provide support, motivation, and accountability. Our digital tools for subscribers include access to a robust suite of apps for iOS and Android devices, and provide access to our considerable database of foods and their ***PointsPlus***® values; a barcode scanner app; great community features; thousands of recipes; interactive cheat sheets; videos; articles and more. All these products are designed to help you toward your goal.

We created the Simply Filling technique for those times when you don't want to track your ***PointsPlus*** values against your budget. To follow it, just eat from the list of satisfying Weight Watchers Power Foods® (they're the foods that help fill you up faster and stay full longer, plus they deliver more nutrients for the ***PointsPlus*** value). Bonus: You don't need to track any of them! Or, enjoy the fact that we've taken the work out of it for you and pick from the list of recipes below that follow Simply Filling:

44 Recipes That Work with the Simply Filling Technique

15 MINUTE MEALS

15 Minute Breakfasts

15 Minute Lunches

15 Minute Dinners

15 Minute Snacks and Sweets

20 MINUTE MEALS

20 Minute Breakfasts

20 Minute Lunches

20 Minute Dinners

20 Minute Snacks and Sweets

30 MINUTE MEALS

30 Minute Breakfasts

30 Minute Lunches

30 Minute Dinners

30 Minute Snacks and Sweets

BONUS—ON THE WEEKEND

Spaghetti with Fresh Tomato Sauce and Meatballs, page 284

Shrimp Salad with Fennel, Red Onion, and Orange, page 117

About Our Recipes

While losing weight isn't only about what you eat, Weight Watchers realizes the critical role it plays in your success and overall good health. That's why our philosophy is to offer simple, straightforward recipes that are nutritious as well as delicious. We make every attempt to use wholesome ingredients and to ensure that our recipes fall within the recommendations of the U.S. Dietary Guidelines for Americans for a diet that promotes health and reduces the risk for disease. If you have special dietary needs, consult with your health-care professional for advice on a diet that is best for you, then adapt these recipes to meet your specific nutritional needs.

To achieve these good-health goals and get the maximum satisfaction from the foods you eat, we suggest you keep the following information in mind while preparing our recipes.

Get Started, Keep Going, and Enjoy Good Nutrition

- Recipes in this book have been developed for Weight Watchers members who are just getting started and for members who are further along toward their goals, including those who are using our ***PointsPlus*** plan, as well as anyone else interested in smart weight loss.

- ***PointsPlus*** values are given for each recipe. They're assigned based on the amount of protein, carbohydrates, fat, and fiber contained in a single serving of a recipe.

- Recipes include approximate nutritional information: they are analyzed for Calories (Cal), Total Fat, Saturated Fat (Sat Fat), Trans Fat, Cholesterol (Chol), Sodium (Sod), Total Carbohydrate (Carb), Dietary Fiber (Fib), Protein (Prot), and Calcium (Calc). The value provided for Total Carb includes sugars, starches, and fiber. The nutritional values are calculated by registered dietitians, using nutrition analysis software.

- Substitutions made to the ingredients will alter the per-serving nutritional information and may affect the ***PointsPlus*** value.

- Our recipes meet Weight Watchers Good Health Guidelines for eating lean proteins and fiber-rich whole grains and for having at least five servings of vegetables and fruits and two servings of low-fat or fat-free dairy products a day, while limiting your intake of saturated fat, sugar, and sodium.

- Health agencies recommend limiting sodium intake. To stay in line with this recommendation, we keep sodium levels in our recipes reasonably low; to boost flavor, we often include fresh herbs or a squeeze of citrus instead of salt. If you don't have to restrict your sodium, feel free to add a touch more salt as desired.
- Cook's Note suggestions have a ***PointsPlus*** value of ***0*** unless otherwise stated.
- Recipes that work with the Simply Filling technique are listed on page xi. Find more details about the Simply Filling technique at your meeting.
- For information about the science behind lasting weight loss and more, please visit **WeightWatchers.com/science.**

PointsPlus value not what you expected?

- You might expect some of the ***PointsPlus*** values in this book to be lower when some of the foods they're made from, such as fruits and vegetables, have no ***PointsPlus*** values. Most fruits and veggies have no ***PointsPlus*** values when served as a snack or part of a meal, like a cup of berries with a sandwich. But if these foods are part of a recipe, their fiber and nutrient content are incorporated into the recipe calculations. These nutrients can affect the ***PointsPlus*** value.
- Alcohol is included in our ***PointsPlus*** calculations. Because alcohol information is generally not included on nutrition labels, it's not an option to include when using the hand calculator or the online calculator. But since we include alcohol information that we get from our nutritionists, you might notice discrepancies between the ***PointsPlus*** values you see in our recipes, and the values you get using the calculator. The ***PointsPlus*** values listed for our recipes are the most accurate values.

Shopping for Ingredients

As you learn to eat healthier and add more Power Foods to your meals, consider the following to help you choose foods wisely:

Lean Meats and Poultry. Purchase lean meats and poultry, and trim them of all visible fat before cooking. When poultry is cooked with the skin on, we recommend removing the skin before eating. Nutritional information for recipes that include meat, poultry, and fish is based on cooked, skinless, boneless portions (unless otherwise stated), with the fat trimmed.

Seafood. Whenever possible, our recipes call for seafood that is sustainable and deemed the most healthful for human consumption so that your choice of seafood is not only good for the oceans but also good for you. For more information about the best seafood choices and to download a pocket guide, go to **environmentaldefensefund.org** or **montereybayaquarium.org.** For information about mercury and seafood go to **weightwatchers.com.**

Produce. For best flavor, maximum nutrient content, and the lowest prices, buy fresh local produce, such as vegetables, leafy greens, and fruits, in season. Rinse them thoroughly before using, and keep a supply of cut-up vegetables and fruits in your refrigerator for convenient healthy snacks.

Whole Grains. Explore your market for whole-grain products such as whole wheat and whole-grain breads and pastas, brown rice, bulgur, barley, cornmeal, whole wheat couscous, oats, and quinoa to enjoy with your meals.

Preparation and Measuring

Read the Recipe. Take a couple of minutes to read through the ingredients and directions before you start to prepare a recipe. This will prevent you from discovering midway through that you don't have an important ingredient or that a recipe requires several hours of marinating. And it's also a good idea to assemble all ingredients and utensils within easy reach before you begin a recipe.

Weighing and Measuring. The success of any recipe depends on accurate weighing and measuring. The effectiveness of the Weight Watchers Program and the accuracy of the nutritional analysis depend on correct measuring as well. Use the following techniques:

- Weigh foods such as meat, poultry, and fish on a food scale.
- To measure liquids, use a standard glass or plastic measuring cup placed on a level surface. For amounts less than ¼ cup, use standard measuring spoons.
- To measure dry ingredients, use metal or plastic measuring cups that come in ¼-, ⅓-, ½-, and 1-cup sizes. Fill the appropriate cup, and level it with the flat edge of a knife or spatula. For amounts less than ¼ cup, use standard measuring spoons.

15 minute meals

15 Minute Breakfasts

15 Minute Lunches

15 Minute Dinners

15 Minute Snacks and Sweets

Spinach-Feta Scramble

SERVES 1

1 large egg

3 large egg whites

1 cup lightly packed baby spinach

2 tablespoons crumbled reduced-fat feta cheese

¼ teaspoon black pepper

1 teaspoon canola or olive oil

1. Whisk together egg and egg whites in medium bowl. Stir in spinach, feta, and pepper.
2. Heat oil in medium nonstick skillet over medium heat. Pour in egg mixture and cook, stirring, until eggs are set and cheese is slightly melted, about 3 minutes.

PER SERVING (1 plate): 197 Cal, 11 g Total Fat, 3 g Sat Fat, 0 g Trans Fat, 218 mg Chol, 432 mg Sod, 4 g Total Carb, 1 g Fib, 20 g Prot, 66 mg Calc.

PointsPlus value: ***5.***

Asparagus and Chive Omelette

1. Whisk together egg substitute, salt, and black pepper in medium bowl.
2. Heat oil in medium nonstick skillet over medium heat. Add egg mixture and cook, stirring gently, until underside is set, about 1 minute.
3. Sprinkle Swiss, asparagus, peas, and bell pepper over half of omelette. Fold unfilled half of omelette over to enclose filling. Cook until cheese is melted, about 2 minutes.
4. Slide omelette onto plate and sprinkle with chives.

PER SERVING (1 omelette): 181 Cal, 6 g Total Fat, 1 g Sat Fat, 0 g Trans Fat, 5 mg Chol, 615 mg Sod, 13 g Total Carb, 4 g Fib, 20 g Prot, 206 mg Calc.

PointsPlus value: ***4.***

SERVES 1

½ cup fat-free egg substitute

⅛ teaspoon salt

⅛ teaspoon black pepper

1 teaspoon canola oil

2 tablespoons shredded low-fat Swiss cheese

¼ cup frozen chopped asparagus, thawed

¼ cup frozen peas, thawed

¼ cup chopped red bell pepper

2 tablespoons chopped fresh chives or scallions

15 minute meals

Provençal Omelette

SERVES 2

2 large eggs

2 large egg whites

1 tablespoon fat-free half-and-half

¼ teaspoon salt

½ teaspoon herbes de Provence

1 teaspoon olive oil

½ cup grape tomatoes, halved

¼ cup shredded fat-free Cheddar cheese

Chopped fresh parsley

2 slices reduced-calorie whole wheat bread, toasted

1. Whisk together eggs, egg whites, half-and-half, salt, and herbes de Provence in medium bowl.
2. Heat oil in medium nonstick skillet over medium heat. Add egg mixture and cook, stirring gently with heatproof rubber spatula, until underside is set, about 2 minutes.
3. Sprinkle tomatoes and Cheddar evenly over half of omelette. Fold unfilled half of omelette over filling and continue to cook until eggs are set, about 1 minute longer.
4. Slide omelette onto plate and cut in half; sprinkle with parsley. Serve with toast.

PER SERVING (½ omelette and 1 slice toast): 213 Cal, 9 g Total Fat, 2 g Sat Fat, 0 g Trans Fat, 215 mg Chol, 745 mg Sod, 18 g Total Carb, 4 g Fib, 17 g Prot, 188 mg Calc.

PointsPlus value: ***6.***

Cook's Note

To dress up the plates and make a delicious partner for the omelette, serve fresh berries in small clear dishes alongside.

Provençal Omelette

15 minute meals

Veggie Breakfast Burrito

SERVES 1

½ cup fat-free egg substitute

⅛ teaspoon salt

⅛ teaspoon black pepper

1 teaspoon canola oil

1 (7-inch) whole wheat tortilla, warmed

3 tablespoons shredded fat-free Cheddar cheese

½ small tomato, chopped

¼ cup diced green bell pepper

2 scallions, thinly sliced

1. Whisk together egg substitute, salt, and black pepper in small bowl.
2. Heat oil in medium nonstick skillet over medium heat. Add eggs to skillet and cook, stirring, until just set, about 2 minutes.
3. Place tortilla on plate and top with egg mixture. Top with Cheddar, tomato, bell pepper, and scallions. Roll up tortilla to enclose filling.

PER SERVING (1 burrito): 233 Cal, 5 g Total Fat, 1 g Sat Fat, 0 g Trans Fat, 4 mg Chol, 923 mg Sod, 29 g Total Carb, 4 g Fib, 23 g Prot, 263 mg Calc.

PointsPlus value: **6.**

Southwestern-Style Huevos Rancheros

SERVES 1

¼ teaspoon canola oil

2 scallions, thinly sliced

1 large egg

3 large egg whites

¼ teaspoon chili powder

¼ cup shredded fat-free Cheddar cheese

1 (6-inch) corn tortilla, warmed

3 tablespoons fat-free salsa

1. Coat small nonstick skillet with oil and set over medium heat. Add scallions and cook, stirring frequently, just until softened, about 2 minutes.
2. Whisk together egg, egg whites, and chili powder in medium bowl. Pour mixture into skillet and add Cheddar. Cook, stirring, until eggs are set and cheese is melted, about 2 minutes.
3. Spoon eggs onto tortilla and top with salsa.

PER SERVING (1 filled tortilla): 272 Cal, 7 g Total Fat, 2 g Sat Fat, 0 g Trans Fat, 218 mg Chol, 835 mg Sod, 23 g Total Carb, 2 g Fib, 29 g Prot, 376 mg Calc.

PointsPlus value: *7.*

Bacon, Cheddar, and
Egg–Topped English Muffins

15 minute meals

Bacon, Cheddar, and Egg-Topped English Muffins

SERVES 2

2 large eggs

1 teaspoon canola oil

2 (1-ounce) slices Canadian bacon

1 whole wheat English muffin, split and toasted

2 (¾-ounce) slices fat-free Cheddar cheese

Snipped fresh chives

Black pepper

1. Fill medium skillet with 1½ inches of water and bring to boil. Reduce heat so water is barely simmering.
2. Break each egg into small cup. Slip eggs, one at time, into water. Cook until yolks just begin to set, about 2 minutes. Using slotted spoon, transfer eggs to paper towels to drain.
3. Pour out water and wipe out skillet. Add oil to skillet and set over medium-high heat. Add Canadian bacon and cook until heated through, about 1½ minutes on each side.
4. Place muffin half on each of 2 plates and top each with slice of Cheddar. Top each with 1 slice of bacon and 1 egg. Sprinkle with chives and pepper.

PER SERVING (1 topped muffin half): 243 Cal, 10 g Total Fat, 3 g Sat Fat, 0 g Trans Fat, 230 mg Chol, 877 mg Sod, 17 g Total Carb, 2 g Fib, 20 g Prot, 265 mg Calc.

PointsPlus value: **6.**

Cook's Note

Top each muffin half with a tomato slice or a few slices of roasted red bell pepper (not oil-packed) before adding the Cheddar, bacon, and egg.

15 minute meals

Waffles with Blueberries and Maple Cream

SERVES 4

2 cups fat-free ricotta cheese

¼ cup maple syrup

½ teaspoon cinnamon

⅛ teaspoon ground nutmeg

4 frozen (4-inch) low-fat whole wheat waffles, toasted

1 pint blueberries

¼ cup pecans, chopped

1. Stir together ricotta, maple syrup, cinnamon, and nutmeg in small bowl.
2. Place waffles on plates and top evenly with ricotta mixture. Sprinkle evenly with blueberries and pecans.

PER SERVING (1 waffle, ½ cup blueberries, and 1 tablespoon pecans): 322 Cal, 6 g Total Fat, 1 g Sat Fat, 0 g Trans Fat, 12 mg Chol, 322 mg Sod, 48 g Total Carb, 4 g Fib, 20 g Prot, 278 mg Calc.

PointsPlus value: ***8.***

Cook's Note

This sweet-spiced ricotta topping is a snap to make and adds a homemade touch to frozen waffles. Substitute any fresh fruit in season for the blueberries and any nuts that you have on hand for the pecans.

Cinnamon French Toast

SERVES 4

2 cups fat-free egg substitute

¼ cup fat-free milk

1 teaspoon cinnamon

½ teaspoon vanilla extract

8 slices whole wheat bread

½ teaspoon canola oil

½ cup reduced-calorie pancake syrup, warmed

1. Whisk together egg substitute, milk, cinnamon, and vanilla in large shallow bowl or pie plate. Dip bread into egg mixture, one slice at a time, until evenly soaked.
2. Coat large nonstick skillet with oil and set over medium heat. Add soaked bread to skillet, in batches, and cook until browned, about 2 minutes on each side.
3. Transfer French toast to plates and serve with warm syrup.

PER SERVING (2 slices toast and 2 tablespoons syrup): 263 Cal, 2 g Total Fat, 0 g Sat Fat, 0 g Trans Fat, 0 mg Chol, 575 mg Sod, 42 g Total Carb, 5 g Fib, 20 g Prot, 287 mg Calc.

PointsPlus value: *7.*

15 minute meals

Breakfast Berry Parfaits

SERVES 2

8 strawberries, hulled and sliced

1 cup vanilla low-fat yogurt

2 tablespoons granola

1 banana, peeled and sliced

½ cup blueberries

Divide strawberries evenly among 2 parfait glasses; top each with ¼ cup of yogurt. Top evenly with granola, then with remaining yogurt, banana slices, and blueberries.

PER SERVING (1 parfait): 213 Cal, 3 g Total Fat, 1 g Sat Fat, 0 g Trans Fat, 6 mg Chol, 91 mg Sod, 42 g Total Carb, 4 g Fib, 8 g Prot, 226 mg Calc.

PointsPlus value: **6.**

Do it Faster

No time to eat breakfast? Layer a parfait in a small plastic container and take it to work to eat at your desk.

Morning Chai

SERVES 4

4 cups cold water

5 regular or decaffeinated black tea bags

1 (3-inch) cinnamon stick, broken in half

8 whole cardamom pods, crushed

12 whole black peppercorns

1½ cups vanilla soy milk

Combine all ingredients except milk in large saucepan and bring to boil. Reduce heat and simmer 5 minutes. Stir in soy milk and cook, stirring, just until heated through, about 1 minute. Pour through sieve into cups or mugs.

PER SERVING (1 cup): 63 Cal, 2 g Total Fat, 0 g Sat Fat, 0 g Trans Fat, 0 mg Chol, 60 mg Sod, 10 g Total Carb, 1 g Fib, 3 g Prot, 118 mg Calc.

PointsPlus value: ***2.***

Cook's Note

If soy milk is not your favorite, chai, a traditional spiced tea drink from southern India, is a delicious way to incorporate soy into your diet. If you prefer it cold, you can let the chai cool slightly, and then serve over ice.

Peanut Butter Blast

SERVES 1

1 small banana

½ cup vanilla fat-free yogurt

½ cup fat-free milk

1 tablespoon creamy peanut butter

¼ teaspoon vanilla extract

Pinch cinnamon

Combine all ingredients except cinnamon in blender and process until smooth. Pour into tall glass and sprinkle with cinnamon.

PER SERVING (about 1 cup): 328 Cal, 9 g Total Fat, 2 g Sat Fat, 0 g Trans Fat, 5 mg Chol, 190 mg Sod, 53 g Total Carb, 6 g Fib, 14 g Prot, 356 mg Calc.

PointsPlus value: ***9.***

Soy-Blueberry Breakfast Shake

SERVES 1

1 cup calcium-fortified plain fat-free soy milk

1 cup frozen unsweetened blueberries

½ banana

2 teaspoons honey

1 teaspoon vanilla extract

Combine all ingredients in blender and process until smooth. Pour into tall glass.

PER SERVING (2 cups): 296 Cal, 1 g Total Fat, 0 g Sat Fat, 0 g Trans Fat, 0 mg Chol, 62 mg Sod, 67 g Total Carb, 7 g Fib, 7 g Prot, 413 mg Calc.

PointsPlus value: **8.**

Ham and Swiss Panini

SERVES 2

4 slices reduced-calorie whole wheat bread

6 (1-ounce) slices lean reduced-sodium ham

2 slices fat-free Swiss cheese

1. Spray ridged grill pan with nonstick spray and set over medium-high heat or heat panini sandwich maker according to manufacturers' instructions.
2. Top 2 bread slices evenly with ham and Swiss cheese. Top with remaining bread slices. Spray sandwiches lightly with olive oil nonstick spray.
3. Place sandwiches in pan and cover with heavy skillet or place in sandwich maker. Grill until bread is well marked and cheese is melted, about 5 minutes. (Turn sandwiches halfway through cooking time if using grill pan.) Cut in half and serve.

PER SERVING (1 sandwich): 203 Cal, 4 g Total Fat, 1 g Sat Fat, 0 g Trans Fat, 35 mg Chol, 949 mg Sod, 21 g Total Carb, 5 g Fib, 22 g Prot, 223 mg Calc.

PointsPlus value: **5.**

Cook's Note

Serve these quick and easy sandwiches with Creamy Tomato Soup, page 199.

Turkey Wraps with Lemon-Yogurt Sauce

15 minute meals

Asian-Style Duck Roll-Ups

SERVES 4

2 cups shredded cooked skinless duck breast or chicken breast

¼ cup hoisin sauce

2 scallions, thinly sliced

4 (7-inch) whole wheat tortillas, warmed

½ small red bell pepper, thinly sliced

8 arugula leaves, trimmed

1. Stir together duck, hoisin sauce, and scallions in medium bowl.
2. Top tortillas evenly with duck mixture, then with bell pepper and arugula. Roll up tortillas and cut in half.

PER SERVING (1 roll-up): 203 Cal, 2 g Total Fat, 1 g Sat Fat, 0 g Trans Fat, 59 mg Chol, 554 mg Sod, 22 g Total Carb, 3 g Fib, 24 g Prot, 34 mg Calc.

PointsPlus value: **5.**

Cook's Note

Packaged cooked duck breast is found in specialty food stores. If it comes with the skin on, be sure to remove it before shredding the duck.

Salmon Salad Sandwich

SERVES 2

1 (7½-ounce) can salmon, drained and flaked

3 tablespoons plain fat-free yogurt

½ cup peeled, seeded, and chopped cucumber

2 scallions, thinly sliced

2 tablespoons chopped fresh dill

1 tablespoon capers, drained

Grated zest and juice of ½ lemon

½ (10-ounce) whole wheat baguette

1. Stir together salmon, yogurt, cucumber, scallions, dill, capers, and lemon zest and juice in medium bowl.
2. Split baguette in half lengthwise and remove soft bready center. Spoon salmon mixture into bottom half of baguette and cover with top of baguette. Cut sandwich in half.

PER SERVING (½ sandwich): 321 Cal, 7 g Total Fat, 1 g Sat Fat, 0 g Trans Fat, 73 mg Chol, 839 mg Sod, 34 g Total Carb, 6 g Fib, 32 g Prot, 389 mg Calc.

PointsPlus value: ***8.***

Quick Turkey Tostadas

Quick Turkey Tostadas

SERVES 2

1 teaspoon canola oil

2 (6-inch) corn tortillas

2 cups thinly sliced romaine lettuce

4 (1-ounce) slices low-sodium skinless deli turkey breast or chicken breast, cut into strips

2 plum tomatoes, chopped

½ avocado, halved, pitted, peeled, and sliced

¼ cup fat-free ranch dressing

¼ cup fat-free salsa

1. Heat oil in small skillet over medium-high heat. Add tortillas to skillet, one at a time, and cook until lightly browned and crisp, about 2 minutes on each side.
2. Place 1 tortilla on each of 2 plates and layer evenly with lettuce, turkey, tomatoes, and avocado.
3. Drizzle dressing evenly over tostadas and serve with salsa.

PER SERVING (1 tostada): 271 Cal, 10 g Total Fat, 1 g Sat Fat, 0 g Trans Fat, 51 mg Chol, 477 mg Sod, 27 g Total Carb, 6 g Fib, 21 g Prot, 77 mg Calc.

PointsPlus value: *7.*

15
minute
meals

Cilantro-Lime Shrimp Salad Pitas

SERVES 4

¼ cup light mayonnaise

¼ cup fresh lime juice

¼ cup chopped fresh cilantro

¼ teaspoon black pepper

½ pound frozen cooked medium shrimp, thawed and chopped

1 small green bell pepper, chopped

1 small red onion, chopped

4 (6½-inch) whole wheat pitas

4 green leaf lettuce leaves

1. Stir together mayonnaise, lime juice, cilantro, and black pepper in large bowl. Add shrimp, bell pepper, and onion to mayonnaise mixture and toss to coat.
2. Cut off top third of each pita and discard. Line each pita with lettuce leaf and fill evenly with shrimp salad.

PER SERVING (1 stuffed pita): 230 Cal, 6 g Total Fat, 1 g Sat Fat, 0 g Trans Fat, 124 mg Chol, 903 mg Sod, 29 g Total Carb, 4 g Fib, 18 g Prot, 74 mg Calc.

PointsPlus value: ***6.***

15 minute meals

California Health Sandwiches

SERVES 2

1 cup thinly sliced romaine lettuce

½ cup shredded carrot

2 tablespoons fat-free Italian dressing

2 tablespoons hummus

4 slices whole-grain bread, toasted

1 tomato, thinly sliced

½ small avocado, thinly sliced

¼ teaspoon salt

⅛ teaspoon black pepper

1. Toss together lettuce, carrot, and dressing in small bowl.
2. Spread hummus evenly on 2 slices of bread. Layer evenly with tomato, avocado, and lettuce mixture. Sprinkle with salt and pepper. Top with remaining 2 slices of bread. Cut each sandwich in half.

PER SERVING: (1 sandwich): 258 Cal, 9 g Total Fat, 1 g Sat Fat, 0 g Trans Fat, 0 mg Chol, 813 mg Sod, 35 g Total Carb, 9 g Fib, 10 g Prot, 101 mg Calc.

PointsPlus value: **6.**

Best BLTs

SERVES 2

4 teaspoons fat-free mayonnaise

2 teaspoons basil pesto

4 slices whole wheat bread

½ cup lightly packed baby arugula

¼ avocado, halved, pitted, peeled, and thinly sliced

1 tomato, sliced

6 slices turkey bacon, crisp-cooked

1. Stir together mayonnaise and pesto in small bowl.
2. Spread mayonnaise mixture evenly on 2 slices of bread. Layer bread evenly with arugula, avocado, tomato, and bacon. Cover sandwiches with remaining slices of bread.

PER SERVING (1 sandwich): 280 Cal, 10 g Total Fat, 2 g Sat Fat, 0 g Trans Fat, 33 mg Chol, 799 mg Sod, 31 g Total Carb, 5 g Fib, 16 g Prot, 105 mg Calc.

PointsPlus value: *7.*

Cook's Note

Cook turkey bacon up to several hours ahead and drain on paper towels. When ready to use, microwave on High just until heated through, about 30 seconds.

Best BLTs

15 minute meals

Avocado, Spinach, and Feta Wrap

SERVES 2

½ avocado, halved, pitted, and peeled

¼ teaspoon salt

¼ teaspoon black pepper

1 (10-inch) spinach tortilla wrap

1 cup lightly packed baby spinach

1 small zucchini, shredded

¼ cup crumbled fat-free feta cheese

1 tablespoon balsamic vinegar

1 teaspoon olive oil

Mash together avocado, salt, and pepper in small bowl. Spread mixture evenly on tortilla. Top with spinach, zucchini, and feta; drizzle with vinegar and oil. Roll up tortilla to enclose filling. Cut wrap in half.

PER SERVING (½ wrap): 250 Cal, 15 g Total Fat, 4 g Sat Fat, 0 g Trans Fat, 13 mg Chol, 577 mg Sod, 26 g Total Carb, 6 g Fib, 7 g Prot, 166 mg Calc.

PointsPlus value: *7.*

Ham and Navy Bean Confetti Soup

SERVES 4

3 cups fat-free reduced-sodium chicken broth

6 ounces cooked lower-sodium lean ham, diced

1 (15½-ounce) can no-salt-added navy beans, rinsed and drained

1 carrot, shredded

1 celery stalk, thinly sliced

½ cup diced red bell pepper

½ cup frozen chopped onion

2 tablespoons chopped fresh parsley

Combine all ingredients except parsley in medium saucepan; cover and bring to boil. Reduce heat and simmer, covered, until vegetables are tender, about 5 minutes. Stir in parsley just before serving.

PER SERVING (1⅓ cups): 200 Cal, 3 g Total Fat, 1 g Sat Fat, 0 g Trans Fat, 23 mg Chol, 849 mg Sod, 25 g Total Carb, 9 g Fib, 18 g Prot, 87 mg Calc.

PointsPlus value: ***4.***

Cook's Note

Enjoy a simple cheese sandwich with this soup to make it a filling meal. Two slices of reduced-calorie whole wheat bread filled with 1 ounce of fat-free Cheddar cheese, tomato slices, and shredded lettuce per serving will increase the ***PointsPlus*** value by ***4.***

Winter Squash Soup
with Lime Cream

Winter Squash Soup with Lime Cream

SERVES 4

2 (12-ounce) boxes frozen squash puree, thawed

2 (14½-ounce) cans reduced-sodium vegetable or chicken broth

1 teaspoon ground cumin

½ teaspoon salt

3 tablespoons fat-free sour cream

Grated zest of 1 lime

2 teaspoons fresh lime juice

2 teaspoons water

1. Combine squash, broth, cumin, and salt in medium saucepan; bring to boil over high heat. Reduce heat and simmer 3 minutes.
2. Meanwhile, stir together sour cream, lime zest and juice, and water in small bowl.
3. Divide soup evenly among 4 bowls and drizzle with lime cream.

PER SERVING (1¼ cups soup and 1 tablespoon lime cream): 91 Cal, 1 g Total Fat, 0 g Sat Fat, 0 g Trans Fat, 1 mg Chol, 789 mg Sod, 19 g Total Carb, 5 g Fib, 5 g Prot, 77 mg Calc.

PointsPlus value: ***2.***

Cook's Note

For a satisfying lunch, serve this quick soup with Hearty Lentil Salad with Radicchio, page 205.

15 minute meals

Southern Vegetable Gumbo

SERVES 4

1½ tablespoons unsalted butter

2 tablespoons all-purpose flour

3 cups reduced-sodium vegetable broth

½ pound frozen okra

1 cup frozen corn kernels

1 cup frozen pearl onions

1 (14½-ounce) can sliced potatoes, drained and rinsed

1 (14½-ounce) can diced tomatoes, drained

2 bay leaves

Hot pepper sauce

1. Melt butter in large saucepan over medium-high heat. Stir in flour and cook, stirring constantly, until mixture becomes golden, 1–2 minutes. Slowly stir in broth, stirring until mixture is smooth.

2. Add okra, corn, onions, potatoes, tomatoes, and bay leaves. Increase heat to high and cook, stirring occasionally, until gumbo is bubbling and vegetables are heated through, about 8 minutes. Discard bay leaves and serve with pepper sauce on side.

PER SERVING (1¾ cups): 179 Cal, 5 g Total Fat, 3 g Sat Fat, 0 g Trans Fat, 11 mg Chol, 574 mg Sod, 33 g Total Carb, 5 g Fib, 4 g Prot, 85 mg Calc.

PointsPlus value: ***5.***

Roast Beef Salad with Creamy Horseradish Dressing

SERVES 4

3 tablespoons fat-free mayonnaise

3 tablespoons plain fat-free Greek yogurt

2 teaspoons bottled horseradish

¼ teaspoon salt

¼ teaspoon black pepper

½ pound thinly sliced lean deli roast beef, cut into strips

1 small head romaine lettuce, thinly sliced (about 6 cups)

1 cup cherry tomatoes, halved

1. To make dressing, whisk together mayonnaise, yogurt, horseradish, salt, and pepper in serving bowl.
2. Add roast beef, lettuce, and tomatoes to dressing; toss to coat.

PER SERVING (about 2 cups): 174 Cal, 9 g Total Fat, 4 g Sat Fat, 0 g Trans Fat, 44 mg Chol, 300 mg Sod, 7 g Total Carb, 2 g Fib, 16 g Prot, 58 mg Calc.

PointsPlus value: ***4.***

15 minute meals

Mexicali Chicken Salad

SERVES 4

¾ cup fat-free salsa

¼ cup fat-free ranch dressing

1 head romaine lettuce, chopped

1 large tomato, diced

1 small jicama, peeled and shredded

1 cup shredded reduced-fat Monterey Jack or pepper Jack cheese

1 cup canned black beans, rinsed and drained

¼ cup diced sweet onion

2 cups diced cooked skinless chicken breast

12 baked tortilla chips, broken up

1. To make dressing, stir together salsa and ranch dressing in large serving bowl. Add lettuce, tomato, jicama, Jack cheese, beans, and onion to bowl and toss to coat.
2. Divide salad evenly among 4 plates. Top salads evenly with chicken and sprinkle with tortilla chips.

PER SERVING (3 cups salad, ½ cup chicken, and 3 tortilla chips): 384 Cal, 10 g Total Fat, 5 g Sat Fat, 0 g Trans Fat, 80 mg Chol, 980 mg Sod, 38 g Total Carb, 12 g Fib, 37 g Prot, 297 mg Calc.

PointsPlus value: ***9.***

Cook's Note

Mild-tasting sweet onions are fantastic for serving in dishes such as this where the onion is eaten raw. Try Walla Walla, Oso Sweet, or Vidalia onions in your favorite salad recipes.

Greek-Style Chicken Salad

SERVES 4

¾ cup plain fat-free yogurt

3 tablespoons chopped fresh mint

3 tablespoons chopped fresh dill

Grated zest and juice of 1 lemon

1 garlic clove, minced

2 teaspoons olive oil

2 cups diced roasted chicken breast

3 cups torn romaine lettuce leaves

2 large tomatoes, cut into wedges

1 cucumber, peeled, seeded, and diced

½ cup chopped red onion

8 pitted Kalamata olives, coarsely chopped

½ cup crumbled fat-free feta cheese

1. To make dressing, whisk together yogurt, mint, dill, lemon zest and juice, garlic, and oil in small bowl.
2. Toss together chicken, lettuce, tomatoes, cucumber, and onion in serving bowl. Drizzle dressing over salad and toss to coat. Sprinkle with olives and feta.

PER SERVING (generous 1½ cups): 230 Cal, 7 g Total Fat, 1 g Sat Fat, 0 g Trans Fat, 59 mg Chol, 514 mg Sod, 14 g Total Carb, 3 g Fib, 28 g Prot, 199 mg Calc.

PointsPlus value: **6.**

Cook's Note

You'll want to make this salad a staple for summer meals. You can vary the salad depending on what's fresh at the farmers' market. Use cherry tomatoes instead of regular tomatoes, zucchini or yellow squash instead of cucumber, and basil and parsley instead of the mint and dill.

15 minute meals

Tropical Turkey Salad

SERVES 4

3 tablespoons fresh lemon juice

2 teaspoons olive oil

½ teaspoon salt

¼ teaspoon black pepper

2 cups diced cooked skinless turkey breast

1 large Granny Smith apple, cored and sliced

1 mango, peeled, pitted, and diced

1 papaya, peeled, halved, seeded, and diced

½ cup chopped red onion

1 jalapeño pepper, seeded and minced

Red leaf lettuce leaves

1. To make dressing, whisk together lemon juice, oil, salt, and black pepper in serving bowl.
2. Add turkey, apple, mango, papaya, onion, and jalapeño to dressing and toss to coat. Line 4 bowls with red leaf lettuce. Top evenly with turkey salad.

PER SERVING (1½ cups): 283 Cal, 6 g Total Fat, 1 g Sat Fat, 0 g Trans Fat, 60 mg Chol, 482 mg Sod, 30 g Total Carb, 11 g Fib, 27 g Prot, 58 mg Calc.

PointsPlus value: ***6.***

Cook's Note

Serve the salad with plain fat-free Greek yogurt topped with fresh berries for dessert (½ cup of plain fat-free Greek yogurt per serving will increase the ***PointsPlus*** value by ***1***).

Tropical Turkey Salad

15 minute meals

Fruity Chicken Salad

SERVES 4

⅔ cup fat-free mayonnaise

¼ cup chopped fresh cilantro

1 tablespoon apple-cider vinegar

2 cups cubed cooked skinless chicken breast

1½ cups fresh pineapple chunks

1 papaya, peeled, seeded, and cut into ¾-inch chunks

1 small orange, peeled and coarsely chopped

½ small red onion, thinly sliced

1. To make dressing, stir together mayonnaise, cilantro, and vinegar in serving bowl.
2. Add chicken, pineapple, papaya, orange, and onion to dressing and toss to coat.

PER SERVING (about 1½ cups): 198 Cal, 2 g Total Fat, 1 g Sat Fat, 0 g Trans Fat, 62 mg Chol, 474 mg Sod, 24 g Total Carb, 4 g Fib, 22 g Prot, 51 mg Calc.

PointsPlus value: ***5.***

Cook's Note

To make this dish more filling, add a chopped apple to the salad and serve each portion on a generous mound of baby arugula.

Chicken Salad with Fennel, Arugula, and Blue Cheese

SERVES 2

1 (5-ounce) bag baby arugula

4 tablespoons fat-free vinaigrette

1½ cups diced cooked skinless chicken breast

1 small fennel bulb, thinly sliced

1 cup cherry tomatoes, halved

½ small red onion, thinly sliced

¼ teaspoon black pepper

¼ cup crumbled blue cheese

2 teaspoons pine nuts

1. Toss together arugula and 2 tablespoons of vinaigrette in large bowl. Divide arugula evenly between 2 plates.
2. Combine chicken, fennel, tomatoes, onion, remaining 2 tablespoons vinaigrette, and pepper in same bowl and toss to coat.
3. Spoon chicken mixture evenly on top of arugula and sprinkle with blue cheese and pine nuts.

PER SERVING (1 salad): 288 Cal, 10 g Total Fat, 4 g Sat Fat, 0 g Trans Fat, 85 mg Chol, 652 mg Sod, 16 g Total Carb, 3 g Fib, 33 g Prot, 211 mg Calc.

PointsPlus value: *7*.

Cook's Note

For more fresh anise flavor, reserve the feathery green tops from the fennel bulb, chop about a tablespoon, and sprinkle over the salads just before serving.

Chinese Chicken Slaw

SERVES 4

1 (1-pound) bag coleslaw mix

3 scallions, sliced

1 (8-ounce) can sliced water chestnuts, drained

1 cup shredded cooked skinless chicken breast

1 cup frozen shelled edamame, thawed

¼ cup chopped fresh cilantro

⅓ cup seasoned rice-wine vinegar

2 tablespoons reduced-sodium soy sauce

1 teaspoon Asian (dark) sesame oil

1 garlic clove, minced

1 teaspoon grated peeled fresh ginger

1. Toss together coleslaw mix, scallions, water chestnuts, chicken, edamame, and cilantro in large bowl.
2. Whisk together vinegar, soy sauce, oil, garlic, and ginger in small bowl. Pour over coleslaw mixture and toss to combine.

PER SERVING (2 cups): 190 Cal, 5 g Fat, 1 g Sat Fat, 0 g Trans Fat, 22 mg Chol, 772 mg Sod, 22 g Total Carb, 7 g Fib, 14 g Prot, 92 mg Calc.

PointsPlus value: ***4.***

Key West-Style Shrimp Salad

SERVES 4

⅓ cup fat-free mayonnaise

⅓ cup sour cream

½ teaspoon salt

¼ teaspoon black pepper

1 pound cooked, peeled, and deveined medium shrimp

2 cups fresh pineapple chunks

2 cups strawberries, hulled and thickly sliced

¼ cup thinly sliced fresh mint

2 scallions, thinly sliced

1 jalapeño pepper, seeded and minced

4 cups mixed baby salad greens

1. To make dressing, whisk together mayonnaise, sour cream, salt, and black pepper in serving bowl.
2. Toss together shrimp, pineapple, strawberries, mint, scallions, and jalapeño pepper in large bowl.
3. Divide salad greens evenly among 4 plates. Top evenly with shrimp mixture. Serve dressing alongside.

PER SERVING (2½ cups salad and 2½ tablespoons dressing): 205 Cal, 2 g Total Fat, 1 g Sat Fat, 0 g Trans Fat, 223 mg Chol, 728 mg Sod, 22 g Total Carb, 5 g Fib, 26 g Prot, 105 mg Calc.

PointsPlus value: **5.**

Maple and Chili-Broiled T-Bone Steaks

SERVES 6

1 canned chipotle en adobo, minced

2 tablespoons maple syrup

2 garlic cloves, minced

Grated zest of ½ orange

1 teaspoon salt

1 teaspoon chili powder

1 teaspoon ground cumin

1 teaspoon onion powder

2 (1½- to 1¾-pound) T-bone steaks, ½ inch thick, trimmed

1. Spray broiler rack with nonstick spray and preheat broiler.
2. Stir together chipotle, maple syrup, garlic, orange zest, salt, chili powder, cumin, and onion powder in small bowl. Rub chipotle mixture on both sides of steaks.
3. Place steaks on broiler rack and broil 4 inches from heat until an instant-read thermometer inserted into side of steak registers 145°F for medium, about 5 minutes on each side. Transfer steaks to cutting board and let stand 5 minutes. Cut each steak into 3 portions.

PER SERVING (1 piece steak): 244 Cal, 9 g Total Fat, 4 g Sat Fat, 0 g Trans Fat, 59 mg Chol, 520 mg Sod, 7 g Total Carb, 0 g Fib, 32 g Prot, 14 mg Calc.

PointsPlus value: **6.**

Cook's Note

Serve the steaks with a side dish of grilled red and yellow bell peppers and spring onions. Use your stovetop grill and grill the vegetables while the steak broils.

Maple and Chili–Broiled
T-Bone Steaks

15 minute meals

Filets Mignons with Cauliflower Puree

SERVES 4

2 (10-ounce) packages frozen cauliflower florets, thawed

½ cup reduced-sodium chicken broth

1 teaspoon unsalted butter

½ teaspoon salt

4 (5-ounce) filets mignons, trimmed

1 tablespoon chopped fresh parsley

1 tablespoon chopped fresh rosemary

1 tablespoon chopped fresh sage

1. Combine cauliflower and broth in food processor and pulse until smooth. Transfer mixture to medium saucepan and cook over medium heat until heated through, about 5 minutes. Add few tablespoons of water if puree seems dry, then stir in butter and ¼ teaspoon of salt.
2. Meanwhile, spray large skillet with nonstick spray and set over medium-high heat. Sprinkle filets mignons with remaining ¼ teaspoon salt. Add steaks to skillet and cook until an instant-read thermometer inserted into side of steak registers 145°F for medium, about 4 minutes on each side. Sprinkle steaks with parsley, rosemary, and sage. Serve with cauliflower puree.

PER SERVING (1 steak and ⅔ cup puree): 226 Cal, 10 g Total Fat, 4 g Sat Fat, 2 g Trans Fat, 74 mg Chol, 457 mg Sod, 7 g Total Carb, 3 g Fib, 27 g Prot, 44 mg Calc.

PointsPlus value: **6.**

Do it Faster

For a fast and flavorful side dish, chop extra amounts of the herbs and toss them with steamed green beans. Season with salt and pepper to taste.

Herb-Crusted Filets Mignons

SERVES 2

½ teaspoon dried basil

¼ teaspoon dried rosemary

¼ teaspoon crushed fennel seeds

¼ teaspoon salt

¼ teaspoon black pepper

2 (¼-pound) filets mignons, trimmed

Lemon wedges

1. Spray broiler rack with nonstick spray and preheat broiler.
2. Stir together basil, rosemary, fennel seeds, salt, and pepper in small bowl. Rub mixture on both sides of filets mignons. Place steaks on broiler rack and broil 5 inches from heat until an instant-read thermometer inserted into side of steak registers 145°F for medium, about 3 minutes on each side. Let steaks stand 5 minutes. Serve with lemon wedges.

PER SERVING (1 steak): 147 Cal, 7 g Total Fat, 3 g Sat Fat, 1 g Trans Fat, 57 mg Chol, 334 mg Sod, 1 g Total Carb, 0 g Fib, 19 g Prot, 18 mg Calc.

PointsPlus value: ***4.***

Cook's Note

For an easy dinner, serve this flavorful steak with steamed broccoli and mashed potatoes (½ pound of red-skinned potatoes, cooked and mashed with salt and pepper to taste will increase the per-serving ***PointsPlus*** value by ***2***).

15 minute meals

Caesar-Style Steak Salad

SERVES 2

6 ounces lean boneless sirloin steak, trimmed

¼ teaspoon black pepper

⅛ teaspoon salt

8 cups chopped romaine lettuce (about 1 medium head)

¼ red onion, thinly sliced

¼ cup fat-free Caesar dressing

¼ cup grated Parmesan cheese

1. Heat ridged grill pan or cast-iron skillet over high heat. Sprinkle steak with pepper and salt. Place steak in pan and cook until an instant-read thermometer inserted into side of steak registers 145°F for medium, about 4 minutes on each side. Transfer to cutting board and let stand 5 minutes.
2. Toss together lettuce, onion, dressing, and Parmesan in large bowl. Divide salad evenly between 2 plates. Cut steak into 10 slices and divide evenly between salads.

PER SERVING (3 cups salad and 5 slices steak): 213 Cal, 6 g Total Fat, 3 g Sat Fat, 1 g Trans Fat, 57 mg Chol, 866 mg Sod, 11 g Total Carb, 4 g Fib, 27 g Prot, 246 mg Calc.

PointsPlus value: ***5.***

Grilled Citrus Pork with Cucumber-Orange Salad

1. Whisk together orange juice, lime juice, garlic, oil, and salt in large bowl. Pour half of mixture into medium bowl and add pork chops. Turn to coat.
2. Spray ridged grill pan with nonstick spray and set over medium-high heat. Remove pork from marinade, discard marinade. Place pork on grill pan. Grill, turning once, until an instant-read thermometer inserted into side of chop registers 145°F, about 4 minutes.
3. Meanwhile, add cucumber, orange, bell pepper, and olives to orange juice mixture in large bowl and toss to coat. Serve salad with pork.

SERVING (1 chop and ⅔ cup salad): 266 Cal, 13 g Total Fat, 3 g Sat Fat, 0 g Trans Fat, 72 mg Chol, 385 mg Sod, 10 g Total Carb, 2 g Fib, 26 g Prot, 39 mg Calc.

PointsPlus value: *7.*

SERVES 4

½ cup fresh orange juice

2 tablespoons fresh lime juice

2 garlic cloves, minced

1 tablespoon canola oil

¾ teaspoon salt

4 (¼-pound) lean boneless center-cut pork loin chops, trimmed

1 cucumber, peeled and diced

1 orange, peeled and diced

1 red bell pepper, diced

¼ cup sliced black olives

15
minute
meals

Lamb and Onion Kebabs with Mint

SERVES 4

1 pound lean lamb loin, trimmed and cut into ¾-inch cubes

1½ cups frozen pearl onions, thawed

2 garlic cloves, minced

1 tablespoon olive oil

1 tablespoon fresh lemon juice

½ teaspoon salt

2 teaspoons grated lemon zest

3 tablespoons chopped fresh mint

1. Spray grill rack with nonstick spray; preheat grill to high or prepare hot fire.
2. Toss together lamb, onions, garlic, oil, lemon juice, and salt in large bowl. Thread lamb and pearl onions alternately on 8 metal skewers. Place on grill rack and cook, turning frequently, until lamb is browned and cooked through, 4–5 minutes.
3. Sprinkle lemon zest and mint over kebabs just before serving.

PER SERVING (2 skewers): 219 Cal, 11 g Fat, 3 g Sat Fat, 1 g Trans Fat, 75 mg Chol, 356 mg Sod, 5 g Total Carb, 1 g Fib, 24 g Prot, 24 mg Calc.

PointsPlus value: **5.**

Superfast Barbecued Chicken

SERVES 4

3 tablespoons ketchup

1 tablespoon hoisin sauce

1 tablespoon apple-cider vinegar

2 teaspoons molasses

2 teaspoons reduced-sodium soy sauce

4 (¼-pound) skinless boneless chicken breasts

¼ teaspoon black pepper

1. Stir together ketchup, hoisin sauce, vinegar, molasses, and soy sauce in small bowl.
2. Spray ridged grill pan with nonstick spray and set over medium heat. Sprinkle chicken with pepper and place in grill pan. Grill, turning often, until chicken is cooked through, about 8 minutes, brushing with ketchup mixture during last 3 minutes of cooking time.

PER SERVING (1 chicken breast): 228 Cal, 5 g Total Fat, 1 g Sat Fat, 0 g Trans Fat, 97 mg Chol, 745 mg Sod, 7 g Total Carb, 0 g Fib, 36 g Prot, 28 mg Calc.

PointsPlus value: **5.**

15 minute meals

Easy Chicken Cutlets Parmesan

SERVES 2

4 (3-ounce) thin-sliced skinless boneless chicken breasts

½ cup fat-free marinara sauce

¾ cup shredded fat-free mozzarella cheese

2 tablespoons grated Parmesan cheese

2 tablespoons chopped fresh basil

1. Spray large skillet with nonstick spray and set over medium heat. Add chicken and cook until browned and cooked through, about 2 minutes on each side.

2. Place chicken in small baking dish in one layer and top evenly with marinara sauce; sprinkle with mozzarella and Parmesan. Microwave on High until cheese is melted, about 2 minutes. Sprinkle with basil.

PER SERVING (2 pieces chicken): 343 Cal, 8 g Total Fat, 3 g Sat Fat, 0 g Trans Fat, 118 mg Chol, 926 mg Sod, 11 g Total Carb, 1 g Fib, 54 g Prot, 493 mg Calc.

PointsPlus value: ***8.***

Turkey Cutlets with Mushroom-Wine Sauce

1. Spray large skillet with nonstick spray and set over medium-high heat. Sprinkle turkey with pepper and ¼ teaspoon of salt; cook until browned and cooked through, about 2 minutes on each side. Transfer to plate and keep warm.
2. Place butter in skillet and swirl so butter melts and coats skillet. Add mushrooms, garlic, and remaining ¼ teaspoon salt; cook, stirring frequently, until mushrooms brown, about 3 minutes. Add wine and thyme; simmer until most of liquid has evaporated, about 4 minutes. Spoon mushrooms over turkey and sprinkle with parsley.

PER SERVING (1 turkey cutlet and ¼ cup mushroom sauce): 174 Cal, 4 g Total Fat, 2 g Sat Fat, 0 g Trans Fat, 84 mg Chol, 351 mg Sod, 4 g Total Carb, 0 g Fib, 28 g Prot, 34 mg Calc.

PointsPlus value: 4.

Cook's Note

If your supermarket has variety packs of mushrooms, use one for this recipe. A blend of different types of mushrooms will intensify the flavor and give sauce dish visual appeal.

SERVES 4

4 (¼-pound) turkey breast cutlets

¼ teaspoon black pepper

½ teaspoon salt

1 tablespoon unsalted butter

2½ cups (6 ounces) thinly sliced fresh cremini mushrooms

2 garlic cloves, minced

¾ cup dry red wine

½ teaspoon dried thyme

2 tablespoons chopped fresh parsley

Grilled Chicken Salad with
Raspberries and Goat Cheese

Grilled Chicken Salad with Raspberries and Goat Cheese

SERVES 4

4 (¼-pound) thin-sliced skinless boneless chicken breasts

¾ teaspoon salt

1 (7-ounce) bag mixed baby salad greens

2 tablespoons raspberry or red-wine vinegar

2 teaspoons olive oil

¼ teaspoon black pepper

½ cup crumbled soft (mild) goat cheese

2 (6-ounce) containers raspberries

3 scallions, thinly sliced

1. Spray ridged grill pan with nonstick spray and set over medium-high heat. Sprinkle chicken with ½ teaspoon of salt. Place chicken in pan and grill until cooked through, about 3 minutes on each side.
2. Meanwhile, combine salad greens, vinegar, oil, remaining ¼ teaspoon salt, and pepper in large bowl; toss to coat.
3. Add goat cheese, raspberries, and scallions to salad and gently toss to combine. Divide salad evenly among 4 plates. Halve chicken breasts and place 2 pieces on top of each salad.

PER SERVING (1 piece chicken and 2 cups salad): 252 Cal, 10 g Total Fat, 4 g Sat Fat, 0 g Trans Fat, 76 mg Chol, 586 mg Sod, 10 g Total Carb, 5 g Fib, 30 g Prot, 85 mg Calc.

PointsPlus value: **6.**

15 minute meals

African-Spiced Turkey and Squash Stew

SERVES 4

1 tablespoon canola oil

1 pound turkey breast cutlets, cut into 1-inch pieces

¾ cup frozen chopped onion, thawed

3 garlic cloves, minced

1 teaspoon ground cumin

½ teaspoon ground coriander

½ teaspoon cinnamon

1 (14½-ounce) can reduced-sodium chicken broth

1 (12-ounce) box frozen squash puree, thawed

1 cup frozen corn kernels

½ teaspoon salt

Chopped fresh cilantro

1. Heat oil in large skillet over medium-high heat. Add turkey and cook, stirring occasionally, until lightly browned, about 5 minutes. Add onion, garlic, cumin, coriander, and cinnamon. Cook, stirring, until fragrant, about 1 minute.
2. Add broth, squash, corn, and salt; bring to boil. Cook, stirring occasionally, until corn is tender, about 2 minutes. Ladle stew into 4 bowls; sprinkle with cilantro.

PER SERVING (1¼ cups): 260 Cal, 8 g Total Fat, 1 g Sat Fat, 0 g Trans Fat, 68 mg Chol, 601 mg Sod, 20 g Total Carb, 4 g Fib, 29 g Prot, 62 mg Calc.

PointsPlus value: *7.*

Cook's Note

Whole wheat couscous makes a fast-cooking accompaniment to this stew (½ cup cooked whole wheat couscous per serving will increase the ***PointsPlus*** value by ***3***).

Grilled Ginger Chicken with Peach Salsa

SERVES 4

2 teaspoons minced peeled fresh ginger

1 garlic clove, minced

2 teaspoons canola oil

½ teaspoon salt

4 (¼-pound) thin-sliced skinless boneless chicken breasts

3 peaches, pitted and diced

1 tomato, diced

½ small red onion, chopped

1 jalapeño pepper, seeded and minced

¼ cup chopped fresh cilantro

2 teaspoons fresh lime juice

1. Combine ginger, garlic, oil, and ¼ teaspoon of salt in small bowl; rub mixture over chicken.
2. Spray ridged grill pan with nonstick spray and set over medium-high heat. Place chicken in pan and grill until cooked through, about 3 minutes on each side.
3. Meanwhile, to make salsa, toss together peaches, tomato, onion, jalapeño, cilantro, lime juice, and remaining ¼ teaspoon salt in serving bowl. Serve chicken with salsa.

PER SERVING (1 piece chicken and 1 cup salsa): 218 Cal, 6 g Total Fat, 1 g Sat Fat, 0 g Trans Fat, 68 mg Chol, 360 mg Sod, 14 g Total Carb, 2 g Fib, 26 g Prot, 27 mg Calc.

PointsPlus value: **5.**

Cook's Note

While you grill the chicken, grill a vegetable side dish, too. Cut 2 zucchini lengthwise into quarters; spray lightly with nonstick spray. Grill, turning occasionally, until crisp-tender, 6–8 minutes. Season to taste with salt and pepper.

Grilled Salmon with
Quick Tomato Tapenade

Grilled Salmon with Quick Tomato Tapenade

SERVES 4

4 (¼-pound) skinless salmon fillets

¼ teaspoon salt

⅛ teaspoon black pepper

¼ cup pitted Kalamata olives

¼ cup coarsely chopped rehydrated sun-dried tomatoes (not packed in oil)

3 tablespoons coarsely chopped fresh basil or parsley

2 tablespoons pine nuts

1. Spray ridged grill pan with nonstick spray and set over medium-high heat. Sprinkle salmon with salt and pepper. Place salmon in pan and cook until just opaque in center, about 4 minutes on each side.
2. Meanwhile, to make tapenade, combine olives, tomatoes, basil, and pine nuts in mini food processor and process until finely chopped. Top salmon evenly with tapenade.

PER SERVING (1 salmon fillet and 2½ tablespoons tapenade): 201 Cal, 9 g Total Fat, 1 g Sat Fat, 0 g Trans Fat, 65 mg Chol, 437 mg Sod, 3 g Total Carb, 1 g Fib, 26 g Prot, 28 mg Calc.

PointsPlus value: **5.**

Cook's Note

Serve the salmon with fresh watercress sprigs.

15 minute meals

Salmon au Poivre with Watercress

SERVES 4

4 (6-ounce) skinless salmon fillets

1 tablespoon mixed peppercorns, cracked

¾ teaspoon salt

3 bunches watercress, trimmed

¼ red onion, thinly sliced

1½ tablespoons fresh lemon juice

1. Sprinkle salmon evenly with peppercorns and ½ teaspoon of salt.
2. Spray large skillet with nonstick spray and set over medium heat. Add salmon and cook until lightly browned and just opaque in center, about 4 minutes on each side.
3. Meanwhile, toss together watercress, onion, lemon juice, and remaining ¼ teaspoon salt in large bowl. Divide watercress salad evenly among 4 plates and top each serving with piece of salmon.

PER SERVING (1 salmon fillet and 1½ cups salad): 266 Cal, 11 g Total Fat, 2 g Sat Fat, 0 g Trans Fat, 94 mg Chol, 584 mg Sod, 3 g Total Carb, 1 g Fib, 37 g Prot, 101 mg Calc.

PointsPlus value: ***6.***

Cook's Note

Before cooking, it's best to run your fingers lightly over surface of salmon fillets to check for any small bones that may be embedded in flesh. If you find any, use clean tweezers or needle-nose pliers to pull them out.

Tuna Steaks with Avocado-Orange Relish

SERVES 4

2 teaspoons canola oil

2 teaspoons reduced-sodium soy sauce

4 (5-ounce) tuna steaks

1 tablespoon red-wine vinegar

2 teaspoons flaxseed oil

1½ teaspoons minced peeled fresh ginger

¼ teaspoon salt

½ avocado, halved, pitted, peeled, and diced

1 (11-ounce) can unsweetened mandarin orange sections, drained

¼ small red onion, chopped

1. Spray broiler rack with nonstick spray and preheat broiler.
2. Whisk together canola oil and soy sauce in small bowl. Brush mixture on both sides of tuna. Place steaks on broiler rack and broil 5 inches from heat, about 3 minutes on each side for medium or until desired doneness.
3. Meanwhile, to make relish, whisk together vinegar, flaxseed oil, ginger, and salt in medium bowl. Add avocado, orange sections, and onion; toss to coat. Serve tuna with relish.

PER SERVING (1 tuna steak and ½ cup relish): 259 Cal, 9 g Total Fat, 1 g Sat Fat, 0 g Trans Fat, 66 mg Chol, 303 mg Sod, 8 g Total Carb, 2 g Fib, 35 g Prot, 32 mg Calc.

PointsPlus value: **6.**

Cook's Note

Flaxseed oil is great source of vitamin E and heart-healthy omega-3 fatty acids. You can use canola oil instead of the flaxseed oil in this recipe if flaxseed oil is not available.

Halibut with Salsa Verde

SERVES 4

4 (6-ounce) skinless halibut fillets

½ teaspoon salt

¼ teaspoon black pepper

2 teaspoons canola oil

1 cup fat-free salsa verde

Cilantro sprigs

Lime wedges

1. Sprinkle halibut with salt and pepper.
2. Heat oil in large skillet over medium-high heat. Add halibut and cook until just opaque in center, about 3 minutes on each side.
3. Place 1 fillet on each of 4 plates and top evenly with salsa verde. Garnish with cilantro sprigs and lime wedges.

PER SERVING (1 fillet and ¼ cup salsa): 198 Cal, 5 g Total Fat, 0 g Sat Fat, 0 g Trans Fat, 90 mg Chol, 634 mg Sod, 5 g Total Carb, 1 g Fib, 33 g Prot, 36 mg Calc.

PointsPlus value: **5.**

Cook's Note

Accompany the halibut with steamed baby carrots and brown rice with a sprinkle of chopped fresh cilantro stirred in (½ cup cooked brown rice per serving will increase the ***PointsPlus*** value by ***3***).

Roast Halibut with Chunky Roasted Pepper Sauce

SERVES 4

4 (6-ounce) halibut steaks, about ¾ inch thick

2 teaspoons olive oil

¼ teaspoon salt

¼ teaspoon black pepper

1 (12-ounce) jar roasted red pepper, drained and chopped (not packed in oil)

16 pitted black and/or green olives, coarsely chopped

¼ cup chopped fresh basil

1 tablespoon sherry vinegar or red-wine vinegar

1 tablespoon drained capers, coarsely chopped

1 garlic clove, minced

1. Preheat oven to 425°F and spray shallow roasting pan with nonstick spray.
2. Place halibut in roasting pan; brush with oil and sprinkle with salt and black pepper. Roast fish until just opaque in center, about 10 minutes.
3. Meanwhile, to make sauce, toss together roasted red pepper, olives, basil, vinegar, capers, and garlic in medium bowl. Serve halibut with sauce.

PER SERVING (1 halibut steak and about ⅓ cup sauce): 215 Cal, 6 g Total Fat, 1 g Sat Fat, 0 g Trans Fat, 90 mg Chol, 662 mg Sod, 6 g Total Carb, 1 g Fib, 33 g Prot, 48 mg Calc.

PointsPlus value: **5.**

15 minute meals

Thai Shrimp and Melon Salad

SERVES 4

Grated zest of 1 lime

3 tablespoons fresh lime juice

2 tablespoons reduced-sodium teriyaki sauce

1 serrano or jalapeño pepper, seeded and minced

1¼ pounds medium cooked, peeled, and deveined shrimp

3 Kirby cucumbers, diced

1 red bell pepper, diced

2 carrots, shredded

¾ cup chopped fresh cilantro

¼ cup thinly sliced fresh mint

1 shallot, very thinly sliced

½ honeydew melon, seeded, peeled, and cut into thin wedges

1. Whisk together lime zest and juice, teriyaki sauce, and serrano pepper in large bowl. Add shrimp, cucumbers, bell pepper, carrots, cilantro, mint, and shallot; toss to coat.
2. Arrange honeydew evenly on 4 plates; top evenly with shrimp salad.

PER SERVING (1¼ cups shrimp salad and about 3 melon wedges): 202 Cal, 1 g Total Fat, 0 g Sat Fat, 0 g Trans Fat, 160 mg Chol, 484 mg Sod, 30 g Total Carb, 6 g Fib, 20 g Prot, 116 mg Calc.

PointsPlus value: ***5.***

Cook's Note

In the summer, you can make this salad with whatever melon is available. Try watermelon, cantaloupe, casaba, Galia, or Persian.

Thai Shrimp and Melon Salad

15 minute meals

Sesame Scallops

SERVES 4

- 1 cup quick-cooking brown rice
- 3 tablespoons sesame seeds
- ¼ teaspoon cracked black pepper
- 1¼ pounds sea scallops
- 2 teaspoons olive oil
- 2 tablespoons reduced-sodium soy sauce
- 2 teaspoons unseasoned rice vinegar
- 2 tablespoons finely chopped fresh chives

1. Prepare rice according to package directions, omitting salt if desired.
2. Meanwhile, combine sesame seeds and pepper on sheet of wax paper. Dip flat sides of each scallop in sesame mixture.
3. Heat oil in large skillet over medium-high heat. Add scallops and cook until browned and just opaque throughout, about 2 minutes on each side.
4. Whisk together soy sauce, vinegar, and chives in small bowl. Serve scallops over rice and drizzle with soy sauce mixture.

PER SERVING (6 scallops, ½ cup rice, and scant 1 tablespoon sauce): 239 Cal, 8 g Total Fat, 1 g Sat Fat, 0 g Trans Fat, 38 mg Chol, 899 mg Sod, 20 g Total Carb, 4 g Fib, 20 g Prot, 98 mg Calc.

***PointsPlus* value 6.**

Sesame Noodles with Green Vegetables

SERVES 4

6 ounces whole wheat capellini

Florets from 2 broccoli crowns

½ pound frozen sugar snap peas

½ pound frozen shelled edamame

3 scallions, trimmed and sliced

2 tablespoons reduced-sodium soy sauce

1 tablespoon Asian (dark) sesame oil

½ garlic clove, minced

1. Cook capellini according to package directions, omitting salt if desired. Four minutes before pasta is done, add broccoli, snap peas, and edamame and cook until pasta and vegetables are tender. Drain, reserving ½ cup of cooking water.
2. Transfer capellini mixture to large bowl; add reserved cooking water, scallions, soy sauce, oil, and garlic and toss to coat.

PER SERVING (1¾ cups): 311 Cal, 7 g Total Fat, 1 g Sat Fat, 0 g Trans Fat, 0 mg Chol, 356 mg Sod, 47 g Total Carb, 12 g Fib, 16 g Prot, 123 mg Calc.

PointsPlus value *7.*

Do it Faster

Thin or small pasta such as capellini, macaroni, mini penne, rotini, and orzo are the quickest cooking. Keep a variety of these on your pantry shelf for fast weeknight meals.

Cottage Cheese and Sun-Dried Tomato Dip

SERVES 4

1 (16-ounce) container fat-free cottage cheese

¼ cup fat-free mayonnaise

¼ cup moist sun-dried tomatoes (not packed in oil), chopped

2 scallions, chopped

1 tablespoon grated Parmesan cheese

2 teaspoons fresh lemon juice

Pinch cayenne pepper

2 tablespoons chopped fresh basil or parsley

Combine all ingredients except basil in food processor and process until smooth. Transfer cheese mixture to serving bowl and stir in basil.

PER SERVING (generous ½ cup): 102 Cal, 1 g Total Fat, 0 g Sat Fat, 0 g Trans Fat, 7 mg Chol, 618 mg Sod, 10 g Total Carb, 1 g Fib, 13 g Prot, 102 mg Calc.

PointsPlus value: ***2***.

Cook's Note

Serve this dip with baked fat-free bagel chips (1 ounce of fat-free bagel chips per serving will increase the ***PointsPlus*** value by ***3***).

Dried Cranberry-Popcorn Mix

SERVES 8

1 tablespoon olive oil

2 teaspoons curry powder

6 cups plain air-popped popcorn

½ cup dried cranberries

⅓ cup dry-roasted peanuts

1. Stir together oil and curry powder in microwavable cup. Microwave on High until fragrant, about 1 minute.
2. Toss together popcorn, cranberries, and peanuts in large bowl. Drizzle curry oil over popcorn mixture and toss to coat.

PER SERVING (¾ cup): 94 Cal, 5 g Total Fat, 1 g Sat Fat, 0 g Trans Fat, 0 mg Chol, 51 mg Sod, 11 g Total Carb, 2 g Fib, 2 g Prot, 10 mg Calc.

PointsPlus value: ***3.***

Chili-Spiced Popcorn and Smoky Pumpkin Seeds, page 247

Chili-Spiced Popcorn

SERVES 6

6 cups plain air-popped popcorn

1 tablespoon chili powder

½ teaspoon paprika

½ teaspoon onion powder

½ teaspoon ground cumin

Place popcorn in large bowl and spray with nonstick spray; toss to coat. Sprinkle remaining ingredients over popcorn and toss to coat evenly.

PER SERVING (1 cup): 36 Cal, 1 g Total Fat, 0 g Sat Fat, 0 g Trans Fat, 0 mg Chol, 14 mg Sod, 7 g Total Carb, 2 g Fib, 1 g Prot, 9 mg Calc.

PointsPlus value: ***1.***

organize your kitchen for speed

If you're not organized, you'll spend too much time in the kitchen looking for ingredients, equipment, and tools. The first step to being a shortcut cook is to set up your kitchen for streamlined cooking. Here's how:

DOWNSIZE AND DECLUTTER. Give away unused kitchen items and unnecessary multiples of tools. You'll probably never use a bagel slicer or a garlic peeler. You need several wooden spoons and spatulas, but only one vegetable peeler, box grater, or salad spinner. For items you rarely use, like a bread machine, waffle baker, muffin pan, or holiday cookie cutters, remove them from the kitchen and store in the attic, garage, or a closet.

CREATE A FUNCTIONAL WORK ZONE. Place wooden and slotted spoons, ladles, spatulas, and tongs in a decorative container near the stove. Place the 6 spices you use most often in a drawer away from the heat of the stove, but close by. Keep a set of stackable dry measuring cups, a liquid measuring cup, and a set of measuring spoons near where you do food prep. Store knives in a knife block or on a wall-mounted magnetized knife rack near a large cutting board.

DIVIDE AND CONQUER STORAGE AREAS. Instead of having kitchen drawers become a jumble of tools, buy shallow containers of different lengths or drawer dividers. Separate tools by size for easy visibility and access. Buy bins or baskets for deep cupboard shelves. You can pull out the bin to find what you're looking for, rather than looking through a whole shelf of bottles or cans. To save space, buy sorter racks to allow you to store cutting boards, baking sheets, and pot lids vertically.

KEEP THE REFRIGERATOR WELL ORGANIZED. Discard foods with expired sell-by dates and odd condiments that you'll never use to free up space. Set up zones on each shelf for the way you and your family cook and eat. Leftovers can go on one shelf, foods you've pre-prepped for future meals on another, and foods that are up for grabs for snacks on another. Keep fruits and vegetables in crisper drawers to keep them fresher longer and all in one place.

USE COUNTER SPACE WISELY. Keep items you use daily on the counter. The microwave, toaster, and coffee pot are in constant use and should be left out all the time. Less frequently used appliances like a stand mixer, blender, or juicer can take their place on a lower shelf in a distant cabinet to free up work space.

MAXIMIZE SHELF SPACE. Buy risers so you can store plates on the shelf and saucers or bowls on the riser above them. Use them in the pantry to double storage space for cans and boxes. Install hooks for hanging cups and mugs to clear out space on the shelf below.

STORE ITEMS IN CLEAR CONTAINERS. Keep pantry staples such as flour, sugar, rice, and pasta in see-through plastic or glass containers so you can instantly see how much you have on hand. These look pretty in your cupboard, too, and will keep you motivated to stay organized.

Open-Faced Roast Beef Sandwich Bites

SERVES 4

3 tablespoons bottled horseradish, drained

3 tablespoons fat-free mayonnaise

20 slices cocktail (party-style) rye bread, toasted

5 (1-ounce) slices lean roast beef, each cut into 4 pieces

10 cherry tomatoes, halved

1. Stir together horseradish and mayonnaise in small bowl. Spread horseradish mayonnaise evenly over slices of toast.
2. Place 1 piece of roast beef on each slice of toast. Thread party toothpick through each tomato half and insert toothpick into each sandwich.

PER SERVING (5 sandwiches): 153 Cal, 3 g Total Fat, 1 g Sat Fat, 0 g Trans Fat, 19 mg Chol, 725 mg Sod, 22 g Total Carb, 3 g Fib, 11 g Prot, 38 mg Calc.

PointsPlus value: ***4.***

15 minute meals

Turkey and Roasted Pepper Lettuce Wraps

SERVES 8

8 green leaf lettuce leaves

8 (1-ounce) slices deli roast turkey breast

8 (¾-ounce) slices Swiss cheese

2 tablespoons coarse-grain Dijon mustard

1 (12-ounce) jar roasted red pepper (not packed in oil), drained and cut into strips

1. Lay out lettuce leaves on work surface. Layer 1 slice of turkey and 1 slice of Swiss on each lettuce leaf. Spread evenly with mustard and top evenly with roasted red pepper.
2. Fold in two opposite sides of filled lettuce leaf, then roll up to enclose filling. Secure with toothpick. Repeat to make total of 8 rolls.

PER SERVING (1 roll): 137 Cal, 6 g Total Fat, 4 g Sat Fat, 0 g Trans Fat, 44 mg Chol, 270 mg Sod, 4 g Total Carb, 1 g Fib, 15 g Prot, 187 mg Calc.

PointsPlus value: ***3.***

Vanilla Yogurt Sundae

SERVES 1

1 (½-cup) scoop frozen vanilla fat-free yogurt

1 tablespoon toasted wheat germ

1 tablespoon chopped walnuts

2 tablespoons thawed frozen fat-free whipped topping

1 fresh sweet cherry or maraschino cherry

Place yogurt in dessert dish. Top with wheat germ, walnuts, whipped topping, and cherry.

PER SERVING (1 sundae): 181 Cal, 6 g Total Fat, 1 g Sat Fat, 0 g Trans Fat, 2 mg Chol, 65 mg Sod, 26 g Total Carb, 2 g Fib, 8 g Prot, 179 mg Calc.

PointsPlus value: ***5.***

Mixed Melon with Honeyed Ricotta

SERVES 4

2 cups fat-free ricotta cheese

1 tablespoon plus 1 teaspoon honey

2 teaspoons vanilla extract

¼ teaspoon ground nutmeg

4 cups cubed cantaloupe

4 cups cubed honeydew

4 cups cubed watermelon

¼ cup toasted wheat germ

1. Stir together ricotta, honey, vanilla, and nutmeg in medium bowl. Toss together cantaloupe, honeydew, and watermelon in large bowl; divide evenly among 4 dessert dishes.
2. Spoon ricotta mixture evenly over fruit and sprinkle evenly with wheat germ.

PER SERVING (3 cups melon cubes, ½ cup ricotta mixture, and 1 tablespoon wheat germ): 211 Cal, 1 g Total Fat, 0 g Sat Fat, 0 g Trans Fat, 8 mg Chol, 101 mg Sod, 38 g Total Carb, 3 g Fib, 14 g Prot, 159 mg Calc.

PointsPlus value: **5.**

Honeydew-Strawberry Soup

SERVES 4

8 cups cubed chilled honeydew

1 teaspoon grated lime zest

2 tablespoons fresh lime juice

2 teaspoons sugar

1 cup sliced strawberries

2 tablespoons sliced fresh mint

1. Puree honeydew in blender or food processor. Pour puree into large bowl and stir in lime zest and juice and sugar.
2. Ladle soup evenly into each of 4 chilled bowls. Top evenly with strawberries and sprinkle with mint.

PER SERVING (1 cup): 92 Cal, 0 g Total Fat, 0 g Sat Fat, 0 g Trans Fat, 0 mg Chol, 11 mg Sod, 30 g Total Carb, 2 g Fib, 1 g Prot, 27 mg Calc.

PointsPlus value: **3.**

Cook's Note

Use leftover mint from this recipe to add refreshing flavor to green salads, stir-fries, or iced tea.

15 minute meals

Pineapple Crush Smoothies

SERVES 3

1 ripe banana, peeled and cut into chunks

1 (8-ounce) can crushed pineapple in juice

½ cup plain low-fat yogurt

½ cup fresh orange juice

1 tablespoon honey

5 ice cubes

Combine all ingredients in blender and process until smooth. Pour into 3 tall glasses.

PER SERVING (1 cup): 148 Cal, 1 g Fat, 0 g Sat Fat, 0 g Trans Fat, 3 mg Chol, 30 mg Sod, 35 g Total Carb, 2 g Fib, 3 g Prot, 90 mg Calc.

PointsPlus value: ***4.***

Do it Faster

If you have any leftover smoothie, pour it into a popsicle mold or a small paper cup and freeze for a healthful treat another day.

Strawberry Colada Cooler

SERVES 1

½ cup halved strawberries

½ cup fresh pineapple chunks

½ cup fat-free milk

½ cup vanilla low-fat yogurt

¼ cup light (reduced-fat) coconut milk

2 ice cubes

Combine all ingredients in blender and process until smooth. Pour into tall glass.

PER SERVING (1 smoothie): 235 Cal, 4 g Total Fat, 2 g Sat Fat, 0 g Trans Fat, 5 mg Chol, 145 mg Sod, 44 g Total Carb, 3 g Fib, 9 g Prot, 332 mg Calc.

PointsPlus value: **6.**

Do it Faster

To quickly remove the hulls of strawberries, use the pointed end of a vegetable peeler, or cut them away with a small paring knife.

20
minute meals

20 Minute Breakfasts

20 Minute Lunches

20 Minute Dinners

20 Minute Snacks and Sweets

Corn and Green Chile Frittata

SERVES 4

6 large eggs

1 cup frozen corn kernels, thawed

1 (4½-ounce) can chopped mild green chiles, drained

¼ cup fat-free milk

2 teaspoons chopped fresh thyme or ½ teaspoon dried

½ teaspoon salt

¼ teaspoon black pepper

3 dashes hot pepper sauce

½ teaspoon canola oil

12 yellow or red cherry tomatoes, halved

1. Whisk together eggs, corn, chiles, milk, thyme, salt, pepper, and pepper sauce in large bowl.
2. Coat medium nonstick skillet with oil and set over medium heat. Add egg mixture and sprinkle with tomatoes. Cover and cook until eggs are set, about 10 minutes. Cut frittata into 4 wedges. Serve hot, warm, or at room temperature.

PER SERVING (1 wedge): 168 Cal, 8 g Total Fat, 3 g Sat Fat, 0 g Trans Fat, 318 mg Chol, 493 mg Sod, 12 g Total Carb, 2 g Fib, 12 g Prot, 74 mg Calc.

PointsPlus value: *4.*

Cook's Note

Half of a toasted whole wheat English muffin makes a crispy partner for the frittata (½ of a whole wheat English muffin per serving will increase the ***PointsPlus*** value by ***2***).

Corn and Green Chile Frittata

Frittata Italiana

SERVES 4

2 teaspoons olive oil

2½ cups fat-free egg substitute

⅛ teaspoon black pepper

1 large tomato, chopped

4 scallions, sliced

2 cups shredded fat-free mozzarella cheese

2 tablespoons grated Parmesan cheese

¼ cup chopped fresh basil

1. Heat oil in large nonstick skillet over medium heat. Add egg substitute and pepper. Cook until eggs are almost set, about 3 minutes, lifting edges frequently with heatproof rubber spatula to allow uncooked egg to flow underneath.
2. Sprinkle eggs with tomato, scallions, and mozzarella. Cover skillet. Reduce heat to low and cook until cheese is melted and eggs are set, about 3 minutes longer.
3. Sprinkle frittata with Parmesan and basil. Cut into 4 wedges. Serve hot, warm, or at room temperature.

PER SERVING (1 wedge): 216 Cal, 4 g Total Fat, 1 g Sat Fat, 0 g Trans Fat, 11 mg Chol, 963 mg Sod, 13 g Total Carb, 2 g Fib, 31 g Prot, 749 mg Calc.

PointsPlus value: **5.**

Do it Faster

Desperate for a superfast dinner idea? Quick egg dishes such as this frittata make fast, filling evening meals, too.

Bell Pepper and Sun-Dried Tomato Omelette

SERVES 2

6 sun-dried tomato halves (not packed in oil)

3 large egg whites

2 large eggs

¼ teaspoon salt

⅛ teaspoon black pepper

2 teaspoons olive oil

¼ cup thinly sliced red onion

¼ cup diced bell pepper

1 garlic clove, minced

1. Place sun-dried tomatoes in bowl and add boiling water to cover by 1 inch. Let stand 5 minutes; drain and cut into thin slices.
2. Meanwhile, whisk together egg whites, eggs, salt, and black pepper in separate bowl.
3. Heat 1 teaspoon of oil in 10-inch nonstick skillet over medium heat. Add sun-dried tomatoes, onion, bell pepper, and garlic; cook, stirring occasionally, until vegetables soften, 4–5 minutes. Transfer vegetables to bowl and set aside.
4. Wipe out skillet and return it to medium heat. Add remaining 1 teaspoon oil. Pour in egg mixture and cook, stirring gently, until underside is set, about 1 minute. Spread bell pepper mixture evenly over half of omelette; with spatula, fold other half over filling. Continue to cook until filling is heated through and eggs are set, 1–2 minutes longer. Cut omelette in half and slide each half onto plate.

PER SERVING (½ omelette): 181 Cal, 10 g Total Fat, 2 g Sat Fat, 0 g Trans Fat, 212 mg Chol, 653 mg Sod, 9 g Total Carb, 2 g Fib, 14 g Prot, 50 mg Calc.

PointsPlus value: **5.**

Cook's Note

Try a plain toasted bagel flat with the omelette (1 plain toasted bagel flat per serving will increase the ***PointsPlus*** value by ***3***).

Pea, Mushroom, and Cherry Tomato Frittata

Cottage Cheese Pancakes

SERVES 6

- 1 cup low-fat cottage cheese
- 1 cup vanilla low-fat yogurt
- 3 large eggs
- 1 teaspoon vanilla extract
- 1 cup all-purpose flour
- ⅓ cup whole wheat flour
- 1 tablespoon sugar
- ¼ teaspoon salt

1. Whisk cottage cheese, yogurt, eggs, and vanilla together in large bowl. Stir in all-purpose flour, whole wheat flour, sugar, and salt.
2. Spray large skillet or griddle with nonstick spray and heat over medium heat. Pour batter by ¼-cup measures onto griddle. Cook until small bubbles just begin to appear on top of pancakes and they are golden brown underneath, about 2 minutes. Flip and cook until second side has browned, about 2 minutes longer.

PER SERVING (2 pancakes): 207 Cal, 4 g Total Fat, 1 g Sat Fat, 0 g Trans Fat, 110 mg Chol, 309 mg Sod, 30 g Total Carb, 1 g Fib, 13 g Prot, 111 mg Calc.

PointsPlus value: **5.**

Cook's Note

If you have leftover pancakes, place them on a wire rack and let cool completely. Stack the pancakes with a sheet of wax paper between each one and place in a heavy zip-close plastic bag. Freeze for up to 3 months. To reheat, wrap two p [illegible] paper towel and microwave on High for 20–30 seconds.

20 minute meals

Breakfast Bruschetta

SERVES 2

1 teaspoon olive oil

1 green bell pepper, chopped

½ onion, chopped

1 carrot, shredded

1 garlic clove, minced

1¼ cups fat-free egg substitute

¼ teaspoon salt

⅛ teaspoon black pepper

2 slices reduced-calorie whole-grain bread, toasted

1. Heat oil in medium nonstick skillet over medium heat. Add bell pepper, onion, carrot, and garlic; cook, stirring frequently, until vegetables are softened, about 5 minutes.
2. Stir in egg substitute, salt, and black pepper. Cook, stirring, just until egg is set. Spoon half of egg on top of each slice of toast.

PER SERVING (1 bruschetta): 186 Cal, 3 g Total Fat, 1 g Sat Fat, 0 g Trans Fat, 0 mg Chol, 716 mg Sod, 21 g Total Carb, 5 g Fib, 19 g Prot, 300 mg Calc.

PointsPlus value: ***4.***

Cook's Note

Add fresh cantaloupe slices to make this a colorful and filling meal.

Breakfast Bruschetta

Quick Quesadillas

SERVES 4

4 (8-inch) whole wheat tortillas

4 thin slices prosciutto

4 thin slices pepper Jack cheese

4 scallions, thinly sliced

¼ cup chopped fresh cilantro

¼ cup fat-free salsa

1. Spray large skillet with nonstick spray and place over medium-high heat.
2. Place tortilla on counter and cover with one fourth of prosciutto and pepper Jack. Sprinkle bottom half with one-fourth of scallions and cilantro. Fold tortilla in half, covering fillings. Repeat with remaining tortillas, prosciutto, pepper Jack, scallions, and cilantro.
3. Place 2 quesadillas in pan and cook, turning once, until tortillas are browned and cheese has melted, about 3 minutes. Repeat with remaining quesadillas. Cut each quesadilla into 3 wedges and serve with salsa on side.

PER SERVING (1 quesadilla and 1 tablespoon salsa): 165 Cal, 7 g Total Fat, 3 g Sat Fat, 0 g Trans Fat, 25 mg Chol, 592 mg Sod, 22 g Total Carb, 3 g Fib, 11 g Prot, 130 mg Calc.

PointsPlus value: **5.**

Do it Faster

Quesadillas are a superquick lunch or light dinner option for weeknights—and both kids and adults love them!

Pan Bagnat

SERVES 4

3 tablespoons red-wine vinegar

3 tablespoons chopped fresh parsley

2 tablespoons reduced-sodium chicken broth

1 tablespoon olive oil

1 garlic clove, minced

¼ teaspoon black pepper

1 (8-ounce) loaf Italian bread

2 (5-ounce) cans chunk light tuna packed in water, drained and flaked

1 small red onion, thinly sliced

2 ripe tomatoes, thinly sliced

4 radishes, thinly sliced

¼ cup pitted Niçoise olives

1. To make dressing, whisk together vinegar, parsley, broth, oil, garlic, and pepper in small bowl.
2. Using serrated knife, split bread loaf in half lengthwise, making bottom of loaf slightly thicker than top. Use your fingers to pull out and discard some of soft interior of bread. Brush inside of loaf with half of dressing.
3. Cover bottom section of bread with tuna, onion, tomatoes, radishes, and olives and drizzle with remaining dressing. Cover with bread top and cut into 4 sandwiches.

PER SERVING (1 sandwich): 254 Cal, 7 g Total Fat, 1 g Sat Fat, 0 g Trans Fat, 19 mg Chol, 559 mg Sod, 27 g Total Carb, 3 g Fib, 21 g Prot, 67 mg Calc.

PointsPlus value: **6.**

Cook's Note

These sandwiches can be eaten immediately or wrapped tightly and chilled for up to 6 hours, so they're perfect for packing for lunch or taking on a picnic.

Chicken and Tzatziki–Stuffed Pitas

Chicken and Tzatziki-Stuffed Pitas

SERVES 2

¾ cup plain fat-free yogurt

⅓ cup shredded cucumber

1 small garlic clove, minced

⅛ teaspoon black pepper

2 (7-inch) whole wheat pitas, halved

1½ cups shredded cooked chicken breast

1 large tomato, cut into 8 slices

4 small romaine lettuce leaves

¼ cup crumbled fat-free feta cheese

1. Stir together yogurt, cucumber, garlic, and pepper in small bowl.
2. Cut each pita in half. Spread half of yogurt mixture inside pitas. Layer chicken, tomato, lettuce, and feta evenly inside pitas. Top with remaining yogurt mixture

PER SERVING (1 sandwich): 464 Cal, 6 g Total Fat, 2 g Sat Fat, 0 g Trans Fat, 88 mg Chol, 783 mg Sod, 54 g Total Carb, 8 g Fib, 48 g Prot, 280 mg Calc.

PointsPlus value: ***11.***

Do it Faster

To make this recipe fuss free, use purchased rotisserie chicken.

9 rules for shortcut cooking

When time is short on busy weeknights, you can still prepare a fresh homemade meal for your family if you follow these rules:

PLAN YOUR MEALS FOR THE WEEK. Jot down a bare-bones menu for every night you'll make dinner for the week. With a plan as simple as "steak fajitas and rice," "spaghetti with meat sauce and salad," and "sautéed chicken, couscous, and green beans" you can organize recipes and create a shopping list in just a few minutes.

KEEP MENUS TO TWO OR THREE SIMPLE ITEMS. Don't try to do too much or get too fancy. Your family will enjoy a quickly prepared homemade meal that's as simple as baked pork chops, mashed potatoes, and salad (from pre-washed greens, of course). Keep seasonings as simple as salt and pepper with a dash of grated lemon zest, minced garlic, or a sprinkle of fresh or dried herbs.

KEEP A WELL-STOCKED FREEZER. Always keep a stash of quick-cooking staples such as boneless skinless chicken breasts, ground beef, and fish fillets on hand for pulling a fast meal together from ingredients you have on hand. Use the defrost setting on the microwave to thaw foods quickly before cooking.

ASSEMBLE INGREDIENTS AND EQUIPMENT BEFORE COOKING. Before you begin to cook, gather the ingredients you need, the measuring cups and spoons, and pots and pans you'll need to prepare the meal. Use pots and pans that look good enough to go straight from oven to table. Once everything is out on the counter or stovetop, you can focus on getting the meal prepared without the distraction of searching for needed items.

START LONG-COOKING FOODS FIRST. For instance, get pasta water on to boil or rice on to cook before you begin what you'll serve with it. Then, start on a pasta sauce or chicken stir-fry.

CLEAN UP AS YOU GO. Keep a trash bowl nearby. If you're preparing a meal that requires peeling and chopping fruits or vegetables, take a tip from chefs and keep a small bowl near the cutting board for peelings, trimmings, and cores. You'll save trips to the trash can and then you can discard all the debris at once.

MULTITASK. If you're waiting on a sauce to simmer or a chop to broil, make a green salad to serve with the meal, cut up some fruit to enjoy for dessert, put dirty dishes in the dishwasher, wipe down kitchen counters, put away any appliances you've used.

ENLIST HELP. Get your spouse and children to help with the meal. When it's crunch time, the smallest task can be helpful. Setting the table, getting out bread or rolls, tossing a salad, or putting away ingredients can shave minutes off your kitchen time.

MAKE WEEKEND COOKING COUNT. Make food in big batches on the weekend to refrigerate or freeze for effortless meals later on. Chilis, soups, and stews freeze perfectly and will be a delicious welcome on nights when you don't have time to cook. Roast a chicken, turkey breast, beef or pork roast, or leg of lamb on the weekend and use the leftovers for another meal or two later in the week.

Pitas Stuffed with Tofu-Egg Salad

SERVES 4

1 (14-ounce) container reduced-fat firm tofu, drained

2 large hard-cooked eggs

1 celery stalk, chopped

1 carrot, shredded

2 tablespoons minced red onion

¼ cup fat-free mayonnaise

1 tablespoon white-wine vinegar

2 teaspoons Dijon mustard

½ teaspoon salt

½ teaspoon hot pepper sauce

4 (6-inch) whole wheat pita breads, halved

2 cups salad greens

1. Crumble tofu onto clean kitchen towel. Roll up towel and twist to remove as much liquid as possible. Mash eggs with fork in large bowl. Add tofu, celery, carrot, onion, mayonnaise, vinegar, mustard, salt, and pepper sauce and mix well.
2. Fill each pita half with ⅓ cup of salad and ¼ cup greens.

PER SERVING (2 filled pita halves): 297 Cal, 9 g Total Fat, 2 g Sat Fat, 0 g Trans Fat, 108 mg Chol, 830 mg Sod, 41 g Total Carb, 9 g Fib, 17 g Prot, 100 mg Calc.

PointsPlus value: **8.**

Cook's Note

You can make the salad up to 2 days ahead and store, refrigerated, for a quick lunch.

Clam and Corn Chowder

SERVES 4

2 (6½-ounce) cans chopped clams

1½ cups frozen corn kernels

¼ teaspoon hot pepper sauce

¼ teaspoon dried thyme

1 (14½-ounce) can reduced-sodium chicken broth

1 (14½-ounce) can sliced potatoes, rinsed and drained

½ cup frozen chopped onion, thawed

½ cup fat-free half-and-half

3 tablespoons chopped fresh parsley

1. Heat clams and their juice, corn, pepper sauce, and thyme in large saucepan over high heat.
2. Meanwhile, puree broth, potatoes, and onion in blender. Add to pot with clams and corn; bring to boil. Reduce heat and simmer, stirring occasionally, about 3 minutes. Stir in half-and-half and heat through. Remove from heat and stir in parsley.

PER SERVING (1½ cups): 190 Cal, 2 g Total Fat, 0 g Sat Fat, 0 g Trans Fat, 29 mg Chol, 501 mg Sod, 29 g Total Carb, 4 g Fib, 16 g Prot, 90 mg Calc.

PointsPlus value: ***5.***

Cook's Note

Rye bread makes a flavorful accompaniment to the creamy chowder (1 rye flat roll per serving will increase the ***PointsPlus*** value by ***3***).

Chickpea Soup

1. Puree broth with chickpeas, in batches, in blender.
2. Heat oil in large saucepan over medium heat. Add carrots, bell pepper, onion, and garlic; cook, stirring, until carrots are crisp-tender, about 5 minutes.
3. Stir in chickpea mixture, rosemary, salt, and black pepper. Stir in a little water if soup is too thick. Cook over medium heat until heated through, about 4 minutes. Serve sprinkled with parsley.

PER SERVING (about 1½ cups): 315 Cal, 6 g Total Fat, 1 g Sat Fat, 0 g Trans Fat, 0 mg Chol, 879 mg Sod, 49 g Total Carb, 11 g Fib, 18 g Prot, 124 mg Calc.

PointsPlus value: ***8.***

Cook's Note

Serve this Mediterranean-inspired soup with rosemary pita bread. Lightly spray a whole wheat pita bread with olive oil nonstick spray and sprinkle with fresh minced rosemary. Broil, turning once, until heated through, 2 minutes (one 1-ounce) whole wheat pita bread per serving will increase the ***PointsPlus*** value by ***2***).

SERVES 4

5 cups reduced-sodium chicken broth

2 (15½-ounce) cans chickpeas, rinsed and drained

2 teaspoons olive oil

2 carrots, thinly sliced

1 red bell pepper, chopped

1 onion, chopped

3 garlic cloves, minced

2 teaspoons fresh rosemary

¼ teaspoon salt

¼ teaspoon black pepper

2 tablespoons chopped fresh parsley

20 minute meals

Black Bean Soup with Rice

SERVES 4

2 teaspoons canola oil

1 onion, chopped

1 celery stalk, chopped

1 green bell pepper, chopped

2 garlic cloves, finely chopped

2 teaspoons chili powder

1½ teaspoons ground cumin

2 (15½-ounce) cans black beans, rinsed and drained

1 (14½-ounce) can reduced-sodium chicken broth or vegetable broth

1 tomato, chopped

¼ cup chopped fresh cilantro

2 cups hot cooked brown rice

1. Heat oil over medium heat in large saucepan. Add onion, celery, bell pepper, and garlic and cook, stirring occasionally, until softened, about 4 minutes. Add chili powder and cumin and cook 1 minute longer.
2. Add beans to saucepan and mash coarsely with potato masher or large fork. Add broth and tomato; increase heat to high and bring soup to boil. Stir in cilantro. Ladle evenly into 4 serving bowls and top with ½ cup rice.

PER SERVING (1½ cups soup and ½ cup rice): 296 Cal, 5 g Total Fat, 0 g Sat Fat, 0 g Trans Fat, 0 mg Chol, 568 mg Sod, 50 g Total Carb, 12 g Fib, 13 g Prot, 84 mg Calc.

PointsPlus value: *7.*

Cook's Note

To preserve fresh cilantro and other herbs, chop them, place in ice cube trays, cover with water, and freeze. Store the frozen cubes in a zip-close bag and pop them into recipes at the end of cooking. The small amount of water in the ice cube won't make a difference in your dish.

Ham and Macaroni Salad–Stuffed Bell Peppers

SERVES 4

1 cup whole wheat macaroni

⅓ cup fat-free mayonnaise

2 tablespoons apple-cider vinegar

¼ teaspoon black pepper

½ pound lean turkey ham, diced

1 (5-ounce) jar roasted red pepper, drained and chopped (not packed in oil)

4 scallions, thinly sliced

2 tablespoons sweet pickle relish

4 red bell peppers, halved lengthwise through stems and seeded

1. Cook macaroni according to package directions, omitting salt. Drain and rinse under cold running water; drain again.
2. Transfer macaroni to large bowl. Add mayonnaise, vinegar, and black pepper; toss to coat. Add turkey ham, roasted red peppers, scallions, and relish; toss to combine.
3. Spoon salad evenly into bell pepper halves.

PER SERVING (2 stuffed pepper halves): 256 Cal, 4 g Total Fat, 1 g Sat Fat, 0 g Trans Fat, 43 mg Chol, 927 mg Sod, 40 g Total Carb, 6 g Fib, 16 g Prot, 42 mg Calc.

PointsPlus value: **6.**

Cook's Note

When you cook the macaroni for this salad, make extra and use it instead of rigatoni to prepare Vegetable Minestrone with Pasta, page 315, on the weekend.

Chicken and Napa Cabbage Salad

SERVES 4

- **2 tablespoons fresh lime juice**
- **2 teaspoons Asian (dark) sesame oil**
- **½ teaspoon salt**
- **¼ teaspoon black pepper**
- **5 cups thinly sliced Napa cabbage**
- **2 cups shredded, cooked skinless chicken breast**
- **1 cup matchstick-cut carrots**
- **1 green bell pepper, thinly sliced**
- **2 scallions, thinly sliced on diagonal**

1. Whisk together lime juice, sesame oil, salt, and black pepper in large serving bowl.
2. Add cabbage, chicken, carrots, bell pepper, and scallions and toss to coat.

PER SERVING (about 2 cups): 173 Cal, 6 g Total Fat, 1 g Sat Fat, 0 g Trans Fat, 57 mg Chol, 653 mg Sod, 8 g Total Carb, 3 g Fib, 23 g Prot, 121 mg Calc.

PointsPlus value: ***4.***

Do it Faster

Wondering what all those blades that came with your food processor actually do? One of them will probably cut matchstick carrots for this recipe in seconds.

Chicken and Napa Cabbage Salad

Gingery Turkey-Couscous Salad

SERVES 2

½ cup whole wheat couscous

5 teaspoons unseasoned rice vinegar

5 teaspoons reduced-sodium soy sauce

1 garlic clove, minced

2 teaspoons minced peeled fresh ginger

1½ cups shredded, cooked, skinless turkey breast

1½ cups small broccoli florets

1 large red bell pepper, cut into ½-inch pieces

3 scallions, thinly sliced

¼ cup chopped fresh cilantro

1. Prepare couscous according to package directions, omitting fat and salt if desired. Transfer to shallow bowl to cool.
2. Meanwhile, whisk together vinegar, soy sauce, garlic, and ginger in serving bowl. Add couscous, turkey, broccoli, bell pepper, scallions, and cilantro and toss to coat.

PER SERVING (2 cups): 357 Cal, 8 g Total Fat, 2 g Sat Fat, 0 g Trans Fat, 86 mg Chol, 279 mg Sod, 34 g Total Carb, 8 g Fib, 39 g Prot, 93 mg Calc.

PointsPlus value: **9.**

Smoked Turkey, Carrot, and Raisin Salad

SERVES 4

⅓ cup light mayonnaise

1 teaspoon grated lemon zest

1 tablespoon fresh lemon juice

½ teaspoon salt

⅛ teaspoon black pepper

1 (6-ounce) piece cooked smoked turkey breast, diced

6 carrots, shredded (about 3 cups)

⅓ cup dark raisins

8 cups lightly packed baby romaine

¼ cup coarsely chopped unsalted peanuts

1. To make dressing, whisk together mayonnaise, lemon zest and juice, salt, and pepper in large bowl.
2. Add turkey, carrots, and raisins to dressing; toss to coat.
3. Divide romaine evenly among 4 plates. Top with turkey mixture and sprinkle evenly with peanuts.

PER SERVING (about 3 cups): 199 Cal, 9 g Total Fat, 2 g Sat Fat, 0 g Trans Fat, 28 mg Chol, 696 mg Sod, 22 g Total Carb, 4 g Fib, 10 g Prot, 75 mg Calc.

PointsPlus value: **5.**

Cook's Note

To add more color and crunch, add 1 diced red or green apple to the salad.

Light and Luscious
Cobb Salad

Light and Luscious Cobb Salad

SERVES 4

3 tablespoons sherry vinegar

2 teaspoons olive oil

¼ teaspoon salt

¼ teaspoon black pepper

6 cups lightly packed torn romaine lettuce

2 cups diced cooked turkey breast

2 large tomatoes, diced

½ avocado, halved, pitted, peeled, and diced

2 large hard-cooked egg whites, chopped

6 slices turkey bacon, crisp-cooked and coarsely crumbled

¼ cup crumbled blue cheese

1. To make dressing, whisk together vinegar, oil, salt, and pepper in small bowl.
2. Spread lettuce on platter. Arrange turkey, tomatoes, and avocado in rows on top of lettuce. Sprinkle with egg whites, bacon, and blue cheese. Serve dressing on side.

PER SERVING (about 1½ cups): 292 Cal, 14 g Total Fat, 4 g Sat Fat, 0 g Trans Fat, 85 mg Chol, 939 mg Sod, 8 g Total Carb, 4 g Fib, 32 g Prot, 94 mg Calc.

PointsPlus value: *7.*

Cook's Note

To save the other half of the avocado, drizzle it with lemon juice, wrap in plastic wrap, and refrigerate for up to 3 days. If the exposed flesh does darken, just cut away a thin layer to reveal the bright green avocado below.

Salmon with Corn, Black Bean, and Tomato Salad

SERVES 6

2 tablespoons fresh lime juice

1 teaspoon olive oil

1 teaspoon salt

¼ teaspoon black pepper

1 (15½-ounce) can black beans, rinsed and drained

2 cups drained canned corn kernels

1 large tomato, diced

½ small red onion, finely chopped

½ cup coarsely chopped fresh cilantro

1 jalapeño pepper, seeded and minced

6 large Boston lettuce leaves

6 (3-ounce) prepared poached salmon fillets

1. To make dressing, whisk together lime juice, oil, salt, and black pepper in large bowl.
2. Add beans, corn, tomato, onion, cilantro, and jalapeño pepper to dressing; toss to coat.
3. Divide lettuce among 6 plates; top with salmon. Spoon bean salad alongside fish.

PER SERVING (1 salmon fillet and about 1¼ cups salad): 311 Cal, 9 g Total Fat, 2 g Sat Fat, 0 g Trans Fat, 83 mg Chol, 635 mg Sod, 26 g Total Carb, 7 g Fib, 33 g Prot, 61 mg Calc.

PointsPlus value: **8.**

Cook's Note

To poach salmon, bring 2 cups of reduced-sodium chicken broth to a simmer in a large skillet. Add 6 (4-ounce) skinless salmon fillets to the broth. Cover and simmer until the salmon is just opaque, 4 to 5 minutes. Serve the salmon warm, at room temperature, or chilled.

Tuna-Potato Salad

1. To make dressing, whisk together mayonnaise, salt, and pepper in large bowl.
2. Add tuna, potatoes, and shallots to dressing and stir to combine well.
3. Divide salad greens evenly among 4 plates. Top evenly with tuna-potato mixture. Serve with lemon wedges.

PER SERVING (1¼ cups): 208 Cal, 1 g Total Fat, 0 g Sat Fat, 0 g Trans Fat, 21 mg Chol, 706 mg Sod, 29 g Total Carb, 4 g Fib, 20 g Prot, 49 mg Calc.

PointsPlus value: **5.**

Cook's Note

To add more delicious veggies to the salad, surround each one with cucumber and plum tomato slices.

SERVES 4

¼ cup fat-free mayonnaise

¼ teaspoon salt

¼ teaspoon black pepper

2 (5-ounce) cans chunk light tuna packed in water, drained and flaked

1 pound packaged cooked diced potatoes

2 large shallots, finely chopped

4 cups mixed baby salad greens

Lemon wedges

20 minute meals

Tuna and White Bean Salad

SERVES 4

½ cup reduced-sodium chicken broth

2 teaspoons olive oil

Grated zest and juice of 1 lemon

½ teaspoon salt

¼ teaspoon black pepper

6 cups torn frisée lettuce

2 different colored bell peppers, chopped

1 large tomato, chopped

3 scallions, thinly sliced

2 (5-ounce) cans chunk light tuna packed in water, drained and flaked

1 (15½-ounce) can cannellini (white kidney) beans, rinsed and drained

1. To make dressing, whisk together broth, oil, lemon zest and juice, salt, and black pepper in serving bowl.
2. Add frisée, bell peppers, tomato, scallions, tuna, and beans to dressing and toss to coat.

PER SERVING (generous 2 cups): 235 Cal, 4 g Total Fat, 1 g Sat Fat, 0 g Trans Fat, 19 mg Chol, 749 mg Sod, 27 g Total Carb, 8 g Fib, 25 g Prot, 82 mg Calc.

PointsPlus value: **6.**

Cook's Note

For a satisfying finish to lunch, enjoy a piece of fresh fruit and a cup of herbal tea for dessert.

Tuna and White Bean Salad

Shrimp Salad with Fennel,
Red Onion, and Orange

Shrimp Salad with Fennel, Red Onion, and Orange

SERVES 4

1 tablespoon fresh lemon juice

2 teaspoons olive oil

½ teaspoon salt

¼ teaspoon black pepper

1¼ pounds cooked, peeled, and deveined medium shrimp

2 large navel oranges, peeled and cut into ¾-inch pieces

1 fennel bulb, trimmed and very thinly sliced

½ small red onion, thinly sliced

12 pitted Kalamata olives

1. To make dressing, whisk together lemon juice, oil, salt, and pepper in serving bowl.
2. Add shrimp, oranges, fennel, onion, and olives and toss to coat.

PER SERVING (about 2 cups): 241 Cal, 5 g Total Fat, 1 g Sat Fat, 0 g Trans Fat, 276 mg Chol, 759 mg Sod, 17 g Total Carb, 5 g Fib, 31 g Prot, 136 mg Calc.

PointsPlus value: **6.**

Cook's Note

Don't be tempted to make this salad ahead. The acid from the lemon juice will cause the shrimp to become rubbery and tough.

20 minute meals

Curried Tuna Salad

SERVES 2

- 1 (5-ounce) can chunk light tuna packed in water, drained and flaked
- 1 celery stalk, chopped
- 2 tablespoons chopped fresh cilantro
- 1 shallot, chopped
- 2 tablespoons golden raisins, chopped
- 2 tablespoons fat-free mayonnaise
- 1 teaspoon curry powder
- 4 red leaf lettuce leaves
- 2 hard-cooked large eggs, peeled and sliced

1. Toss together tuna, celery, cilantro, shallot, raisins, mayonnaise, and curry powder in small bowl.
2. Divide lettuce evenly between 2 plates. Mound tuna salad evenly on lettuce and surround with eggs.

PER SERVING (2 lettuce leaves, ½ cup tuna salad, and 1 egg): 212 Cal, 7 g Total Fat, 2 g Sat Fat, 0 g Trans Fat, 207 mg Chol, 428 mg Sod, 14 g Total Carb, 2 g Fib, 24 g Prot, 67 mg Calc.

PointsPlus value: ***5.***

Cook's Note

To quickly add more flavor to this tuna salad, stir in a teaspoon of grated lime zest.

White Bean Salad with Feta-Pita Crisps

20 minute meals

1. Preheat broiler. Line baking sheet with foil.
2. Lay pitas on baking sheet and sprinkle evenly with feta. Broil 5 inches from heat until cheese is melted and pitas are crisp, about 3 minutes. Cut each pita into 6 wedges.
3. Meanwhile, toss together beans, bell pepper, onion, parsley, oil, lemon zest and juice, and black pepper in large bowl. Serve salad with pita wedges.

PER SERVING (1 cup salad and 6 pita wedges): 371 Cal, 7 g Total Fat, 2 g Sat Fat, 0 g Trans Fat, 10 mg Chol, 945 mg Sod, 62 g Total Carb, 11 g Fib, 19 g Prot, 208 mg Calc.

PointsPlus value: ***9.***

Cook's Note

To remove about 40 percent of the sodium in canned beans, always rinse and drain them before using in a recipe.

SERVES 4

4 (7-inch) whole wheat pitas

1 cup crumbled reduced-fat feta cheese

1 (15½-ounce) can Great Northern or other white beans, rinsed and drained

1 red or green bell pepper, chopped

½ small red onion, chopped

¼ cup chopped fresh parsley

2 teaspoons olive oil

Grated zest and juice of 1 lemon

¼ teaspoon black pepper

20 minute meals

Crab Salad–Stuffed Tomatoes

SERVES 2

- ⅓ cup orzo
- 2 large tomatoes
- 1 cup crabmeat, picked over for pieces of shell
- ⅓ cup chopped black or green olives
- 2 tablespoons crumbled reduced-fat feta cheese
- 2 tablespoons chopped fresh dill
- 2 teaspoons balsamic vinegar
- ⅛ teaspoon salt
- ⅛ teaspoon black pepper

1. Cook orzo according to package directions, omitting salt if desired. Drain and rinse under cold water; drain again.
2. Meanwhile, cut thin slice off tops of tomatoes; reserve tops. Using spoon, carefully scoop out seeds and pulp; reserve for another use.
3. Gently toss together crabmeat, olives, feta, dill, vinegar, salt, and pepper in medium bowl. Spoon crabmeat mixture evenly into tomato shells and cover with reserved tomato tops.

PER SERVING (1 stuffed tomato): 279 Cal, 10 g Total Fat, 2 g Sat Fat, 0 g Trans Fat, 67 mg Chol, 795 mg Sod, 30 g Total Carb, 2 g Fib, 19 g Prot, 130 mg Calc.

PointsPlus value: *7.*

Cook's Note

Scoop the seeds and pulp from the tomatoes into a storage container. Cover and freeze up to 4 months and toss them into a soup or stew.

Crab Salad–Stuffed Tomatoes

Maui Tortilla Pizzas

SERVES 4

4 (7-inch) whole wheat tortillas

¼ pound piece lean deli ham, diced

4 (1-ounce) slices reduced-fat Swiss cheese

½ red bell pepper, chopped

1 (8-ounce) can well-drained unsweetened pineapple chunks, chopped

3 tablespoons chopped macadamia nuts or almonds

1. Preheat oven to 400°F. Line baking sheet with foil.
2. Lay tortillas on baking sheet. Layer evenly with ham, Swiss, and bell pepper. Bake until cheese is melted and bubbling, about 10 minutes. Sprinkle evenly with pineapple and macadamia nuts.

PER SERVING (1 pizza): 226 Cal, 8 g Total Fat, 2 g Sat Fat, 0 g Trans Fat, 25 mg Chol, 493 mg Sod, 23 g Total Carb, 4 g Fib, 17 g Prot, 294 mg Calc.

PointsPlus value: ***6.***

Cook's Note

Because of their high fat content, nuts can become rancid quickly if stored at room temperature. To keep them fresh longer, place nuts in an airtight container and store in the freezer.

Steak Fajitas

SERVES 4

1 (1¼-pound) lean flank steak, trimmed

½ teaspoon salt

2 teaspoons canola oil

1 green bell pepper, thinly sliced

1 red bell pepper, thinly sliced

1 onion, thinly sliced

2 garlic cloves, minced

¼ teaspoon black pepper

4 (7-inch) whole wheat tortillas, warmed

2 tablespoons taco sauce

1. Spray ridged grill pan with nonstick spray and set over medium-high heat. Sprinkle steak with ¼ teaspoon of salt. Place steak in grill pan and cook until an instant-read thermometer inserted into side of steak registers 145°F for medium, about 5 minutes on each side.
2. Meanwhile, heat oil in large nonstick skillet over medium heat. Add bell peppers, onion, and garlic; sprinkle with remaining ¼ teaspoon salt and black pepper. Cook, stirring, until softened, about 8 minutes.
3. Transfer steak to cutting board and let stand 5 minutes. Cut steak across grain into 20 slices.
4. Lay tortillas on work surface and top evenly with steak and bell pepper mixture; drizzle with taco sauce. Fold tortillas in half.

PER SERVING (1 fajita): 375 Cal, 15 g Total Fat, 5 g Sat Fat, 2 g Trans Fat, 68 mg Chol, 542 mg Sod, 30 g Total Carb, 4 g Fib, 31 g Prot, 121 mg Calc.

PointsPlus value: ***10.***

Cook's Note

To get an accurate measure of the temperature of a steak or other thin cut of meat or poultry, insert the thermometer sideways into the food. Make sure beef, pork, and lamb reach at least 145°F, ground meats reach 160°F, and all poultry, including ground poultry, reaches 165°F.

Thai-Style Beef Salad

SERVES 4

- 3 teaspoons canola oil
- 2 (¼-pound) filet mignon steaks, trimmed
- ¼ cup fresh lime juice
- 2 teaspoons Asian fish sauce
- 2 teaspoons packed light brown sugar
- ¼ teaspoon red pepper flakes
- 3 cups mixed baby greens
- 1 cup fresh mint leaves
- 1 cup fresh cilantro leaves
- 1 cup thinly sliced cucumber
- ½ red onion, thinly sliced

1. Heat 2 teaspoons of oil in medium skillet over medium-high heat. Add beef and cook, turning once, until instant-read thermometer inserted into side of each steak registers 145°F for medium, 8–10 minutes. Transfer meat to cutting board and let stand 5 minutes.
2. Meanwhile, whisk together lime juice, fish sauce, sugar, red pepper flakes, and remaining 1 teaspoon oil in large bowl.
3. Just before serving, add greens, mint, cilantro, cucumber, and onion to bowl with dressing. Cut the steaks into ¼-inch-thick slices, then slice in half again lengthwise. Toss warm beef with salad.

PER SERVING (2 cups): 157 Cal, 8 g Fat, 2 g Sat Fat, 0 g Trans Fat, 25 mg Chol, 271 mg Sod, 8 g Total Carb, 2 g Fib, 15 g Prot, 54 mg Calc.

PointsPlus value: ***4.***

Orange Beef with Broccoli

1. Combine steak, soy sauce, garlic, ginger, and red pepper flakes in large shallow dish; toss to coat.
2. Heat large deep skillet or wok over high heat until drop of water sizzles in pan. Add oil and swirl to coat skillet. Add beef and stir-fry until lightly browned, about 3 minutes. Using slotted spoon, transfer beef to plate. Add broccoli and onion to skillet and stir-fry until broccoli is bright green, about 3 minutes.
3. Stir together orange zest and juice and cornstarch in small cup until smooth; add to skillet. Stir-fry until sauce thickens and bubbles, about 1 minute. Stir in beef and stir-fry until heated through, about 2 minutes longer.

PER SERVING (1¾ cups): 244 Cal, 7 g Total Fat, 2 g Sat Fat, 0 g Trans Fat, 73 mg Chol, 334 mg Sod, 13 g Total Carb, 3 g Fib, 33 g Prot, 60 mg Calc.

PointsPlus value: **6.**

Cook's Note

To quickly add more flavor to this stir-fry, stir in a handful of chopped fresh basil or cilantro just before serving.

SERVES 4

1 pound lean sirloin steak, trimmed and cut into thin strips

2 tablespoons reduced-sodium soy sauce

2 garlic cloves, minced

2 teaspoons minced peeled fresh ginger

⅛ teaspoon red pepper flakes

2 teaspoons canola oil

5 cups small broccoli florets

1 onion, thinly sliced

1 tablespoon grated orange zest

¼ cup fresh orange juice

1 teaspoon cornstarch

got 5 minutes?

Have a few moments to spare? Add a fast flourish to your meals with one of these speedy suggestions.

- Grate a little **orange zest** or **tangerine zest** over your morning oatmeal, pancakes, or French toast for a hit of bright flavor.
- Instead of eating your morning yogurt with a spoon, throw it in the blender with a few ice cubes and half a cup of chopped fruit for a **satisfying smoothie** you can enjoy with a straw.
- Stir a little **grated fresh ginger** into unsweetened applesauce or fruit preserves for a hint of exotic flavor.
- Slice or dice **fresh apples or pears** and add them to a sandwich or salad for natural sweetness and crunch.
- Toss a handful of **fresh whole basil, mint, or parsley leaves** into a green salad to add a punch of fresh flavor.
- Thin **fat-free Greek yogurt** with a little water and drizzle it over bowls of soup or chili for a touch of richness and color contrast.
- Add a hint of deep, smoky flavor to baked or pan-seared meat, fish, or poultry with a sprinkle of **smoked paprika or smoked sea salt**.
- Chop parsley, garlic, and lemon zest together for a **quick gremolata** to use as a garnish for stews or roast meats.
- Finely chop a **hard-cooked egg white** and use it as a protein-rich topping for side dishes, salads, or soups.
- Sprinkle an **exotic spice blend** like za'atar, Berber seasoning, or Cajun spice on steamed vegetables or cooked whole grains to wake up their flavor.
- Use a vegetable peeler to make **long strips of raw carrot, zucchini, or yellow squash** to add color and texture to your next salad.
- Perk up bottled salad dressing with some **chopped fresh herbs and minced shallot**—it will taste almost as good as homemade.
- Add half a **diced onion and a bay leaf** to the water when you cook whole grains to give them pilaf-like flavor.
- Add a few **sliced strawberries and mint leaves** to glasses of seltzer for a refreshing accompaniment to meals or snacks.
- Split open a **pomegranate** and use the seeds as a crunchy, flavorful garnish for salads or desserts.
- Shave or grate a little antioxidant-rich **dark chocolate** over desserts, fruits, or yogurt and you'll have a healthful fix for a chocolate craving.

20 minute meals

Ginger Steak and Broccoli Stir-Fry

SERVES 2

2 teaspoons Asian (dark) sesame oil

10 ounces lean sirloin steak, trimmed and cut into thin strips

1 tablespoon minced peeled fresh ginger

2 garlic cloves, minced

2 cups small broccoli florets

4 scallions, cut into 1-inch lengths

1 tablespoon reduced-sodium soy sauce

½ teaspoon hot chili paste (optional)

1. Heat large deep skillet or wok over high heat until drop of water sizzles in pan. Add oil and swirl to coat skillet. Add steak and stir-fry until lightly browned, about 2 minutes. Transfer to plate.
2. Add ginger and garlic to skillet and stir-fry until fragrant, about 30 seconds. Add broccoli and scallions and stir-fry until just softened, about 2 minutes longer.
3. Return steak to skillet along with soy sauce and chili paste, if using. Stir-fry until beef is just cooked through, about 2 minutes longer.

PER SERVING (1½ cups): 262 Cal, 11 g Total Fat, 3 g Sat Fat, 1 g Trans Fat, 80 mg Chol, 400 mg Sod, 10 g Total Carb, 5 g Fib, 32 g Prot, 113 mg Calc.

PointsPlus value: **6.**

Cook's Note

To easily cut the steak into thin strips, put it in the freezer for about 30 minutes before slicing.

20 minute meals

Summer Squash Stuffed with Beef and Olives

SERVES 4

2 large (½ pound) yellow summer squash

½ teaspoon salt

1½ teaspoons canola oil

¾ pound lean ground beef (7% fat or less)

½ cup frozen chopped onion

3 garlic cloves, chopped

½ teaspoon Italian seasoning

¼ cup chopped black olives

¼ cup fat-free sour cream

3 tablespoons plain dried bread crumbs

1. Cut each squash in half lengthwise. Using small spoon, scoop out and discard most of flesh, leaving ¼-inch border all around. Place squash halves on microwavable plate, sprinkle insides of squash with salt, and cover loosely with wax paper. Microwave on High until squash is very tender but still holds its shape, 2–3 minutes; set aside.
2. Meanwhile, preheat broiler and line baking sheet with foil.
3. Heat oil in large skillet over high heat. Add beef, onion, garlic, and Italian seasoning and cook, breaking meat up, until meat is no longer pink and vegetables are tender, about 4 minutes. Stir in olives, sour cream, and 2 tablespoons of bread crumbs and remove from heat.
4. Mound beef mixture into squash halves and sprinkle tops with remaining 1 tablespoon bread crumbs. Broil 5 inches from heat until tops are browned, about 2 minutes.

PER SERVING (1 stuffed squash half): 201 Cal, 8 g Total Fat, 3 g Sat Fat, 0 g Trans Fat, 49 mg Chol, 465 mg Sod, 13 g Total Carb, 2 g Fib, 19 g Prot, 75 mg Calc.

PointsPlus value: **5.**

Do it Faster

Italian seasoning is a time-saving herb blend to keep on hand. It contains oregano, thyme, and basil—all the herbs you would usually add to an Italian dish, but in one container.

Pork with Sweet Coconut-Peanut Sauce

SERVES 4

⅓ cup light (reduced-fat) coconut milk

⅓ cup reduced-sodium chicken broth

2 tablespoons peanut butter

1 tablespoon packed light brown sugar

2 teaspoons grated peeled fresh ginger

4 (¼-pound) lean boneless pork loin chops, trimmed

¼ teaspoon cayenne pepper

¼ teaspoon salt

1 tablespoon peanut or canola oil

3 scallions, thinly sliced

1. Combine coconut milk, broth, peanut butter, sugar, and ginger in small bowl and stir until smooth. Set aside.
2. Sprinkle pork with cayenne and salt. Heat oil in large nonstick skillet over medium heat. Add pork and cook, turning once, until an instant-read thermometer inserted into side of each chop registers 145°F, 6–8 minutes. Transfer pork to plate and cover loosely with foil to keep warm.
3. Add coconut milk mixture to same skillet; set over medium heat and cook, stirring, until sauce is slightly thickened, about 2 minutes. Pour over chops and sprinkle with scallions.

PER SERVING (1 chop and 2 tablespoons sauce): 290 Cal, 17 g Total Fat, 5 g Sat Fat, 0 g Trans Fat, 70 mg Chol, 288 mg Sod, 7 g Total Carb, 1 g Fib, 27 g Prot, 22 mg Calc.

PointsPlus value: **8.**

Cook's Note

Cayenne pepper adds spice to this dish, but if you're making it for young ones, you can omit it. This dish is also delicious made with skinless boneless chicken breasts instead of the pork chops.

Pork Chops with Ginger and Snow Peas

Pork Chops with Ginger and Snow Peas

SERVES 4

4 (5-ounce) lean bone-in pork loin chops, trimmed

¼ teaspoon salt

2 teaspoons canola oil

½ cup reduced-sodium chicken broth

2 tablespoons hoisin sauce

2 tablespoons matchstick-thin strips peeled fresh ginger

2 garlic cloves, sliced

2 teaspoons reduced-sodium soy sauce

1 teaspoon Asian (dark) sesame oil

1½ cups frozen snow peas, thawed

1 teaspoon toasted sesame seeds

1. Sprinkle pork with salt. Heat canola oil in large nonstick skillet over medium heat. Add pork and cook, turning once, until an instant-read thermometer inserted into side of each chop registers 145°F, 6–8 minutes. Transfer pork to plate and cover loosely with foil to keep warm.
2. Add broth, hoisin sauce, ginger, garlic, soy sauce, and sesame oil to same skillet. Cook, scraping up any browned bits from bottom of pan with wooden spoon, until mixture is slightly thickened, 2–3 minutes. Stir in snow peas and cook until heated through, 1 minute.
3. Sprinkle snow peas with sesame seeds and serve with chops.

PER SERVING (1 chop and ⅓ cup snow peas): 260 Cal, 13 g Total Fat, 3 g Sat Fat, 0 g Trans Fat, 70 mg Chol, 483 mg Sod, 9 g Total Carb, 2 g Fib, 27 g Prot, 36 mg Calc.

PointsPlus value: *7.*

Do it Faster

To quickly make matchstick-thin strips of peeled ginger, thinly slice a piece of ginger, keeping the slices in a neat stack. Then, cut the slices into thin strips.

Chicken Piccata

SERVES 4

2 tablespoons all-purpose flour

¾ teaspoon salt

¼ teaspoon black pepper

4 (¼-pound) thin-sliced skinless boneless chicken breasts

2 tablespoons unsalted butter

½ cup reduced-sodium chicken broth

¼ cup fresh lemon juice

1 tablespoon drained capers

2 tablespoons chopped fresh parsley

1. Combine flour, ½ teaspoon of salt, and ⅛ teaspoon of pepper in large bowl. Working one at a time, dip both sides of chicken into flour mixture and shake off excess. Place on large plate.
2. Melt 1 tablespoon of butter in large skillet over medium-high heat. Add chicken and cook until lightly browned and cooked through, 3–4 minutes on each side; transfer chicken to plate and cover to keep warm.
3. Add broth, lemon juice, and capers into skillet and bring to boil. Reduce heat and simmer until slightly reduced, about 2 minutes. Remove from heat, then swirl in parsley and remaining 1 tablespoon butter, ¼ teaspoon salt, and ⅛ teaspoon pepper. Pour sauce over chicken.

PER SERVING (1 piece chicken and 2 tablespoons sauce): 211 Cal, 9 g Total Fat, 5 g Sat Fat, 0 g Trans Fat, 84 mg Chol, 635 mg Sod, 4 g Total Carb, 0 g Fib, 26 g Prot, 22 mg Calc.

PointsPlus value: ***5.***

Cook's Note

Serve this classic quick dish with whole wheat angel hair pasta (½ cup cooked whole wheat angel hair pasta per serving will increase the ***PointsPlus*** value by ***2***).

Chicken in Coconut-Curry Sauce

SERVES 4

2 teaspoons olive oil

1 onion, diced

2 teaspoons curry powder

1 cup light (reduced-fat) coconut milk

1 (14½-ounce) can diced tomatoes

2 tablespoons tomato paste

1 pound skinless boneless chicken breast, cut into 1-inch cubes

¼ teaspoon salt

1 (5-ounce) bag baby spinach

1 cup frozen peas

1. Heat oil in large nonstick skillet over medium heat. Add onion and cook, stirring occasionally, until softened, about 4 minutes. Stir in curry powder. Add coconut milk, tomatoes, and tomato paste and bring to boil.

2. Add chicken and salt to skillet and cook until chicken is no longer pink in center, about 4 minutes. Add spinach and peas and cook until spinach is wilted and peas are tender, about 2 minutes.

PER SERVING (1½ cups): 272 Cal, 9 g Total Fat, 4 g Sat Fat, 0 g Trans Fat, 63 mg Chol, 440 mg Sod, 21 g Total Carb, 7 g Fib, 28 g Prot, 75 mg Calc.

PointsPlus value: *7.*

Cook's Note

Brown basmati rice is the perfect accompaniment to this quick curry dish. It takes about 50 minutes to cook, so make a batch on the weekend to serve with meals throughout the week (½ cup cooked brown basmati rice will increase the ***PointsPlus*** value by **3**).

Chicken Tikka with Cucumber Raita

SERVES 4

1 cup plain fat-free yogurt

Juice of ½ lemon

2 garlic cloves, peeled

1 tablespoon peeled minced fresh ginger

¾ teaspoon salt

½ teaspoon garam masala

½ teaspoon ground coriander

½ teaspoon ground turmeric

Pinch cayenne pepper

1¼ pounds skinless boneless chicken breasts, cut into 1-inch pieces

1 cucumber, finely diced

¼ cup chopped fresh mint

Pappadam or other flatbread, toasted (optional)

1. Preheat broiler. Line baking sheet with foil and spray foil with nonstick spray.
2. Stir together ⅓ cup of yogurt, lemon juice, garlic, ginger, ½ teaspoon of salt, garam masala, coriander, turmeric, and cayenne in large bowl; add chicken and toss to coat.
3. Thread chicken on 8 (12-inch) metal skewers. Place skewers on baking sheet. Broil 5 inches from heat until chicken is browned and cooked through, about 4 minutes on each side.
4. Meanwhile, to make raita, stir together remaining ⅔ cup yogurt, cucumber, mint, and remaining ¼ teaspoon salt in serving bowl. Serve raita with chicken and pappadam, if using.

PER SERVING (2 skewers and ⅓ cup raita without pappadam): 181 Cal, 3 g Total Fat, 1 g Sat Fat, 0 g Trans Fat, 79 mg Chol, 461 mg Sod, 6 g Total Carb, 1 g Fib, 31 g Prot, 90 mg Calc.

PointsPlus value: ***4.***

Cook's Note

Serve the chicken skewers arranged on a bed of brown rice (½ cup cooked brown rice per serving will increase the ***PointsPlus*** value by ***3***).

Chicken Tikka with Cucumber Raita

20 minute meals

Braised Bok Choy and Chicken with Soba Noodles

SERVES 4

1 (8-ounce) package soba noodles

1 pound skinless boneless chicken breast, thinly sliced

¼ teaspoon salt

4 scallions, sliced

1 tablespoon grated peeled fresh ginger

2 garlic cloves, minced

2 tablespoons hoisin sauce

8 heads baby bok choy, quartered

2 teaspoons Asian (dark) sesame oil

1. Cook noodles according to package directions; drain, reserving ½ cup of cooking liquid.
2. Meanwhile, spray large skillet with nonstick spray and set over medium heat. Sprinkle chicken with salt; add to skillet and cook, stirring frequently, until lightly browned, about 3 minutes. Add scallions, ginger, and garlic and cook, stirring occasionally, 1 minute. Stir in hoisin sauce. Add bok choy and ½ cup of pasta cooking liquid. Cover skillet and cook until bok choy is tender, 4 minutes.
3. Add noodles and oil to skillet and toss until combined.

PER SERVING (2 cups): 243 Cal, 6 g Total Fat, 1 g Sat Fat, 0 g Trans Fat, 63 mg Chol, 422 mg Sod, 20 g Total Carb, 4 g Fib, 29 g Prot, 183 mg Calc.

PointsPlus value: **6.**

Do it Faster

Soba noodles are thin buckwheat noodles that are a smart addition to your weeknight cooking rotation. They cook in about 5 minutes and are perfect for serving with stir-fries when you don't have cooked rice on hand.

Turkey Cutlets Milanese

SERVES 4

8 cups baby romaine

1 cup cherry tomatoes, halved

3 tablespoons fat-free balsamic dressing

½ teaspoon salt

½ teaspoon black pepper

1 large egg white

1 tablespoon fresh lemon juice

¼ cup yellow cornmeal

2 tablespoons grated Parmesan cheese

4 (¼-pound) turkey breast cutlets

4 teaspoons olive oil

1. Toss together romaine, tomatoes, dressing, ¼ teaspoon of salt, and ¼ teaspoon of pepper in large bowl; set aside.
2. Whisk together egg white and lemon juice in large shallow bowl. Mix together cornmeal, Parmesan, remaining ¼ teaspoon salt, and ¼ teaspoon pepper on sheet of wax paper.
3. Dip each cutlet into egg white mixture, then coat with cornmeal mixture, pressing lightly so it adheres.
4. Heat oil in large nonstick skillet over medium heat. Add cutlets and cook until browned and cooked through, about 3 minutes on each side.
5. Transfer cutlets to 4 plates; top evenly with salad.

PER SERVING (1 turkey cutlet and about 1½ cups salad): 251 Cal, 7 g Total Fat, 2 g Sat Fat, 0 g Trans Fat, 77 mg Chol, 570 mg Sod, 15 g Total Carb, 3 g Fib, 31 g Prot, 116 mg Calc.

PointsPlus value: **6.**

Turkey Cutlets with Orange Sauce

SERVES 4

2 teaspoons olive oil

4 (¼-pound) turkey breast cutlets

½ teaspoon salt

¼ teaspoon black pepper

1 shallot, minced

2 teaspoons grated orange zest

⅓ cup fresh orange juice

⅓ cup reduced-sodium chicken broth

1 tablespoon cornstarch

2 tablespoons chopped fresh chives

1. Heat oil in large skillet over medium-high heat. Sprinkle turkey with salt and pepper. Add cutlets to skillet and cook until lightly browned and cooked through, about 3 minutes on each side. Transfer to plate and cover to keep warm.
2. Reduce heat to medium and add shallot to skillet. Cook, stirring, until softened, about 2 minutes.
3. Whisk together orange zest and juice, broth, and cornstarch in cup until smooth. Add cornstarch mixture to skillet and cook, stirring, until sauce thickens and bubbles, about 1 minute.
4. Transfer turkey to 4 plates; drizzle evenly with sauce. Sprinkle with chives.

PER SERVING (1 turkey cutlet and 2½ tablespoons sauce): 166 Cal, 3 g Total Fat, 1 g Sat Fat, 0 g Trans Fat, 75 mg Chol, 347 mg Sod, 5 g Total Carb, 0 g Fib, 28 g Prot, 20 mg Calc.

PointsPlus value: **4.**

Cook's Note

If you don't have chives on hand, add some thinly sliced scallion tops to add color and flavor to this dish.

Mediterranean Turkey Burgers

SERVES 4

1 pound ground skinless turkey breast

¾ teaspoon dried oregano

¼ teaspoon black pepper

½ cup finely crumbled feta cheese

2 teaspoons olive oil

2 large whole wheat pitas, halved

1 (5-ounce) jar roasted red peppers, drained (not packed in oil)

2 cups mixed baby salad greens

1. Mix together turkey, oregano, and black pepper in large bowl. With damp hands, shape mixture into 8 thin patties.
2. Place 2 tablespoons of feta in middle of each of 4 patties. Top with remaining patties and pinch edges to enclose cheese and to seal patties.
3. Heat oil in large skillet over medium heat. Add burgers and cook until an instant-read thermometer inserted into side of burger (without touching cheese) registers 165°F, 5 minutes on each side.
4. Place each burger in pita half. Top evenly with roasted red pepper and salad greens.

PER SERVING (1 stuffed pita): 317 Cal, 8 g Total Fat, 4 g Sat Fat, 0 g Trans Fat, 91 mg Chol, 717 mg Sod, 25 g Total Carb, 3 g Fib, 34 g Prot, 139 mg Calc.

PointsPlus value: ***8.***

Cook's Note

The feta cheese should be in small crumbles for stuffing inside the burgers. This is easiest to do when the cheese is cold, so take it from the refrigerator and immediately break it into fine crumbles.

Cod with Tomato-Oregano Sauce

SERVES 4

2 teaspoons olive oil

2 scallions, chopped

1 garlic clove, minced

1 (14½-ounce) can diced tomatoes

¼ teaspoon dried oregano

1 (1½-pound) cod fillet, about 1 inch thick, cut into 4 pieces

½ teaspoon salt

¼ teaspoon black pepper

1. Stir together oil, scallions, and garlic in large shallow glass bowl or casserole dish. Cover with wax paper and microwave on High until fragrant, about 1 minute. Stir in tomatoes and oregano. Cover and microwave on High 3 minutes.
2. Spray shallow microwavable dish with nonstick spray. Place cod in dish in one layer. Sprinkle fish with salt and pepper. Cover dish with wax paper and microwave on High until fish is just opaque in center, about 6 minutes. Spoon tomato sauce over fish.

PER SERVING (1 fillet cod and ⅓ cup sauce): 194 Cal, 6 g Total Fat, 1 g Sat Fat, 0 g Trans Fat, 65 mg Chol, 614 mg Sod, 6 g Total Carb, 1 g Fib, 28 g Prot, 43 mg Calc.

PointsPlus value: ***5.***

Cook's Note

Serve the fish with a side of steamed green beans and some whole wheat orzo to soak up the flavorful tomato sauce (½ cup cooked whole wheat orzo per serving will increase the ***PointsPlus*** value by ***2***).

Cod with Tomato-Oregano Sauce

20 minute meals

Sweet-and-Spicy Salmon with Broccoli Slaw

SERVES 4

2 tablespoons packed light brown sugar

1 teaspoon five-spice powder

¼ teaspoon salt

4 (¼-pound) pieces skinless salmon fillet

2 tablespoons reduced-sodium soy sauce

2 tablespoons rice vinegar

2 teaspoons Asian (dark) sesame oil

1 (12-ounce) package broccoli slaw

¼ cup chopped fresh cilantro

3 scallions, thinly sliced

1. Preheat broiler. Spray broiler pan with nonstick spray and place about 6 inches from heat until pan is hot.
2. Meanwhile, stir together brown sugar, five-spice powder, and salt in small bowl. Sprinkle mixture over tops of salmon fillets.
3. Carefully place salmon fillets on hot broiler pan and broil until salmon is just opaque in center, about 7 minutes.
4. Meanwhile, whisk together soy sauce, vinegar, and oil in large bowl. Add broccoli slaw, cilantro, and scallions and toss to combine. Serve salmon with slaw.

PER SERVING (1 salmon fillet and 1 cup slaw): 224 Cal, 7 g Total Fat, 1 g Sat Fat, 0 g Trans Fat, 65 mg Chol, 561 mg Sod, 13 g Total Carb, 4 g Fib, 27 g Prot, 77 mg Calc.

PointsPlus value: **5.**

Cook's Note

A package of broccoli slaw or regular cabbage slaw is a great item to keep on hand for weeknight meals. You can, of course, use it to make slaw, but you can also quickly sauté it for a side dish, add some to a stir-fry, or use it as a crunchy sandwich topping.

Arctic Char with Cranberry Couscous

SERVES 4

1¼ cups water

1 cup whole wheat couscous

⅓ cup dried cranberries or cherries

1 teaspoon olive oil

1 teaspoon salt

¼ teaspoon black pepper

2 scallions, chopped

⅓ cup chopped fresh parsley

4 (¼-pound) arctic char fillets

1. Bring water to boil in medium saucepan. Stir in couscous, cranberries, oil, ½ teaspoon of salt, and pepper. Remove saucepan from heat. Cover and let stand 5 minutes, then fluff couscous mixture with fork. Spoon couscous mixture into serving bowl and stir in scallions and parsley.
2. Meanwhile, sprinkle arctic char with remaining ½ teaspoon salt. Spray large skillet with nonstick spray and set over medium-high heat. Add fish and cook until just opaque in center, about 3 minutes on each side. Serve with couscous.

PER SERVING (1 piece arctic char and scant 1 cup couscous): 317 Cal, 10 g Total Fat, 2 g Sat Fat, 0 g Trans Fat, 65 mg Chol, 657 mg Sod, 31 g Total Carb, 5 g Fib, 28 g Prot, 83 mg Calc.

PointsPlus value: **8.**

Cook's Note

Most Arctic char sold in the United States is farmed sustainably, so it is a good choice to make at the seafood counter. If it is unavailable, you can substitute salmon in this recipe.

California Fish Tacos

California Fish Tacos

SERVES 4

2 (6-ounce) skinless halibut fillets

½ teaspoon salt

¼ teaspoon ground cumin

8 small taco shells

1 cup tender watercress sprigs

1 avocado, halved, pitted, peeled, and diced

¼ cup chopped fresh cilantro

½ cup fat-free salsa

Lime wedges

1. Spray broiler rack with nonstick spray and preheat broiler.
2. Sprinkle halibut with salt and cumin. Place fillets on broiler rack and broil 5 inches from heat until fish is just opaque throughout, about 3 minutes on each side. Transfer fish to plate and use fork to flake fish.
3. Divide fish evenly among taco shells. Top evenly with watercress, avocado, and cilantro. Serve with salsa and lime wedges.

PER SERVING (2 tacos and 2 tablespoons salsa): 295 Cal, 12 g Total Fat, 2 g Sat Fat, 0 g Trans Fat, 60 mg Chol, 685 mg Sod, 23 g Total Carb, 5 g Fib, 25 g Prot, 66 mg Calc.

PointsPlus value: *7.*

Cook's Note

Halibut has a firm texture that you can break into large flakes that are perfect for tacos. Other good options are cod, tilapia, or catfish.

20 minute meals

Shrimp and Spaghetti Arrabbiata

SERVES 4

8 ounces whole wheat spaghetti

4 teaspoons olive oil

1 pound large peeled and deveined shrimp

¾ teaspoon salt

3 garlic cloves, minced

1 (15-ounce) can crushed tomatoes

3 tablespoons tomato paste

½ teaspoon dried oregano

¼ teaspoon red pepper flakes

6 large basil leaves, thinly sliced

1. Cook spaghetti according to package directions, omitting salt if desired; drain and keep warm.
2. Meanwhile, heat 2 teaspoons of oil in large nonstick skillet over medium heat. Sprinkle shrimp with ½ teaspoon of salt. Add half of shrimp to skillet and cook until just opaque in center, about 2 minutes on each side. Transfer to plate. Repeat with remaining shrimp.
3. Add remaining 2 teaspoons oil to skillet. Add garlic and cook, stirring, until fragrant, about 30 seconds. Stir in tomatoes, tomato paste, oregano, and red pepper flakes; cook until slightly thickened, about 5 minutes. Add shrimp, basil, and remaining ¼ teaspoon salt; cook, stirring occasionally, just until shrimp are heated through, about 1 minute.
4. Divide pasta evenly among 4 plates and top evenly with shrimp and sauce.

PER SERVING (1 cup pasta and about ½ cup shrimp with sauce): 367 Cal, 7 g Total Fat, 1 g Sat Fat, 0 g Trans Fat, 168 mg Chol, 782 mg Sod, 52 g Total Carb, 10 g Fib, 29 g Prot, 102 mg Calc.

PointsPlus value: **9.**

Cook's Note

An Italian-inspired salad is the perfect accompaniment to this traditional dish. Toss together romaine lettuce, halved cherry tomatoes, thinly sliced pepperoncini, sliced red onion, and your favorite fat-free Italian dressing.

Shrimp and Spaghetti Arrabbiata

Shrimp with Cherry Tomatoes and Feta

SERVES 4

⅔ cup whole wheat couscous

2 teaspoons olive oil

¾ pound medium shrimp, peeled and deveined

¼ teaspoon salt

1 pint cherry tomatoes, halved

2 garlic cloves, finely chopped

1 teaspoon dried oregano

¼ cup reduced-sodium chicken broth

¼ cup chopped fresh dill

3 tablespoons crumbled feta cheese

1. Prepare couscous according to package directions, omitting salt if desired.
2. Meanwhile, heat oil in large skillet over medium-high heat. Add shrimp and salt and cook, stirring, until shrimp begin to turn pink, 1–2 minutes.
3. Add tomatoes, garlic, and oregano and cook until tomatoes soften, about 1 minute. Add broth and cook until most of liquid has evaporated, 1–2 minutes. Stir in dill and feta and cook 1 minute longer. Serve over couscous.

PER SERVING (1 cup shrimp mixture and ½ cup couscous): 263 Cal, 5 g Total Fat, 2 g Sat Fat, 0 g Trans Fat, 132 mg Chol, 415 mg Sod, 35 g Total Carb, 6 g Fib, 21 g Prot, 87 mg Calc.

PointsPlus value: *7.*

Do it Faster

It saves time to buy shrimp already peeled and deveined, but to do it yourself as efficiently as possible, peel the shrimp, then use kitchen scissors to slit the flesh on the back of each shrimp. Hold each shrimp under cold running water to rinse away the vein.

Vegetable Fried Rice

SERVES 6

1 teaspoon canola oil

4 scallions, trimmed and sliced

2 garlic cloves, finely chopped

1 tablespoon grated peeled fresh ginger

¼ pound snow peas, sliced lengthwise

1 red bell pepper, chopped

2 cups cooked white rice

2 cups cooked brown rice

1 (10-ounce) package frozen mixed vegetables, thawed

8 ounces firm tofu, diced

2 large eggs, beaten

3 tablespoons reduced-sodium soy sauce

2 teaspoons Asian (dark) sesame oil

1. Heat canola oil in large skillet over medium-high heat. Add scallions, garlic, and ginger and cook, stirring, until fragrant, about 30 seconds. Add snow peas and bell pepper and cook until bell pepper softens, about 1 minute. Add white and brown rice, mixed vegetables, and tofu and cook, stirring, until heated through, about 5 minutes.
2. Push rice mixture to edge of skillet, making hollow in center. Pour in eggs and cook, stirring, until eggs are cooked. Stir eggs into rice, drizzle with soy sauce and sesame oil, and toss to combine.

PER SERVING (1¼ cups): 293 Cal, 8 g Total Fat, 2 g Sat Fat, 0 g Trans Fat, 71 mg Chol, 358 mg Sod, 42 g Total Carb, 5 g Fib, 14 g Prot, 307 mg Calc.

PointsPlus value: *7.*

Cook's Note

If picky eaters at your house are not sold on the idea of healthy brown rice, this recipe is a good start. With a blend of white and brown rice, this flavor-packed dish might win them over.

Blackened Scallops with Lemon-Caper Mayonnaise

Blackened Scallops with Lemon-Caper Mayonnaise

20 minute meals

SERVES 4

3 tablespoons fat-free mayonnaise

2 teaspoons drained capers, chopped

½ teaspoon grated lemon zest

1 teaspoon fresh lemon juice

1 teaspoon paprika

¾ teaspoon dried oregano

½ teaspoon ground coriander

½ teaspoon salt

12 large sea scallops (about ¾ pound)

2 teaspoons olive oil

1. Combine mayonnaise, capers, zest, and lemon juice in small bowl; cover and refrigerate.
2. Combine paprika, oregano, coriander, and salt on sheet of wax paper. Dip one side of each scallop into spice mixture and set them on plate, spice side up.
3. Heat oil in large skillet over medium-high heat until very hot. Add scallops, spice side down, and cook until scallops are browned and opaque in center, 2–3 minutes on each side.
4. Stick small wooden skewer into side of each scallop so that it looks like a lollipop; serve with sauce on side.

PER SERVING (3 scallops and scant tablespoon sauce): 80 Cal, 3 g Total Fat, 1 g Sat Fat, 0 g Trans Fat, 24 mg Chol, 536 mg Sod, 2 g Total Carb, 1 g Fib, 10 g Prot, 57 mg Calc.

PointsPlus value: ***2***.

Cook's Note

Make these scallops the centerpiece of a "small plates" dinner by serving them with Black Bean–Tomatillo Dip with fresh vegetables, page 156, and plates of roasted red bell peppers (not oil-packed) sprinkled with crumbled fat-free feta cheese (1 ounce of fat-free feta per serving will increase the ***PointsPlus*** value by ***1***).

10 essential kitchen time-savers

If you're determined to make healthy, home-cooked meals for your family in minimal time, these tools can make cooking a pleasure.

FOOD PROCESSOR. Of course you can use this essential kitchen appliance for making pureed soups, hummus, pesto, and bread crumbs. But, with the basic blade attachments, you can slice, shred, or chop large amounts of vegetables or cheese in seconds.

HANDHELD ELECTRIC MIXER. For making small-batch cake and cookie batters and whipping up the fluffiest mashed potatoes ever, a lightweight, easy-to-clean mixer is a must-have. Some models also have attachments for making smoothies and kneading bread dough.

IMMERSION BLENDER. With this handy appliance, you can blend soups and puree sauces right in the pot, saving the time it takes to transfer foods to a blender or food processor. Choose a model that does double-duty with an ice crushing attachment.

SLOW COOKER. Yes, a slow cooker can help you make fast meals! With a few minutes prep in the morning, you can come home to a ready-made dinner. All you have to do is set the table. See the section "Slow Cookers Save Time" on page 293 for 19 delicious slow-cooker dishes.

RICE COOKER. A rice cooker doesn't cook rice any faster, but this ingenious appliance saves you the time and stress of constantly checking rice to see if it's done while keeping watch over other parts of the meal. With a rice cooker, you add rice and water, turn it on, and then focus on preparing the rest of your dinner.

KITCHEN SHEARS. Once you keep a pair of these handy scissors in a kitchen drawer, you'll put them to use every day. They make fast work of peeling and deveining shrimp, trimming fat from steaks and chops, snipping herbs, cutting up dried fruit, and cutting up whole tomatoes right in the can.

STOVETOP GRILL PAN. When you're craving the smoky flavor of a grilled dinner, but don't want to spend the time it takes to fire up the grill—not to mention clean up—a stovetop grill pan is the answer. These pans are perfect to grill favorites like steaks, burgers, skinless boneless chicken breasts and thighs, pork chops, shrimp, and salmon fillets.

HANDHELD GRATER. Our favorite is the super-sharp Microplane grater, which creates thin shards of citrus zest, hard cheese, nutmeg, chocolate, or coconut in seconds. For cleanup, just toss it in the dishwasher.

SILICONE BRISTLE BRUSH. Cooking healthy meals means making a little fat go a long way. With one of these dishwasher-safe brushes, you can coat a baking pan or skillet with a tiny amount of oil in just seconds. Unlike other brushes, these are heat resistant and dishwasher safe—no more laborious hand washing to remove stubborn oils from the bristles!

PARCHMENT PAPER. If you hate the time and hard work of scrubbing baking pans, parchment paper will free you from this tedious task. Not only is it good for cake and cookie pans, but use it to line the pan when you bake lasagna, meatballs, or chicken, or when you roast vegetables. Cleanup takes seconds instead of minutes.

Linguine with White Bean Puttanesca

1. Cook linguine according to package directions, omitting salt if desired; drain and place in large serving bowl.
2. Meanwhile, heat oil in large skillet over medium-high heat. Add onion, garlic, oregano, and crushed red pepper flakes; cook, stirring occasionally, until onion softens, 2–3 minutes. Stir in tomatoes, olives, and capers; simmer, stirring occasionally, until sauce thickens, 6–7 minutes. Add beans and salt; cook until heated through, about 1 minute.
3. Pour beans and sauce over linguine, sprinkle with parsley.

PER SERVING (1½ cups): 324 Cal, 6 g Total Fat, 1 g Sat Fat, 0 g Trans Fat, 0 mg Chol, 897 mg Sod, 57 g Total Carb, 10 g Fib, 15 g Prot, 139 mg Calc.

PointsPlus value: **8.**

SERVES 4

6 ounces whole wheat linguine

1 tablespoon olive oil

1 onion, chopped

3 garlic cloves, minced

1 teaspoon dried oregano

¼ teaspoon red pepper flakes

1 (14½-ounce) can diced tomatoes

12 pimiento-stuffed olives, sliced

1 tablespoon drained capers, chopped

1 (15½-ounce) can small white beans, rinsed and drained

¼ teaspoon salt

2 tablespoons chopped fresh parsley

20 minute meals

Fettuccine with Goat Cheese, Arugula, and Tomatoes

SERVES 4

1 (9-ounce) package fresh fettuccine

1 (4-ounce) log goat cheese, crumbled

1 (5-ounce) bag baby arugula

1½ cups cherry or grape tomatoes, quartered

½ teaspoon black pepper

1. Cook fettuccine according to package directions; drain, reserving 1 cup of cooking water.
2. Return pasta to pot with ½ cup of cooking water and place over low heat. Add goat cheese, arugula, tomatoes, and pepper; toss until cheese melts and arugula just begins to wilt, about 1 minute. Add more cooking water if pasta is too dry.

PER SERVING (1¼ cups): 270 Cal, 9 g Total Fat, 5 g Sat Fat, 0 g Trans Fat, 49 mg Chol, 323 mg Sod, 36 g Total Carb, 3 g Fib, 12 g Prot, 119 mg Calc.

PointsPlus value: *7.*

Cook's Note

For a milder dish, you can make this recipe using baby spinach instead of the peppery arugula.

Fettuccine with Goat Cheese,
Arugula, and Tomatoes

Black Bean–Tomatillo Dip

SERVES 6

2 (15½-ounce) cans black beans, rinsed and drained

1 (12-ounce) can tomatillos, drained and coarsely chopped

1 (4½-ounce) can chopped green chiles, drained

3 scallions, chopped

½ cup chopped fresh cilantro

2–4 tablespoons water

3 tablespoons fresh lime juice

2 teaspoons chili powder

2 teaspoons ground cumin

½ teaspoon salt

½ teaspoon black pepper

1. Combine beans and tomatillos in food processor and pulse until chunky puree forms.
2. Transfer bean mixture to large bowl and add remaining ingredients; stir until well combined.

PER SERVING (⅓ cup): 102 Cal, 1 g Total Fat, 0 g Sat Fat, 0 g Trans Fat, 0 mg Chol, 390 g Sod, 17 g Total Carb, 7 g Fib, 6 g Prot, 38 mg Calc.

PointsPlus value: ***2.***

Cook's Note

For a satisfying vegetarian lunch, start with this dip paired with any fresh vegetables you have on hand. Then enjoy a bowl of Winter Squash Soup with Lime Cream, page 35.

Sun-Dried Tomato Hummus

SERVES 4

6 sun-dried tomatoes (not packed in oil)

1 (15½-ounce) can chickpeas, rinsed and drained

2 tablespoons tahini

1 tablespoon fresh lemon juice

1 garlic clove, chopped

¼ teaspoon salt

Pinch cayenne pepper

1. Put tomatoes in small bowl and add boiling water to cover. Let stand 10 minutes; remove tomatoes and reserve liquid.
2. Combine tomatoes and remaining ingredients in food processor and pulse until smooth, adding some of reserved liquid if hummus seems too thick.

PER SERVING (¼ cup): 56 Cal, 5 g Total Fat, 3 g Sat Fat, 0 g Trans Fat, 14 mg Chol, 176 mg Sod, 2 g Total Carb, 0 g Fib, 2 g Prot, 19 mg Calc.

PointsPlus value: ***2.***

Cook's Note

Hummus is a handy condiment to have on hand. Serve it with celery and carrot sticks for a snack, spread it on bread and top with tomato slices for a lunchtime sandwich, or serve it alongside grilled chicken or salmon for dinner.

From top, clockwise:
Chunky Guacamole, Black Bean-Tomatillo Dip, page 156, and Crispy Green Plantains, page 162

Chunky Guacamole

SERVES 6

2 Hass avocados, halved, pitted, and peeled

1 small tomato, seeded and chopped

¼ cup chopped fresh cilantro

¼ cup finely chopped onion

1½ tablespoons fresh lime or lemon juice

½ teaspoon salt

¼ teaspoon black pepper

4 drops hot pepper sauce

Coarsely mash avocados in medium bowl. Add remaining ingredients and stir until combined. Serve at once or press piece of plastic wrap directly onto surface to prevent guacamole from browning. Refrigerate up to 3 hours.

PER SERVING (2 tablespoons): 82 Cal, 7 g Total Fat, 1 g Sat Fat, 0 g Trans Fat, 0 mg Chol, 204 mg Sod, 5 g Total Carb, 3 g Fib, 1 g Prot, 10 mg Calc.

PointsPlus value: ***2.***

Cook's Note

Serve this classic Tex-Mex dish with fresh cut-up vegetables for a snack or with grilled shrimp for an easy, yet flavorful main dish.

Red Pepper and Sun-Dried Tomato Dip

SERVES 12

1 (8-ounce) package light cream cheese (Neufchâtel)

½ cup jarred roasted red pepper (not packed in oil), drained

6 moist sun-dried tomatoes (not packed in oil), sliced

1 small garlic clove, crushed with a press

1 teaspoon Italian seasoning or dried oregano

¼ teaspoon salt

⅛ teaspoon black pepper

Combine all ingredients in food processor and puree.

PER SERVING (about 2 tablespoons): 111 Cal, 4 g Total Fat, 3 g Sat Fat, 0 g Trans Fat, 14 mg Chol, 141 mg Sod, 1 g Total Carb, 0 g Fib, 2 g Prot, 16 mg Calc.

PointsPlus value: ***1.***

Cook's Note

Serve the dip with any fresh vegetables that you have on hand. Try small white mushrooms or cherry tomatoes, cucumber spears, broccoli florets, or celery sticks.

Spicy Cereal and Pretzel Snack Mix

SERVES 10

2 tablespoons unsalted butter, melted

1 tablespoon curry powder

1 tablespoon reduced-sodium soy sauce

1½ teaspoons sugar

1½ teaspoons paprika

1 teaspoon ground cumin

¼ teaspoon salt

⅛–¼ teaspoon cayenne pepper

2½ cups crispy rice cereal squares

2½ cups crispy corn cereal squares

½ cup tiny pretzel twists

3 tablespoons lightly salted peanuts

1. Stir together butter, curry powder, soy sauce, sugar, paprika, cumin, salt, and cayenne in small bowl.
2. Toss together rice cereal, corn cereal, and pretzel twists in large bowl. Add butter mixture to cereal mixture and toss until evenly coated. Stir in peanuts. Store in an airtight container at room temperature up to 2 weeks.

PER SERVING (about ½ cup): 100 Cal, 4 g Total Fat, 2 g Sat Fat, 0 g Trans Fat, 6 mg Chol, 273 mg Sod, 15 g Total Carb, 1 g Fib, 2 g Prot, 53 mg Calc.

PointsPlus value: **3.**

Crispy Green Plantains

SERVES 4

4 teaspoons olive oil

2 green plantains, peeled and cut on diagonal into ½-inch slices (about 20 pieces)

1 teaspoon salt

1. Heat oil in large nonstick skillet over medium heat. Cook plantains, in batches, until tender and golden brown, about 5 minutes on each side. Transfer plantain slices to double thickness of paper towels to drain. With bottom of heavy plate or saucepan, gently press down on slices, one at time, to flatten to ¼-inch thickness.
2. Spray same skillet with olive oil nonstick spray and set over medium heat. Add plantain slices, in batches, and cook until nicely browned, about 1 minute on each side. Sprinkle with salt while hot.

PER SERVING (about 5 pieces): 185 Cal, 3 g Total Fat, 0 Sat Fat, 0 g Trans Fat, 0 Chol, 153 mg Sod, 44 g Total Carb, 3 g Fiber, 1 g Prot, 4 mg Calc.

PointsPlus value: ***5.***

Cook's Note

Here's how to peel a plantain: cut off both ends, then cut it crosswise in half. Using small knife, slit the skin along its ridges, cutting down to the flesh, then peel off the skin.

Microwave Apple-Pear Crisp

SERVES 6

2 Golden Delicious apples, peeled, cored, and thinly sliced

2 Bartlett pears, peeled, cored, and thinly sliced

¼ cup dried cherries or cranberries

4 tablespoons packed light brown sugar

¾ teaspoon cinnamon

1 cup low-fat granola

2 tablespoons unsalted butter, melted

1. Spray microwavable 8-inch square dish with nonstick spray.
2. Stir together apples, pears, dried cherries, 3 tablespoons of brown sugar, and ½ teaspoon of cinnamon in large bowl. Spread evenly in baking dish.
3. Toss together granola, butter, and remaining 1 tablespoon brown sugar and ¼ teaspoon cinnamon in small bowl. Sprinkle granola mixture evenly over fruit mixture. Microwave on High until apples and pears are tender, about 8 minutes. Serve warm or at room temperature.

PER SERVING (⅙ of crisp): 202 Cal, 5 g Total Fat, 3 g Sat Fat, 0 g Trans Fat, 10 mg Chol, 72 mg Sod, 41 g Total Carb, 4 g Fib, 2 g Prot, 27 mg Calc.

PointsPlus value: **6.**

Brown Sugar Plums

SERVES 4

- ¼ cup plus 1 tablespoon sliced almonds
- 3 tablespoons packed brown sugar
- 2 teaspoons unsalted butter, melted
- 6 ripe red or purple plums, halved and pitted
- ½ cup plain fat-free Greek yogurt
- 1 tablespoon honey

1. Preheat oven to 425°F. Spray large baking sheet with nonstick spray.
2. Combine ¼ cup of almonds and brown sugar in food processor and pulse until almonds are finely ground. Add butter and process just until combined.
3. Arrange plums, cut side up, on baking sheet. Fill cavity of each plum half with level ½ teaspoon of almond mixture; reserve remaining mixture. Roast until almond mixture is browned and plums are softened, about 15 minutes.
4. Meanwhile, stir together yogurt and honey in small bowl.
5. Stir together remaining ground almond mixture with remaining 1 tablespoon almonds in small bowl. Place 3 plum halves on each of 4 plates. Spoon generous 2 tablespoons of yogurt mixture on each plate and sprinkle evenly with remaining almond mixture.

PER SERVING (3 plum halves and 1 tablespoon almond mixture): 176 Cal, 6 g Total Fat, 2 g Sat Fat, 0 g Trans Fat, 6 mg Chol, 28 mg Sod, 29 g Total Carb, 2 g Fib, 4 g Prot, 94 mg Calc.

PointsPlus value: **5.**

Cook's Note

Brown sugar is made by combining white granulated sugar with molasses. Light brown and dark brown sugar can be used interchangeably in most recipes, though dark brown sugar has a slightly more robust flavor.

Bananas Foster

SERVES 6

- 1½ tablespoons unsalted butter
- ¼ cup packed dark brown sugar
- 2 teaspoons lemon juice
- 1 teaspoon vanilla extract
- ¼ teaspoon cinnamon
- 2 firm-ripe bananas, cut on an angle into ¼-inch-thick slices
- 2 tablespoons orange liqueur
- 2 cups fat-free vanilla frozen yogurt

1. Heat medium nonstick skillet over medium-low heat. Add butter, sugar, lemon juice, vanilla, and cinnamon; cook, stirring, until butter melts and sugar dissolves, about 1 minute. Add bananas and cook, stirring occasionally, until bananas soften, 3–4 minutes.
2. Pour in orange liqueur. Touch lit match to surface of skillet to ignite; cook, shaking pan, until flame goes out, about 30 seconds. Remove skillet from heat.
3. Place ⅓ cup scoop of frozen yogurt into each of 6 bowls. Top with warm banana mixture and serve at once.

PER SERVING (⅓ cup bananas and ⅓ cup frozen yogurt): 188 Cal, 3 g Total Fat, 2 g Sat Fat, 0 g Trans Fat, 9 mg Chol, 50 mg Sod, 37 g Total Carb, 1 g Fib, 3 g Prot, 127 mg Calc.

PointsPlus value: **5.**

Cook's Note

Use long match or long-handled sparker to safely ignite the liqueur. If you'd prefer not to use alcohol, substitute 2 tablespoons orange juice and skip this step.

30 minute meals

30 Minute Breakfasts

30 Minute Lunches

30 Minute Dinners

30 Minute Snacks and Sweets

Spanish Frittata

SERVES 4

½ teaspoon canola oil

1 small red bell pepper, diced

½ cup diced onion

1 (14½-ounce) can sliced potatoes, rinsed and drained

6 large eggs

6 large egg whites

¼ teaspoon black pepper

Paprika

2 tablespoons chopped fresh parsley

1. Preheat broiler.
2. Coat 10-inch ovenproof nonstick skillet with oil and place over medium heat. Add bell pepper and onion and cook until softened, about 8 minutes. Add potatoes, breaking up larger slices with side of wooden spoon.
3. Whisk together eggs, egg whites, and pepper in medium bowl. Pour over vegetables in pan and stir gently. Cook, lifting edges frequently with spatula to let any uncooked egg flow underneath, until eggs are almost set, about 5 minutes.
4. Place skillet under broiler 5 inches from heat and broil until eggs are set and top is lightly browned, 4 minutes. Invert frittata onto plate, sprinkle with paprika and parsley, and cut into 4 wedges.

PER SERVING (1 wedge): 203 Cal, 8 g Total Fat, 3 g Sat Fat, 0 g Trans Fat, 318 mg Chol, 651 mg Sod, 15 g Total Carb, 3 g Fib, 17 g Prot, 56 mg Calc.

PointsPlus value: ***5.***

Cook's Note

Serve the frittata with reduced-calorie whole wheat toast (1 slice of reduced-calorie whole wheat toast per serving will increase the ***PointsPlus*** value by ***1***).

Florentine Frittata

SERVES 4

2 teaspoons olive oil

1 small onion, chopped

1 (10-ounce) package frozen chopped spinach, thawed and squeezed dry

3 large eggs

5 large egg whites

¼ cup crumbled reduced-fat feta cheese

¼ teaspoon salt

½ cup shredded part-skim mozzarella cheese

1 cup grape tomatoes, halved

1. Heat 1 teaspoon of oil in 10-inch ovenproof nonstick skillet over medium heat. Add onion and cook, stirring frequently, until softened, about 5 minutes.
2. Preheat broiler. Scrape onion into large bowl and add spinach, eggs, egg whites, feta, salt, and ¼ cup of mozzarella. Mix with fork until well blended.
3. Heat remaining 1 teaspoon oil in same skillet over medium heat. Pour egg mixture into skillet and scatter tomatoes on top. Cover skillet and cook until eggs are just set around edges, 5 minutes.
4. Place skillet under broiler 5 inches from heat and broil until frittata is lightly browned and just set in center, about 4 minutes. Sprinkle with remaining ¼ cup mozzarella; broil until cheese melts, about 1 minute longer. Cut into 4 wedges.

PER SERVING (1 wedge). 191 Cal, 10 g Total Fat, 4 g Sat Fat, 0 g Trans Fat, 170 mg Chol, 494 mg Sod, 9 g Total Carb, 3 g Fib, 17 g Prot, 240 mg Calc.

PointsPlus value: ***5.***

Do it Faster

To quickly thaw frozen spinach, remove it from the package, place in a microwavable bowl, cover with wax paper, and microwave on the defrost setting for 2 to 3 minutes, breaking spinach up halfway through defrosting.

Mini Mexican Frittatas

SERVES 6

4 large eggs

¼ cup low-fat (1%) milk

¼ cup mild salsa

¼ cup shredded reduced-fat Cheddar cheese

¼ teaspoon ground cumin

¼ teaspoon salt

1. Preheat oven to 350°F. Spray 6-cup muffin pan with nonstick spray.
2. Whisk together eggs, milk, salsa, Cheddar cheese, cumin, and salt in medium bowl. Ladle mixture evenly into muffin cups.
3. Bake until egg mixture puffs up and edges are golden brown, about 20 minutes. Remove pan from oven, run knife around edge of each cup, and lift frittatas out.

PER SERVING (1 frittata): 71 Cal, 5 g Total Fat, 2 g Sat Fat, 0 g Trans Fat, 145 mg Chol, 218 mg Sod, 2 g Total Carb, 0 g Fib, 6 g Prot, 63 mg Calc.

PointsPlus value: ***2.***

Cook's Note

Freshen up the flavor of purchased salsa by stirring in chopped fresh cilantro and a squeeze of lime before using it in recipes.

Ranch-Style Eggs over Polenta

SERVES 4

1 (16-ounce) tube fat-free polenta, cut into 12 slices

1 (15½-ounce) can pinto beans, rinsed and drained

1 cup fat-free chunky salsa

½ teaspoon ground cumin

½ teaspoon canola oil

4 large eggs

½ cup shredded reduced-fat Cheddar cheese

2 tablespoons chopped fresh cilantro

1. Preheat oven to 425°F. Spray baking sheet with nonstick spray.
2. Arrange polenta slices in single layer on baking sheet. Spray polenta lightly with nonstick spray. Bake until hot, about 15 minutes.
3. Meanwhile, combine beans, salsa, and cumin in small saucepan; bring to boil. Reduce heat and simmer, covered, about 10 minutes.
4. Coat large nonstick skillet with oil. Crack eggs into skillet; set over medium heat and cook until yolks just begin to set, 2–3 minutes. Remove skillet from heat and sprinkle eggs with Cheddar cheese and cilantro. Cover skillet and let stand until cheese melts, about 2 minutes.
5. To serve, place 3 polenta slices on each of 4 plates. Spoon beans over polenta and top with an egg.

PER SERVING (3 slices polenta, ½ cup beans, and 1 egg): 301 Cal, 9 g Total Fat, 3 g Sat Fat, 0 g Trans Fat, 215 mg Chol, 945 mg Sod, 37 g Total Carb, 6 g Fib, 19 g Prot, 177 mg Calc.

PointsPlus value: ***8.***

Do it Faster

Prepared polenta is a must-have staple for quick meals. It's delicious for breakfast with eggs or drizzled with a touch of syrup or honey, at lunch it's a great way to serve topped with sautéed veggies, or enjoy it for dinner with a quick Bolognese sauce.

Brown Rice and Honey Pancakes

Brown Rice and Honey Pancakes

SERVES 2

½ cup cooked brown rice

1 cup fat-free milk

2 tablespoons honey

⅓ cup all-purpose flour

3 tablespoons wheat germ

1 teaspoon baking powder

¼ teaspoon salt

¼ cup fat-free egg substitute

½ teaspoon canola oil

1 cup unsweetened applesauce

2 tablespoons ground flaxseed

1. Combine rice, milk, and honey in small saucepan and bring to boil over medium-high heat. Reduce heat and simmer 5 minutes. Transfer mixture to shallow bowl and let cool about 10 minutes.
2. Meanwhile, whisk together flour, wheat germ, baking powder, and salt in medium bowl. Stir in lukewarm rice mixture and egg substitute.
3. Coat nonstick griddle or large nonstick skillet with oil and set over medium heat. Drop batter by ¼ cupfuls onto griddle and cook pancakes until bubbles appear and edges look dry, about 3 minutes. Turn and cook until deep golden brown, about 2 minutes longer.
4. Transfer pancakes to 2 plates and top evenly with applesauce and flaxseed.

PER SERVING (3 pancakes and ½ cup applesauce): 379 Cal, 5 g Total Fat, 1 g Sat Fat, 0 g Trans Fat, 2 mg Chol, 792 mg Sod, 73 g Total Carb, 7 g Fib, 15 g Prot, 373 mg Calc.

PointsPlus value: ***10.***

Cook's Note

Top the pancakes with sliced banana or a handful of fresh berries.

30 minute meals

Wild Blueberry and Cornmeal Pancakes

SERVES 4

1 cup reduced-fat all-purpose baking mix

1 cup yellow cornmeal

1¼ cups low-fat (1%) milk

1 large egg, beaten

3 tablespoons sugar

1¼ cups fresh or frozen wild blueberries

½ teaspoon canola oil

1. Stir together baking mix, cornmeal, milk, egg, and sugar in large bowl just until moistened. Gently stir in blueberries.
2. Coat nonstick griddle or large nonstick skillet with oil and set over medium heat. Drop batter by heaping ¼ cupfuls onto griddle and cook pancakes until bubbles appear and edges look dry, about 3 minutes. Turn and cook until browned, about 2 minutes longer.

PER SERVING (3 pancakes): 341 Cal, 5 g Total Fat, 2 g Sat Fat, 0 g Trans Fat, 56 mg Chol, 388 mg Sod, 64 g Total Carb, 4 g Fib, 10 g Prot, 136 mg Calc.

PointsPlus value: ***9.***

Cook's Note

Wild blueberries are often available in the freezer section of large supermarkets. They are appreciated for their intense sweet-tart flavor. You can substitute regular blueberries if you wish.

Peach Muesli with Almonds

SERVES 6

2 cups rolled (old-fashioned) oats

1 cup fat-free milk

¾ cup chopped dried peaches

¼ cup golden raisins

¼ cup apple juice

1 cup plain fat-free yogurt

2 tablespoons honey

¼ cup sliced almonds

1. Stir together oats, milk, peaches, raisins, and apple juice in medium bowl; let stand 25 minutes, stirring occasionally.
2. Meanwhile, stir together yogurt and honey in small bowl.
3. Divide oat mixture evenly among 6 bowls. Top evenly with yogurt mixture and almonds.

PER SERVING (½ cup): 255 Cal, 4 g Total Fat, 1 g Sat Fat, 0 g Trans Fat, 2 mg Chol, 53 mg Sod, 48 g Total Carb, 5 g Fib, 10 g Prot, 165 mg Calc.

PointsPlus value: *7.*

Cook's Note

Make the muesli a more filling breakfast by topping it with a small sliced banana or if you like a little crunch, a chopped fresh apple.

30 minute meals

Creamy Couscous Breakfast Pudding

SERVES 6

1½ cups water

1 cup whole wheat couscous

Pinch salt

3 cups fat-free milk

2 tablespoons packed brown sugar

½ teaspoon grated orange zest

¼ cup fat-free egg substitute

¼ cup toasted wheat germ

¾ teaspoon vanilla extract

1. Bring water to boil in large heavy saucepan over high heat. Stir in couscous and salt. Reduce heat and simmer until water is absorbed, about 2 minutes. Remove saucepan from heat and fluff couscous with fork. Cover and let stand about 5 minutes.
2. Whisk milk, brown sugar, and orange zest into couscous. Bring to boil over medium-high heat, whisking frequently to break up any lumps. Reduce heat to medium-low and cook, stirring frequently, until mixture is slightly thickened, about 5 minutes. Remove saucepan from heat.
3. Whisk together ½ cup of couscous mixture and egg substitute in small bowl. Return mixture to saucepan and cook over low heat, stirring, until pudding is thick and creamy, about 5 minutes longer. Stir in wheat germ and vanilla.

PER SERVING (generous ¾ cup): 152 Cal, 1 g Total Fat, 0 g Sat Fat, 0 g Trans Fat, 2 mg Chol, 123 mg Sod, 28 g Total Carb, 3 g Fib, 9 g Prot, 190 mg Calc.

PointsPlus value: ***4.***

Cook's Note

Top the pudding with fresh raspberries and sliced almonds (1 tablespoon sliced almonds per serving will increase the ***PointsPlus*** value by ***1***).

Creamy Couscous
Breakfast Pudding

30 minute meals

Spice-Roasted Pears with Yogurt

SERVES 4

4 ripe Bartlett or Comice pears, peeled, halved lengthwise, and cored

1 tablespoon fresh lemon juice

¾ teaspoon cinnamon

⅛ teaspoon ground allspice

¼ cup plain fat-free yogurt

1. Preheat oven to 450°F. Spray baking sheet with nonstick spray.
2. Combine pears, lemon juice, cinnamon, and allspice in medium bowl; toss well.
3. Using sharp knife, cut each pear half lengthwise almost through to base into ¼-inch-thick slices, keeping base intact. Carefully transfer sliced pear halves cut side down to baking sheet with spatula. Gently press down on each half to fan slices open slightly. Bake until pears are tender, about 20 minutes.
4. Using spatula, transfer 2 pear halves to each of 4 dessert plates. Top each serving with 1 tablespoon yogurt.

PER SERVING (1 pear and 1 tablespoon yogurt): 107 Cal, 0 g Total Fat, 0 g Sat Fat, 0 g Trans Fat, 0 mg Chol, 14 mg Sod, 27 g Total Carb, 6 g Fib, 2 g Prot, 51 mg Calc.

PointsPlus value: **3.**

Cook's Note

Enjoy the pears with a toasted light multigrain English muffin (1 light multigrain English muffin per serving will increase the ***PointsPlus*** value by **3**).

Philly Cheese Steak Sandwiches

SERVES 4

1 teaspoon canola oil

2 large onions, thinly sliced

2 Italian frying peppers, sliced

2 garlic cloves, finely chopped

¼ teaspoon salt

¾ pound lean boneless sirloin steak, trimmed and thinly sliced

4 (¾-ounce) slices reduced-fat provolone cheese

1 dill pickle, sliced

4 small (2-ounce) crusty whole wheat rolls, split lengthwise

1. Heat oil in large skillet over medium-high heat. Add onions, peppers, and garlic and sprinkle with ⅛ teaspoon of salt. Cook, stirring occasionally, until onions are browned, about 10 minutes. Transfer to small bowl and set aside.
2. Wipe out skillet and spray with nonstick spray. Place over medium-high heat. Sprinkle steak with remaining ⅛ teaspoon salt and place half of steak in skillet. Cook until browned on both sides, about 2 minutes; transfer to plate. Repeat with remaining steak.
3. Place 1 slice of provolone and few pickle slices on each roll. Divide beef and onion mixture among rolls.

PER SERVING (1 sandwich): 352 Cal, 12 g Total Fat, 4 g Sat Fat, 0 g Trans Fat, 59 mg Chol, 755 mg Sod, 37 g Total Carb, 6 g Fib, 29 g Prot, 348 mg Calc.

PointsPlus value: **9.**

Do it Faster

To remove the papery peel from a clove of garlic, put the garlic on a cutting board, place the flat side of the blade of a chef's knife on the clove, and carefully press down on the knife.

Open-Faced Garlicky
Steak Sandwiches

Open-Faced Garlicky Steak Sandwiches

1. Spray broiler rack with nonstick spray and preheat broiler.
2. Sprinkle steak with oregano, salt, and pepper. Broil steak 5 inches from heat until an instant-read thermometer inserted into side of steak registers 145°F, about 5 minutes on each side. Transfer to cutting board and let stand 5 minutes. Cut steak across grain into thin slices.
3. Meanwhile, combine water and garlic in small saucepan and bring to boil over high heat. Reduce heat and simmer until garlic is very tender, about 10 minutes; drain and rinse under cold running water. Peel garlic; place in small bowl and mash with fork.
4. To make salsa, stir together tomatoes, cucumber, onion, cilantro, jalapeño, vinegar, and oil in medium bowl.
5. Spread mashed garlic evenly over bread. Top bread evenly with steak and salsa.

PER SERVING (1 sandwich): 303 Cal, 9 g Total Fat, 2 g Sat Fat, 0 g Trans Fat, 73 mg Chol, 474 mg Sod, 20 g Total Carb, 4 g Fib, 35 g Prot, 72 mg Calc.

PointsPlus value: *7.*

SERVES 4

1 (1-pound) lean boneless sirloin steak, trimmed

2 teaspoons dried oregano

½ teaspoon salt

½ teaspoon black pepper

2 cups water

6 garlic cloves, unpeeled

1 pint cherry or grape tomatoes, halved

½ large English (seedless) cucumber, peeled and diced

½ red onion, thinly sliced

¼ cup chopped fresh cilantro

1 jalapeño pepper, seeded and minced

3 tablespoons apple-cider vinegar

1 tablespoon olive oil

4 (½-inch) slices whole-grain country-style bread, toasted

30 minute meals

Cuban Beef Lettuce Wraps

SERVES 4

1 large onion, chopped

4 garlic cloves, minced

1 pound ground lean beef (7% fat or less)

¼ teaspoon salt

1 (14½-ounce) can diced tomatoes

½ (4-ounce) can tomato paste

⅓ cup sliced pitted green olives

⅓ cup raisins

2 teaspoons dried oregano

2 teaspoons ground cumin

8 large Boston or butter lettuce leaves

1. Spray large skillet with nonstick spray and set over medium-high heat. Add onion and garlic and cook, stirring occasionally, until softened, about 4 minutes.
2. Add beef and salt; cook, breaking meat up with wooden spoon, until browned, about 3 minutes. Stir in tomatoes, tomato paste, olives, raisins, oregano, and cumin. Simmer over medium-low heat, stirring occasionally, until mixture is thickened, about 8 minutes.
3. To serve, spoon into lettuce leaves.

PER SERVING (1¼ cups picadillo and 2 lettuce leaves): 264 Cal, 7 g Total Fat, 2 g Sat Fat, 1 g Trans Fat, 62 mg Chol, 650 mg Sod, 24 g Total Carb, 3 g Fib, 27 g Prot, 103 mg Calc.

PointsPlus value: *7.*

Do it Faster

To core a head of Boston or iceberg lettuce in a few seconds, rap the core of the lettuce on the counter to loosen it from the leaves and pull it out in one neat piece.

Beef and Black Bean Burgers

SERVES 6

1 (14½-ounce) can black beans, rinsed and drained

¾ pound ground lean beef (5% fat or less)

¼ cup fat-free mild salsa

¼ cup chopped fresh parsley

¼ teaspoon salt

6 reduced-calorie whole wheat hamburger buns

1. Preheat broiler. Spray broiler pan with nonstick spray.
2. Place beans in large bowl and mash coarsely with potato masher or large fork (some beans should remain whole for texture). Add beef, salsa, parsley, and salt and mix with spoon or your hands until blended.
3. Shape into 6 patties and place patties on broiler pan. Broil, turning once, until cooked through and browned, about 10 minutes. Serve in buns.

PER SERVING (1 sandwich): 239 Cal, 6 g Total Fat, 2 g Sat Fat, 0 g Trans Fat, 38 mg Chol, 497 mg Sod, 29 g Total Carb, 6 g Fib, 19 g Prot, 66 mg Calc.

PointsPlus value: ***6.***

Cook's Note

Quick-cooking baby potatoes are a perfect accompaniment to these hearty burgers (3 ounces baked baby potatoes per serving will increase the ***PointsPlus*** value by ***2***).

express shopping

Grocery shopping is one of the most time-consuming household tasks, yet it has to be done at least once a week. Be sure to take the few extra minutes to read labels and choose sustainably raised meats, poultry, seafood, and eggs. Visit local farmers' markets or shop at supermarkets that support local farmers for your produce. And use these tips to streamline the time you spend in the aisles.

ALWAYS SHOP WITH A LIST. Create a list based on what you'll be cooking for the entire week, including any special events like a family potluck or cupcakes you need to bake to donate to the school fundraiser. Organize the list by food category and the layout of the supermarket aisles. This way, you'll get everything you need in one aisle of the store before moving on to the next. Use an online grocery list template, a grocery list app, or your own paper list.

SHOP ONLY ONCE A WEEK. Making fewer trips to the store is one of the best timesaving tricks there is. That's why it's so important to make a comprehensive weekly shopping list so you're not stopping by the store after work wasting half an hour to buy the one thing you forgot. This saves money, too, because you're sure to pick up more than one thing once you're inside the store.

GO AT OFF-PEAK TIMES. If your schedule allows, try hitting the store early in the morning or mid-afternoon before the after-work rush. Nights are less crowded, but the shelves may not be as well-stocked as they are during the day. Avoid weekends whenever possible.

SHOP ALONE. You'll get through the aisles faster without the distraction of children asking for sugar-sweetened cereal or a spouse leading you to the sausage sampling station set up at the meat counter.

STAY FOCUSED. Skip going down aisles with food that is not on your list, say "no thank you" to anyone offering food samples, and if you run into anyone you know, say a quick hello and be on your way.

BE A LOYAL CUSTOMER. Decide which one or two supermarkets are your favorites and always do your shopping there. You'll become familiar with where items are located in the aisles, cutting down on backtracking for forgotten items. You'll also get to know the staff of the store and learn to identify which cashiers will get you through the checkout lane the quickest.

QUESTION COUPONING. Keep track of how much money you save using coupons versus how much time you spend searching for them online or in magazines and newspapers, keeping them organized, and the extra time it takes in the checkout lane. Unless you're a coupon pro, it's probably not worth your time. A quicker way to save money is to scope out weekly specials at the supermarket and stock up when pantry staples are on sale.

BE A CLEVER CLICKER. Many supermarkets offer timesaving online shopping and grocery delivery for a nominal fee. Check the cost at your market and decide if the time saved is worth the money. If you feel you need to choose fresh produce, meats, and seafood in person, you'll still save time if you get pantry staples delivered and shop for fresh food yourself.

Honey-Mustard Turkey Sandwiches

SERVES 4

¼ cup Dijon mustard

2 tablespoons honey

1½ teaspoons reduced-sodium soy sauce

¾ cup plain dried bread crumbs

4 (¼-pound) turkey breast cutlets

4 whole wheat ciabatta rolls, split and toasted

4 leaf lettuce leaves

2 plum tomatoes, sliced

1. Preheat oven to 400°F. Spray baking sheet with nonstick spray.
2. Whisk together mustard, honey, and soy sauce in small bowl. Place bread crumbs on plate. Dip turkey into mustard mixture, then into bread crumbs. Place on baking sheet. Spray turkey lightly with nonstick spray and bake, turning once, until cooked through, about 20 minutes.
3. Serve turkey in rolls topped with lettuce leaves and tomato slices.

PER SERVING (1 sandwich): 388 Cal, 5 g Total Fat, 1 g Sat Fat, 0 g Trans Fat, 76 mg Chol, 818 mg Sod, 48 g Total Carb, 5 g Fib, 34 g Prot, 105 mg Calc.

PointsPlus value: **9.**

Do it Faster

To make cleanup easy, lightly spray the measuring spoon with nonstick spray before measuring the honey.

30 minute meals

Dilled Salmon Sandwiches with Caper Sauce

SERVES 4

1 (14½-ounce) can red sockeye salmon, drained, skin and bones discarded

½ cup plain dried bread crumbs

½ cup chopped red onion

¼ cup plus 3 tablespoons fat-free mayonnaise

1 large egg, lightly beaten

2 tablespoons chopped fresh dill

¼ teaspoon black pepper

½ teaspoon canola oil

½ cup roasted red bell peppers (not packed in oil)

⅛ teaspoon hot pepper sauce

2 tablespoons drained capers

4 whole wheat sandwich rolls, split and toasted

½ English (seedless) cucumber, peeled and sliced

1. To make salmon patties, combine salmon, bread crumbs, onion, ¼ cup mayonnaise, egg, dill, and black pepper in medium bowl. Stir, breaking up any large chunks of salmon, until just combined. Form mixture into 4 patties.
2. Coat large nonstick skillet with oil placed over medium heat. Add patties and cook until browned and heated through, about 5 minutes on each side.
3. Meanwhile, to make sauce, combine remaining 3 tablespoons mayonnaise, bell peppers, and hot pepper sauce in blender; puree. Add capers and pulse until just combined.
4. Spread cut sides of rolls with sauce; fill with salmon patties and cucumber slices.

PER SERVING (1 sandwich): 305 Cal, 8 g Total Fat, 2 g Sat Fat, 0 g Trans Fat, 113 mg Chol, 984 mg Sod, 32 g Total Carb, 5 g Fib, 27 g Prot, 300 mg Calc.

PointsPlus value: ***8.***

Do it Faster

If peeling cucumbers and other vegetables is taking longer than it should, it could be that you need to replace the blade on your vegetable peeler or buy a new one.

Tuna Steak Sandwiches with Roasted Pepper Relish

SERVES 4

4 (6-ounce) tuna steaks

½ teaspoon paprika

½ teaspoon ground cumin

¼ teaspoon black pepper

2 teaspoons canola oil

¼ teaspoon salt

1 cup thinly sliced roasted red bell peppers (not packed in oil)

2 tablespoons chopped fresh basil

2 teaspoons grated lemon zest

2 teaspoons fresh lemon juice

4 (½-inch) slices crusty whole wheat bread, toasted

1. Sprinkle tuna with paprika, cumin, and ⅛ teaspoon black pepper; cover and refrigerate 10 minutes.
2. Heat oil in large skillet over high heat. Sprinkle tuna with ⅛ teaspoon salt. Add tuna to skillet and cook until seared and cooked to desired doneness, about 2 minutes on each side for medium.
3. Meanwhile, stir together bell peppers, basil, lemon zest, lemon juice, remaining ⅛ teaspoon salt, and remaining ⅛ teaspoon black pepper in small bowl.
4. Place bread on 4 plates; top with tuna steaks. Top sandwiches evenly with bell pepper mixture.

PER SERVING (1 open-faced sandwich): 365 Cal, 12 g Total Fat, 3 g Sat Fat, 0 g Trans Fat, 59 mg Chol, 515 mg Sod, 21 g Total Carb, 4 g Fib, 42 g Prot, 70 mg Calc.

PointsPlus value: **9.**

Do it Faster

Set aside a new toothbrush to use in the kitchen specifically for quickly removing all the citrus zest and fresh ginger from your grater. This quick extra step prevents waste and speeds cleanup.

30 minute meals

Crunchy Fish Sliders

SERVES 4

¾ pound cod fillet

¼ cup all-purpose flour

½ cup buttermilk

¾ cup whole wheat cracker crumbs

1 tablespoon finely chopped fresh parsley

¼ teaspoon salt

¼ teaspoon garlic powder

2 teaspoons olive oil

4 mini whole wheat buns

1. Cut fish into 4 equal squares. Place flour in shallow bowl and buttermilk in another bowl. Stir together crumbs, parsley, salt, and garlic powder in third bowl. Coat each piece of fish first with flour, then with buttermilk, and finally with crumb mixture.
2. Heat oil in medium nonstick skillet over medium heat. Add fish and cook, turning once, until browned and just opaque in center, about 8 minutes total. Place each piece in bun.

PER SERVING (1 sandwich): 277 Cal, 8 g Total Fat, 1 g Sat Fat, 0 g Trans Fat, 34 mg Chol, 477 mg Sod, 34 g Total Carb, 4 g Fib, 19 g Prot, 85 mg Calc.

PointsPlus value: *7.*

Cook's Note

Fill the sandwiches with ***0 PointsPlus*** value toppings of your choice. Try lettuce leaves, tomato slices, red onion rings, or dill pickles.

Quesadillas with Guacamole and Pepper Jack

1. Spread beans evenly over 4 tortillas. Sprinkle evenly with pepper Jack, tomato, onion, and cilantro. Cover with remaining 4 tortillas, pressing down lightly.
2. Spray medium skillet with nonstick spray and set over medium heat. Cook quesadillas, one at a time, until crisp and heated through, about 2 minutes on each side. Cut each quesadilla into 4 wedges and arrange on platter. Serve with guacamole and salsa.

PER SERVING (1 quesadilla, ¼ cup guacamole, and ¼ cup salsa): 253 Cal, 8 g Total Fat, 2 g Sat Fat, 0 g Trans Fat, 6 mg Chol, 982 mg Sod, 36 g Total Carb, 9 g Fib, 12 g Prot, 147 mg Calc.

PointsPlus value: **6.**

Cook's Note

To make a filling lunch, serve the quesadillas with a crunchy slaw. Toss together 1 cup each shredded jicama and green cabbage, 2 large shredded carrots, and a handful of chopped fresh cilantro with fresh lime juice and salt and pepper to taste.

SERVES 4

1 cup canned fat-free refried beans

8 (6-inch) whole wheat tortillas

½ cup shredded reduced-fat pepper Jack cheese

1 small tomato, chopped

¼ small red onion, chopped

2 tablespoons chopped fresh cilantro

1 cup purchased guacamole

1 cup fat-free refrigerated salsa

30 minute meals

Asian-Style Pork, Mushroom, and Noodle Soup

SERVES 4

4 ounces whole wheat capellini or spaghetti

4 cups reduced-sodium chicken broth

2 cups water

3 cups thinly sliced Napa cabbage

8 shiitake mushrooms, stems removed and caps sliced

4 scallions, sliced on diagonal

1 large tomato, seeded and diced

1 cup frozen baby peas

1 tablespoon minced peeled fresh ginger

1 tablespoon reduced-sodium soy sauce

6 ounces cooked lean boneless center-cut pork loin chops, trimmed and cut into thin strips

3 drops hot pepper sauce

1. Cook pasta according to package directions, omitting salt if desired; drain.
2. Meanwhile, bring broth and water to boil in large pot. Add cabbage, mushrooms, scallions, tomato, peas, ginger, and soy sauce; reduce heat and simmer until cabbage is tender, about 5 minutes.
3. Add pasta, pork, and hot pepper sauce to soup; simmer until pork is heated through, about 2 minutes.

PER SERVING (about 2½ cups): 270 Cal, 5 g Total Fat, 2 g Sat Fat, 0 g Trans Fat, 35 mg Chol, 866 mg Sod, 35 g Total Carb, 6 g Fib, 24 g Prot, 106 mg Calc.

PointsPlus value: *7*.

Cook's Note

For an easy, elegant dessert, serve thinly sliced fresh mango sprinkled with grated lime zest.

Asian-Style Pork, Mushroom, and Noodle Soup

30 minute meals

Manhattan Clam Chowder

SERVES 4

2 teaspoons olive oil

1 onion, finely chopped

1 carrot, finely chopped

1 celery stalk, finely chopped

1½ cups water

1 (14½-ounce) can petite diced tomatoes

1 (8-ounce) bottle clam juice

1 large all-purpose potato, peeled and chopped

½ teaspoon dried thyme

¼ teaspoon black pepper

2 (6½-ounce) cans chopped clams, undrained

1. Heat oil in large saucepan over medium heat. Add onion, carrot, and celery; cook, stirring, until softened, about 3 minutes.
2. Add water, tomatoes, clam juice, potato, thyme, and pepper; bring to boil over medium-high heat. Reduce heat and simmer, partially covered, until vegetables are tender, about 12 minutes.
3. Add clams and simmer just until heated through, about 2 minutes.

PER SERVING (about 1¾ cups): 174 Cal, 3 g Total Fat, 0 g Sat Fat, 0 g Trans Fat, 25 mg Chol, 358 mg Sod, 25 g Total Carb, 4 g Fib, 12 g Prot, 99 mg Calc.

PointsPlus value: ***4***.

Cook's Note

This soup calls for a crusty roll to serve alongside (a 1½-ounce light roll per serving will increase the ***PointsPlus*** value by ***2***).

Smoky Vegetarian Chili

30 minute meals

SERVES 4

2 teaspoons olive oil

1 onion, chopped

1 red bell pepper, chopped

3 garlic cloves, minced

1 tablespoon chili powder

1 teaspoon ground cumin

1 teaspoon dried oregano

1 (28-ounce) can diced tomatoes

1 (15½-ounce) can pinto beans, rinsed and drained

1 (15½-ounce) can red kidney beans, rinsed and drained

⅛ teaspoon salt

3 drops liquid smoke

4 scallions, sliced

½ cup shredded reduced-fat Cheddar cheese

½ cup fat-free sour cream

1. Heat oil in large saucepan over medium-high heat. Add onion, bell pepper, garlic, chili powder, cumin, and oregano; cook until vegetables are softened, about 5 minutes.
2. Stir in tomatoes, pinto beans, kidney beans, salt, and liquid smoke; bring to boil. Reduce heat and simmer until chili thickens slightly, about 15 minutes.
3. Divide chili evenly among 4 bowls and top evenly with scallions, Cheddar, and sour cream.

PER SERVING (1 cup chili, about 2 tablespoons scallions, 2 tablespoons cheese, and 2 tablespoons sour cream): 337 Cal, 5 g Total Fat, 1 g Sat Fat, 0 g Trans Fat, 6 mg Chol, 854 mg Sod, 57 g Total Carb, 16 g Fib, 20 g Prot, 298 mg Calc.

PointsPlus value: ***8.***

Do it Faster

Use your kitchen shears to make quick work of slicing scallions or chives.

30 minute meals

Hearty Corn Chowder

SERVES 4

2 teaspoons olive oil

1 red or green bell pepper, diced

1 onion, chopped

3 cups frozen corn kernels

¾ pound red potatoes, scrubbed and diced

1 cup reduced-sodium chicken broth

¼ teaspoon black pepper

3 cups fat-free milk

4 slices turkey bacon, crisp-cooked and coarsely crumbled

1. Heat oil in large saucepan over medium heat. Add bell pepper and onion; cook, stirring, until softened, about 5 minutes. Add corn, potatoes, broth, and black pepper; bring to boil over medium-high heat. Reduce heat and simmer, covered, until potatoes are tender, about 10 minutes.
2. Puree ½ cup of vegetable mixture with 1 cup of milk in blender until almost smooth. Stir puree along with remaining 2 cups milk back into soup. Cook over medium heat, stirring occasionally, until heated through, about 5 minutes. Serve sprinkled with bacon.

PER SERVING (about 2 cups): 319 Cal, 7 g Total Fat, 2 g Sat Fat, 0 g Trans Fat, 17 mg Chol, 552 mg Sod, 52 g Total Carb, 6 g Fib, 16 g Prot, 266 mg Calc.

PointsPlus value: ***8.***

Cook's Note

Pureeing some of the soup takes a bit of extra time and effort, but it's worth it for the creaminess and body it adds to this satisfying chowder.

Potato-Watercress Soup

SERVES 4

- 2 teaspoons olive oil
- 1 onion, chopped
- 4 Yukon Gold potatoes, peeled and coarsely chopped
- 1 bunch watercress, tender sprigs only
- 4 cups reduced-sodium chicken broth
- 1 cup fat-free half-and-half
- ⅛ teaspoon salt
- ⅛ teaspoon black pepper

1. Heat oil in large saucepan over medium heat. Add onion and cook, stirring, until softened, about 3 minutes. Add potatoes, watercress, and broth; bring to boil over medium-high heat. Reduce heat and simmer, covered, until potatoes are tender, about 12 minutes. Let cool 5 minutes.

2. Puree potato mixture, in batches, in blender. Return soup to saucepan and stir in half-and-half, salt, and pepper. Cook over medium heat until heated through, about 2 minutes; do not boil.

PER SERVING (about 1¼ cups): 230 Cal, 3 g Total Fat, 1 g Sat Fat, 0 g Trans Fat, 3 mg Chol, 738 mg Sod, 43 g Total Carb, 4 g Fib, 8 g Prot, 123 mg Calc.

PointsPlus value: ***6.***

Cook's Note

Serve this comforting soup with a salad made with fresh baby spinach, sliced mushrooms, thinly sliced red onion, white wine vinegar, and salt and pepper to taste.

Creamy Tomato Soup
and Ham and Swiss Panini,
page 18

Creamy Tomato Soup

SERVES 4

2 teaspoons olive oil

1 onion, chopped

2 garlic cloves, minced

4 large tomatoes, coarsely chopped

1 cup reduced-sodium chicken broth

4 teaspoons chopped fresh thyme or 1 teaspoon dried

½ teaspoon salt

¼ teaspoon black pepper

3 cups fat-free milk

¼ cup tomato paste

1. Heat oil in large saucepan over medium heat. Add onion and garlic; cook, stirring, until softened, about 5 minutes.
2. Stir in tomatoes, broth, thyme, salt, and pepper. Cover and simmer until vegetables are tender, about 5 minutes longer. Let cool 5 minutes.
3. Puree tomato mixture, in batches, in blender. Return mixture to saucepan.
4. Whisk together milk and tomato paste in small bowl; whisk mixture into soup. Cook, stirring occasionally, just until heated through, about 5 minutes; do not boil.

PER SERVING (1¼ cups): 198 Cal, 6 g Total Fat, 1 g Sat Fat, 0 g Trans Fat, 4 mg Chol, 574 mg Sod, 29 g Total Carb, 4 g Fib, 11 g Prot, 263 mg Calc.

PointsPlus value: **5.**

Cook's Note

For an update on a classic menu, serve the soup with Ham and Swiss Panini, page 18, and crisp celery stalks.

30 minute meals

Cremini Mushroom, Tomato, and Rice Soup

SERVES 4

2 teaspoons olive oil

2 leeks cleaned and chopped, white and light green parts only

1 pound cremini mushrooms, sliced

2½ cups reduced-sodium chicken broth

1 (14½-ounce) can fire-roasted diced tomatoes

¼ teaspoon salt

⅛ teaspoon black pepper

½ cup quick-cooking brown rice

1. Heat oil in large saucepan over medium-high heat. Add leeks and cook, stirring, until softened, about 5 minutes. Add mushrooms and cook, stirring, until tender, about 5 minutes.
2. Add broth, tomatoes, salt, and pepper; simmer 5 minutes. Stir in rice and cook until tender, about 10 minutes longer.

PER SERVING (1½ cups): 145 Cal, 3 g Total Fat, 0 g Sat Fat, 0 g Trans Fat, 0 mg Chol, 657 mg Sod, 24 g Total Carb, 4 g Fib, 8 g Prot, 78 mg Calc.

PointsPlus value: ***4.***

Cook's Note

Cheese toast is an easy partner for this comforting soup. To make it, top 1 slice of reduced-calorie whole wheat bread with 1 slice of fat-free Swiss cheese and broil until the cheese melts (1 cheese toast per serving will increase the ***PointsPlus*** value by *2*).

Edamame Salad with Basil Vinaigrette

SERVES 4

1 cup frozen shelled edamame

3 tablespoons red-wine vinegar

1 tablespoon olive oil

1 garlic clove, minced

¼ teaspoon salt

1 (15½-ounce) can cannellini (white kidney) beans, rinsed and drained

1 large tomato, diced

1 celery stalk, sliced

½ red onion, diced

½ cup chopped fresh basil

1. Bring small pot of water to boil. Add edamame and cook 5 minutes; drain, rinse under cold water, and pat dry.
2. Combine vinegar, oil, garlic, and salt in large bowl. Add edamame, cannellini beans, tomato, celery, onion, and basil; mix well. Let stand at room temperature about 15 minutes before serving.

PER SERVING (generous 1 cup): 206 Cal, 6 g Total Fat, 2 g Sat Fat, 0 g Trans Fat, 0 mg Chol, 395 mg Sod, 27 g Total Carb, 8 g Fib, 12 g Prot, 143 mg Calc.

PointsPlus value: ***5.***

Cook's Note

Serve this salad with mixed fresh fruit for dessert. Try sliced kiwifruit and nectarines sprinkled with blueberries for a fresh, colorful finish.

30 minute meals

Pasta Salad with Apple and Chicken

SERVES 4

6 ounces whole wheat penne

⅓ cup fresh orange juice

3 tablespoons balsamic vinegar

1 tablespoon Dijon mustard

1 tablespoon pure maple syrup

1 cup diced cooked skinless chicken breast

1 (5-ounce) bag baby arugula

1 small Granny Smith apple, cored and diced

1 large shallot, finely chopped

¼ cup pecans, coarsely chopped

1. Cook penne according to package directions, omitting salt if desired. Drain and rinse under cold running water; drain again.
2. To make dressing, whisk together orange juice, vinegar, mustard, and maple syrup in large bowl. Add pasta, chicken, arugula, apple, shallot, and pecans to dressing; toss to coat.

PER SERVING (about 2 cups): 315 Cal, 8 g Total Fat, 1 g Sat Fat, 0 g Trans Fat, 29 mg Chol, 284 mg Sod, 46 g Total Carb, 5 g Fib, 19 g Prot, 100 mg Calc.

PointsPlus value: ***8.***

Cook's Note

If you like the robust flavor of whole-grain mustard, it's a delicious option for using in this recipe.

Pasta Salad with Apple and Chicken

Tabbouleh with Shrimp

SERVES 4

1¼ cups water

1 cup bulgur

1 pound cooked, peeled, and deveined medium shrimp

1 small cucumber, peeled, seeded, and chopped

2 tomatoes, cut into ½-inch pieces

2 scallions, chopped

½ cup chopped fresh parsley

¼ cup chopped fresh mint

3 tablespoons fresh lemon juice

2 teaspoons olive oil

½ teaspoon salt

¼ teaspoon black pepper

1. Pour water over bulgur in medium bowl. Cover and let stand until water is absorbed, about 25 minutes. Fluff bulgur with fork; transfer to serving bowl.
2. Add remaining ingredients to bulgur; toss to combine.

PER SERVING (about 2 cups): 246 Cal, 4 g Total Fat, 1 g Sat Fat, 0 g Trans Fat, 161 mg Chol, 501 mg Sod, 32 g Total Carb, 8 g Fib, 23 g Prot, 80 mg Calc.

PointsPlus value: **6.**

Cook's Note

Serve the salad with pita bread, the traditional Mediterranean accompaniment (a 100% whole wheat pita bread per serving will increase the ***PointsPlus*** value by ***3***).

Hearty Lentil Salad with Radicchio

SERVES 4

1½ cups brown lentils, picked over and rinsed

1 bay leaf

6 cups water

1 large head radicchio, quartered, cored, and very thinly sliced

1 cup cherry tomatoes, halved

4 scallions, chopped

1 carrot, shredded

½ cup chopped fresh basil

2½ tablespoons red-wine vinegar

1 tablespoon olive oil

¾ teaspoon salt

¼ teaspoon black pepper

1. Combine lentils, bay leaf, and water in medium saucepan and bring to boil over medium-high heat. Reduce heat and simmer, covered, until lentils are tender but still hold their shape, about 20 minutes; drain. Discard bay leaf and rinse lentils under cold running water; drain again.
2. Meanwhile, combine remaining ingredients in large serving bowl. Add lentils and toss again.

PER SERVING (1⅔ cups): 292 Cal, 4 g Total Fat, 1 g Sat Fat, 0 g Trans Fat, 0 mg Chol, 482 mg Sod, 46 g Total Carb, 14 g Fib, 19 g Prot, 86 mg Calc.

PointsPlus value: *7.*

30 minute meals

Greek Pita Pizzas with Spinach and Feta

SERVES 4

1 teaspoon olive oil

1 onion, chopped

3 garlic cloves, minced

¼ teaspoon dried oregano

1 (10-ounce) package frozen chopped spinach, thawed and squeezed dry

⅓ cup crumbled reduced-fat feta cheese

4 (6-inch) whole wheat pita breads

1 cup grape tomatoes, halved

¾ cup shredded part-skim mozzarella cheese

1. Preheat oven to 425°F.
2. Heat oil in large nonstick skillet over medium heat. Add onion and cook, stirring frequently, until softened, about 4 minutes. Stir in garlic and oregano; cook, stirring, about 1 minute. Stir in spinach and cook until hot, about 2 minutes. Remove skillet from heat and stir in feta.
3. Arrange pitas on baking sheet. Top with spinach mixture, spreading it to edges. Arrange tomatoes on top. Bake until pitas are crisp, 8–10 minutes.
4. Sprinkle pizzas with mozzarella; bake until melted, about 3 minutes.

PER SERVING (1 pizza): 281 Cal, 8 g Total Fat, 4 g Sat Fat, 0 g Trans Fat, 15 mg Chol, 596 mg Sod, 40 g Total Carb, 7 g Fib, 15 g Prot, 296 mg Calc.

PointsPlus value: *7.*

Do it Faster

To quickly squeeze the water out of thawed spinach, separate it into small handfuls and squeeze it as tightly as you can over the sink. If it still seems wet, blot the spinach with paper towels to remove more moisture.

Filets Mignons with Tomato-Bean Salsa

SERVES 4

4 (¼-pound) lean filets mignons, trimmed

½ teaspoon ground cumin

¼ teaspoon black pepper

1 (15½-ounce) can small white beans, rinsed and drained

2 tomatoes, seeded and chopped

1 Kirby cucumber, peeled and chopped

¼ cup finely chopped red onion

¼ cup diced avocado

2 tablespoons chopped fresh basil

1 tablespoon red-wine vinegar

½ teaspoon salt

1½ teaspoons olive oil

1. Sprinkle filets mignons with cumin and pepper; cover and refrigerate 10 minutes.
2. Meanwhile, to make salsa, toss together beans, tomatoes, cucumber, onion, avocado, basil, vinegar, and ¼ teaspoon of salt in serving bowl.
3. Heat oil in large skillet over medium-high heat. Sprinkle steaks with remaining ¼ teaspoon salt. Add steaks to skillet and cook until an instant-read thermometer inserted into side of steak registers 145°F for medium, about 2 minutes on each side. Serve with salsa.

PER SERVING (1 steak and about 1 cup salsa): 323 Cal, 11 g Total Fat, 3 g Sat Fat, 0 g Trans Fat, 46 mg Chol, 567 mg Sod, 24 g Total Carb, 7 g Fib, 33 g Prot, 90 mg Calc.

PointsPlus value: ***8.***

Sliced Steak with Crispy Polenta

Sliced Steak with Crispy Polenta

SERVES 4

1 (1-pound) lean flank steak, trimmed

½ teaspoon ancho or regular chili powder

½ teaspoon salt

1 (16-ounce) tube fat-free polenta, cut into 12 slices

1½ cups fresh or thawed frozen corn kernels

1 red bell pepper, chopped

½ red onion, chopped

1 jalapeño pepper, seeded and minced

2 tablespoons chopped fresh cilantro

1. Spray ridged grill pan with nonstick spray and set over medium-high heat. Sprinkle steak with chili powder and salt. Place steak in pan and cook until an instant-read thermometer inserted into side of steak registers 145°F for medium, about 5 minutes on each side. Transfer steak to cutting board and let stand 5 minutes. Cut on diagonal into 16 slices.
2. Meanwhile, spray broiler rack with nonstick spray and preheat broiler. Arrange slices of polenta on rack and broil 5 inches from heat until crispy and heated through, about 2 minutes on each side.
3. Spray medium skillet with nonstick spray and set over medium heat. Add corn, bell pepper, onion, and jalapeño pepper; cook, stirring, until softened, about 5 minutes. Remove skillet from heat and stir in cilantro.
4. Place 3 slices of polenta on each of 4 plates and top each serving with 4 slices of steak. Divide corn mixture evenly among plates.

PER SERVING (4 slices steak, 3 slices polenta, and ¾ cup corn mixture): 312 Cal, 5 g Total Fat, 2 g Sat Fat, 1 g Trans Fat, 83 mg Chol, 345 mg Sod, 29 g Total Carb, 3 g Fib, 37 g Prot, 16 mg Calc.

PointsPlus value: ***8.***

Do it Faster

To neatly and quickly remove the kernels from an ear of corn, place a bowl in the sink, stand the corn on end inside the bowl, and cut off the kernels with a knife. Any fly-away kernels will end up in the sink.

you *can* make it quick

Fast, convenient, and economical, canned foods can be a real time-saver and a smart way to supplement fresh and frozen ingredients in your meals. Better yet, they will last for years, so you'll practically never have to worry about them going bad. Here are our top picks for canned staples that combine quality with good nutrition.

BEANS. No pantry should be without an assortment of ready-to-eat beans. Beans are a classic example of foods that do beautifully in cans, and no-salt-added varieties are a terrific option for lowering the sodium in home-cooked meals.

BROTHS. Canned or packaged broths can flavor everything from soups to stews to pilafs. Look for broths labeled low-sodium or no-salt-added to avoid excess sodium.

COCONUT PRODUCTS. Many coconut products are sold in convenient and economical cans or shelf-stable cartons. Keep lite (reduced-fat) coconut milk and coconut water as pantry staples. A splash of coconut milk adds tropical flavor to a smoothie and coconut water makes a refreshing drink for only ***1 PointsPlus*** value per cup.

FRUITS. Avoid fruits canned in sugary syrups, but keep water-packed or juice-packed favorites such as pineapple, pears, peaches, and mandarin oranges on hand. They're a great addition to sweet and savory recipes, or you can enjoy them on their own for snacks and desserts.

SEAFOOD. Canned salmon, tuna, and sardines are great to have on hand for quick salads and sandwiches. Make sure the fish is packed in water (not oil) to avoid excess fat, and look for no-salt-added options when possible. Canned clams are excellent for adding to pasta dishes or as a pizza topping.

SOUPS. Keep a few cans of low-fat, low-sodium soup around for days when you have no time to cook. Cans and cartons of vegetable-based soups such as tomato, butternut squash, or red bell pepper can also be handy for composing soups on the fly: add some diced leftover chicken or tofu and leftover rice or pasta and you'll have a superquick, filling meal.

TOMATOES. Canned tomatoes are tops when it comes to getting big, bold, consistent tomato flavor year-round. Canned tomato sauce is also a healthy time-saver—just be sure to read the label and make sure the product does not contain added sugar.

VEGETABLES. Veggies from a can can be a smart alternative to fresh. Canned corn kernels, cream-style corn, sauerkraut, lima beans, beets, artichoke hearts, and hearts of palm are delicious, convenient options for recipes.

A note about BPA

The chemical Bisphenol A (BPA) is sometimes used as an interior coating on cans to keep food from coming in contact with metal. There is evidence that the chemical may leach into food. Although the FDA has concluded that amounts are too minimal to pose a health risk, if you're concerned you can look for cans or cartons labeled as BPA-free, or rinse and drain canned foods like beans and corn to minimize exposure.

Grilled Flank Steak with Tomato-Fennel Salad

SERVES 4

4 plum tomatoes, each cut into 6 wedges

2 tablespoons chopped fresh flat-leaf parsley

2 teaspoons grated lemon zest

1 tablespoon lemon juice

¾ teaspoon salt

¼ teaspoon black pepper

1 (1-pound) flank steak, trimmed

1 fennel bulb, cut lengthwise into ½-inch-thick slices

1. Spray grill rack with nonstick spray; preheat grill to medium-high or prepare medium-high fire.
2. Combine tomatoes, parsley, lemon zest and juice, ¼ teaspoon of salt, and 1/8 teaspoon of pepper in medium bowl. Set aside.
3. Sprinkle steak with remaining ½ teaspoon salt and remaining ⅛ teaspoon pepper. Lightly spray fennel with nonstick spray. Place steak and fennel on grill rack. Grill, turning fennel occasionally, and turning steak once, until fennel is tender and instant-read thermometer inserted into center of steak registers 145°F, about 10 minutes. Remove core from fennel; coarsely chop fennel. Stir fennel into tomato mixture. Cut steak into 12 slices and serve with salad.

PER SERVING: (3 slices steak with 1 cup salad): 191 Cal, 7 g Total Fat, 3 g Sat Fat, 0 g Trans Fat, 42 mg Chol, 519 mg Sod, 7 g Total Carb, 2 g Sugar, 3 g Fib, 25 g Prot, 55 mg Calc.

PointsPlus value: ***5.***

Cook's Note

To make this meal more filling and nutritious, serve the steak and salad over a bed of curly endive or mixed baby greens along with corn-on-the-cob (½ of a small ear of corn will increase the ***PointsPlus*** value by ***1***).

30 minute meals

Curried Beef Kebabs with Basmati Rice

SERVES 4

1 cup basmati rice

1¼ pound lean boneless sirloin steak, trimmed and cut into 1-inch chunks

1 red onion, quartered and separated into slices

1 yellow squash, thickly sliced

4 baby pattypan squash, halved

2 teaspoons canola oil

2½ teaspoons curry powder

⅛ teaspoon salt

¼ cup whole fresh cilantro leaves

1. Prepare rice according to package directions, omitting salt if desired.
2. Spray broiler rack with nonstick spray and preheat broiler.
3. Combine beef, onion, squashes, oil, curry powder, and salt in large bowl; toss to coat.
4. Thread beef, onion, and squashes alternately on 8 (12-inch) metal skewers. Place skewers on broiler rack and broil 5 inches from heat, turning occasionally, until an instant-read thermometer inserted into chunk of beef registers 145°F for medium, about 10 minutes. Serve with rice and sprinkle with cilantro.

PER SERVING (2 skewers and ¾ cup rice): 435 Cal, 8 g Total Fat, 2 g Sat Fat, 0 g Trans Fat, 92 mg Chol, 675 mg Sod, 46 g Total Carb, 2 g Fib, 42 g Prot, 39 mg Calc.

PointsPlus value: ***11.***

Do it Faster

No time to thread skewers? Simply place the steak and vegetables directly on the broiler pan and broil as directed.

Curried Beef Kebabs with Basmati Rice

Hearty Steak and Vegetables

SERVES 4

1½ cups quick-cooking brown rice

1 pound lean beef top round steak, trimmed and thinly sliced

¾ teaspoon chili powder

¼ teaspoon salt

2 teaspoons olive oil

2 zucchini, halved lengthwise and sliced

2 red bell peppers, sliced

1 onion, sliced

½ teaspoon ground cumin

1. Cook rice according to package directions, omitting salt if desired.
2. Meanwhile, toss together steak, chili powder, and ⅛ teaspoon of salt in large bowl.
3. Heat oil in large skillet over high heat. Add steak and cook, stirring frequently, until lightly browned, about 5 minutes. Transfer to plate.
4. Reduce heat to medium-high. Add zucchini, bell peppers, onion, cumin, and remaining ⅛ teaspoon salt to skillet; cook, stirring frequently, until vegetables are softened, about 5 minutes.
5. Return steak to skillet and cook just until heated through, about 2 minutes. Serve over rice.

PER SERVING (2 cups steak and vegetables and ¾ cup rice): 385 Cal, 9 g Total Fat, 2 g Sat Fat, 0 g Trans Fat, 84 mg Chol, 647 mg Sod, 38 g Total Carb, 7 g Fib, 39 g Prot, 45 mg Calc.

PointsPlus value: ***9.***

Cook's Note

To enjoy even more veggies with this healthy dinner, make a salad of plum tomato wedges and sliced cucumbers tossed with a pinch of cumin, fresh lime juice, and salt and pepper to taste.

Spaghetti with Quick Bolognese Sauce

SERVES 4

8 ounces whole wheat spaghetti

1 pound lean ground beef (5% fat or less)

1 onion, chopped

1 green bell pepper, chopped

2 garlic cloves, minced

1 (28-ounce) can diced tomatoes

2 teaspoons dried basil

¼ teaspoon salt

Pinch red pepper flakes

1. Cook spaghetti according to package directions, omitting salt if desired.
2. Meanwhile, cook beef in large skillet over medium-high heat, breaking it apart with wooden spoon, until lightly browned, about 4 minutes. Stir in onion, bell pepper, and garlic; cook, stirring occasionally, until vegetables are softened, about 5 minutes. Stir in tomatoes, basil, salt, and red pepper flakes; bring mixture to boil. Reduce heat and simmer, stirring occasionally, until slightly thickened, about 10 minutes. Toss pasta with sauce.

PER SERVING (1½ cups spaghetti and sauce): 413 Cal, 8 g Total Fat, 3 g Sat Fat, 0 g Trans Fat, 64 mg Chol, 693 mg Sod, 56 g Total Carb, 8 g Fib, 33 g Prot, 114 mg Calc.

PointsPlus value: ***11.***

Cook's Note

To make a ***0 PointsPlus*** value tossed salad to serve with the pasta, toss together chopped romaine, halved cherry tomatoes, sliced cucumber, thinly sliced red onion, red-wine vinegar, and salt and pepper to taste.

Stir-Fried Beef with Asparagus

Stir-Fried Beef with Asparagus

SERVES 4

1 cup quick-cooking brown rice

2 teaspoons canola oil

1 pound lean beef top round steak, trimmed and cut into thin strips

4 garlic cloves, thinly sliced

1 tablespoon minced peeled fresh ginger

1 pound asparagus spears, trimmed and cut into 2-inch pieces

1 red bell pepper, thinly sliced

4 scallions, thinly sliced

1 (5-ounce) can sliced water chestnuts, drained

¾ cup reduced-sodium chicken broth

1 tablespoon reduced-sodium soy sauce

1. Cook rice according to package directions, omitting salt if desired.
2. Meanwhile, heat large skillet or wok over high heat until drop of water sizzles in pan. Add oil and swirl to coat skillet. Add beef and stir-fry until browned and cooked through, about 4 minutes. Using slotted spoon, transfer beef to plate.
3. Add garlic and ginger to skillet and stir-fry until fragrant, about 30 seconds. Add asparagus and bell pepper and stir-fry until crisp-tender, about 2 minutes longer. Return beef to skillet and add remaining ingredients. Stir-fry until liquid is almost evaporated, about 3 minutes longer. Serve with rice.

PER SERVING (1⅓ cups stir-fry and ½ cup rice): 354 Cal, 8 g Total Fat, 2 g Sat Fat, 0 g Trans Fat, 84 mg Chol, 810 mg Sod, 30 g Total Carb, 6 g Fib, 39 g Prot, 53 mg Calc.

***PointsPlus* value: 8.**

Cook's Note

To serve the stir-fry with an Asian salad, toss together thinly sliced Napa cabbage, shredded carrots, thinly sliced scallions, and reduced-sodium soy sauce to taste. For a touch of spice, add a tiny bit of chili-garlic paste.

Roast Pork Tenderloin with Black Bean Salsa

SERVES 2

½ teaspoon ground cumin

½ teaspoon ancho or regular chili powder

¼ teaspoon salt

1 (¾-pound) lean pork tenderloin, trimmed

1 cup black beans, rinsed and drained

½ cup thawed frozen corn kernels

3 scallions, thinly sliced

1 plum tomato, chopped

½ jalapeño pepper, seeded and minced

2 tablespoons chopped fresh cilantro

1½ tablespoons fresh lime juice

1. Preheat oven to 425°F.
2. Mix together cumin, chili powder, and salt in cup; sprinkle all over pork.
3. Spray large ovenproof skillet with nonstick spray and set over medium-high heat. Add pork and cook until browned on all sides, about 5 minutes.
4. Transfer skillet to oven and roast until an instant-read thermometer inserted into center of pork registers 145°F, about 10 minutes. Transfer to cutting board and let stand 5 minutes. Cut tenderloin into 12 slices.
5. Meanwhile, to make salsa, toss together remaining ingredients in serving bowl. Serve with pork.

PER SERVING (6 slices pork and 1 cup salsa): 385 Cal, 8 g Total Fat, 2 g Sat Fat, 0 g Trans Fat, 106 mg Chol, 386 mg Sod, 32 g Total Carb, 10 g Fib, 47 g Prot, 60 mg Calc.

PointsPlus value: ***9.***

Cook's Note

Steamed kale or mustard greens make an easy side dish for the pork tenderloin.

Cajun-Spiced Roast Pork Tenderloin

1. Preheat oven to 400°F.
2. On sheet of wax paper, combine paprika, cumin, sugar, salt, and cayenne. Roll pork in mixture until evenly coated.
3. Spray large ovenproof skillet with nonstick spray and set over medium-high heat. Add pork and cook until lightly browned on all sides, about 5 minutes.
4. Transfer skillet to oven and roast until an instant-read thermometer inserted into center of tenderloin registers 145°F, about 12 minutes.
5. Transfer pork to cutting board and let stand 5 minutes. Cut into 16 slices.

SERVES 4

1 tablespoon paprika

½ teaspoon ground cumin

½ teaspoon sugar

½ teaspoon salt

⅛ teaspoon cayenne pepper

1 (1-pound) lean pork tenderloin, trimmed

PER SERVING (4 slices pork): 139 Cal, 4 g Total Fat, 1 g Sat Fat, 0 g Trans Fat, 63 mg Chol, 337 mg Sod, 2 g Total Carb, 0 g Fib, 23 g Prot, 10 mg Calc.

PointsPlus value: **3**.

Cook's Note

To accompany the pork tenderloin, make microwave-baked sweet potatoes. Prick 4 (5-ounce) sweet potatoes in several places with a small knife, wrap in paper towels, and microwave on High until tender, 8 to 10 minutes, turning once (a 5-ounce baked sweet potato per serving will increase the ***PointsPlus*** value by **3**).

Saucy Pan-Roasted Pork Chops with Ziti

SERVES 4

- 4 ounces whole wheat ziti or penne
- 2 garlic cloves, minced
- 1 (14½-ounce) can tomato puree
- ¾ teaspoon Italian seasoning
- Pinch red pepper flakes
- 4 (¼-pound) lean bone-in pork loin chops, trimmed
- ¼ teaspoon black pepper
- ⅛ teaspoon salt
- ¼ cup shredded fat-free mozzarella cheese
- 2 tablespoons chopped fresh basil

1. Cook ziti according to package directions, omitting salt if desired.
2. Meanwhile, spray medium saucepan with olive oil nonstick spray and set over medium heat. Add garlic and cook, stirring, until fragrant, about 20 seconds. Add tomato puree, Italian seasoning, and red pepper flakes and bring to boil; reduce heat and simmer, stirring occasionally, 10 minutes.
3. Spray large skillet with nonstick spray and set over high heat. Sprinkle pork with black pepper and salt. Add chops to skillet and cook until lightly browned, about 2 minutes on each side. Reduce heat to medium-low and sprinkle chops evenly with mozzarella. Cover skillet and cook until cheese is melted and an instant-read thermometer inserted into side of chop registers 145°F, about 4 minutes.
4. Divide ziti evenly among 4 plates and top with tomato sauce and pork chop. Sprinkle with basil.

PER SERVING (1 cup linguine, 1 pork chop, and scant ½ cup sauce): 357 Cal, 11 g Total Fat, 4 g Sat Fat, 0 g Trans Fat, 75 mg Chol, 717 mg Sod, 33 g Total Carb, 4 g Fib, 34 g Prot, 108 mg Calc.

PointsPlus value: **9.**

Cook's Note

For a quick green vegetable side dish, make steamed spinach tossed with lemon juice and salt and pepper to taste.

Saucy Pan-Roasted Pork Chops with Ziti

30 minute meals

Pork and Mushroom Stir-Fry

SERVES 6

- 1 tablespoon peanut or canola oil
- 1 pound lean boneless pork loin, trimmed and cut into 1 × ¼-inch strips
- 1 red bell pepper, thinly sliced
- ¼ pound snow peas, trimmed
- 4 scallions, cut into 1-inch pieces
- 1 tablespoon grated peeled fresh ginger
- 1 tablespoon minced garlic
- 1 (15-ounce) can straw mushrooms, drained
- 1 cup drained canned baby corn
- ¼ cup reduced-sodium vegetable broth
- 3 tablespoons reduced-sodium teriyaki sauce
- 1 teaspoon cornstarch
- 3 cups hot cooked brown rice

1. Heat large skillet or wok over medium-high heat until drop of water sizzles in pan. Add 1½ teaspoons of oil and swirl to coat skillet. Add pork, in batches, and stir-fry until browned and cooked through, about 4 minutes. Transfer to plate.
2. Add remaining 1½ teaspoons oil to skillet. Add bell pepper, snow peas, scallions, ginger, and garlic; stir-fry 2 minutes. Add mushrooms and corn and stir-fry until heated through, about 1 minute longer. Return pork to skillet.
3. Stir together broth, teriyaki sauce, and cornstarch in cup until smooth, then add to skillet. Stir-fry until sauce thickens and bubbles, about 2 minutes. Serve with rice.

PER SERVING (1½ cups pork mixture and ½ cup rice): 347 Cal, 10 g Total Fat, 3 g Sat Fat, 0 g Trans Fat, 48 mg Chol, 972 mg Sod, 41 g Total Carb, 8 g Fib, 24 g Prot, 51 mg Calc.

PointsPlus value: ***9.***

Cook's Note

Cooked brown rice will keep in the refrigerator for up to 5 days, so cook a batch on the weekend to enjoy with meals all week long.

Ham with Apples and Mustard

SERVES 4

4 (3-ounce) slices reduced-sodium lean deli ham, trimmed

1 small onion, chopped

3 red apples, cored and cut into ½-inch wedges

1½ cups apple cider

2 teaspoons Dijon mustard

1 tablespoon cornstarch

2 tablespoons cold water

1. Spray large skillet with nonstick spray and set over medium heat. Add ham and cook until lightly browned, about 2 minutes on each side. Transfer to plate.
2. Add onion to skillet and cook, stirring frequently, until softened, about 5 minutes. Add apples, cider, and mustard; cook, stirring frequently, until apples are tender, about 5 minutes longer.
3. Stir together cornstarch and water in cup until smooth, then add to skillet. Cook, stirring constantly, until sauce thickens and bubbles, about 2 minutes. Return ham to skillet and cook until heated through, about 1 minute longer.

PER SERVING (1 slice ham and about ½ cup apple mixture): 254 Cal, 5 g Total Fat, 2 g Sat Fat, 0 g Trans Fat, 45 mg Chol, 890 mg Sod, 34 g Total Carb, 4 g Fib, 19 g Prot, 28 mg Calc.

PointsPlus value: **6.**

Cook's Note

If you prefer, you can use a ¾-pound ham steak for this recipe and cut it into 4 pieces before cooking.

30 minute meals

Minted Lamb Chops with Lemony Bulgur

SERVES 4

1 cup bulgur

4 tablespoons chopped fresh mint

2 garlic cloves, minced

2 teaspoons olive oil

½ teaspoon salt

4 (¼-pound) lean boneless lamb loin chops, trimmed

1 large tomato, coarsely chopped

Grated zest and juice of 1 lemon

2 tablespoons chopped fresh chives

1. Prepare bulgur according to package directions, omitting salt if desired.
2. Meanwhile, spray broiler rack with nonstick spray and preheat broiler.
3. Stir together 2 tablespoons of mint, garlic, oil, and salt in large shallow bowl. Add lamb and turn to coat evenly. Place lamb on broiler rack. Broil 5 inches from heat until an instant-read thermometer inserted into side of chop registers 145°F for medium, about 5 minutes on each side.
4. Stir tomato, lemon zest and juice, remaining 2 tablespoons mint, and chives into bulgur. Serve with lamb.

PER SERVING (1 lamb chop and ¾ cup bulgur): 319 Cal, 10 g Total Fat, 3 g Sat Fat, 0 g Trans Fat, 74 mg Chol, 367 mg Sod, 30 g Total Carb, 7 g Fib, 29 g Prot, 37 mg Calc.

PointsPlus value: ***8.***

Cook's Note

To broil a vegetable side dish while you broil the chops, arrange 2 thinly sliced red or yellow bell peppers on the broiler rack alongside the chops. Lightly spray with olive oil nonstick spray. Broil, turning occasionally, until crisp-tender, 6 to 8 minutes. Season to taste with salt and pepper.

Grilled Lamb Chops and Asparagus with Lemon-Garlic Mayonnaise

SERVES 4

¼ cup fat-free mayonnaise

1 small garlic clove, minced

1 teaspoon grated lemon zest

1 teaspoon fresh lemon juice

½ teaspoon olive oil

4 (5-ounce) lean lamb loin chops, about 1 inch thick, trimmed

1 pound thick asparagus spears, trimmed

½ teaspoon salt

½ teaspoon black pepper

1. Spray grill rack with nonstick spray. Preheat grill to medium-high or prepare medium-high fire.
2. Stir together mayonnaise, garlic, lemon zest, lemon juice, and oil in small bowl; cover and refrigerate until ready to serve.
3. Sprinkle lamb and asparagus with salt and pepper. Spray asparagus with olive oil nonstick spray. Place lamb and asparagus on grill rack. Grill lamb until an instant-read thermometer inserted into center of chop registers 145°F for medium, about 4 minutes on each side, and until asparagus is browned in spots and crisp-tender, about 5 minutes. Serve lamb and asparagus with garlic sauce.

PER SERVING (1 lamb chop, 5 asparagus spears, and 1 tablespoon mayonnaise): 260 Cal, 11 g Total Fat, 4 g Sat Fat, 0 g Trans Fat, 94 mg Chol, 505 mg Sod, 8 g Total Carb, 3 g Fib, 31 g Prot, 44 mg Calc.

PointsPlus value: ***6.***

Cook's Note

Serve the chops with a side of whole wheat orzo tossed with grated lemon zest and chopped fresh mint (½ cup of cooked whole wheat orzo per serving will increase the ***PointsPlus*** value by ***2***).

30 minute meals

Moroccan-Style Chicken

SERVES 4

4 (5-ounce) skinless boneless chicken breasts, cut into 1-inch pieces

2 teaspoons canola oil

1 teaspoon ground cumin

1 teaspoon salt

1 (3-inch) cinnamon stick

4 carrots, sliced

1 red onion, chopped

2 garlic cloves, minced

2 yellow squash, diced

1 (14½-ounce) can petite diced tomatoes, drained

1 cup reduced-sodium vegetable broth

1 cup canned chickpeas, rinsed and drained

¼ cup dark raisins

1. Stir together chicken, 1 teaspoon of oil, cumin, salt, and cinnamon stick in medium bowl.
2. Stir together carrots, onion, garlic, and remaining 1 teaspoon oil in microwavable 3-quart casserole with lid. Cover and microwave on High until onion is softened, about 4 minutes.
3. Add squash, tomatoes, broth, and chicken to casserole. Cover and microwave on High until chicken is almost cooked through, about 3 minutes, stirring once halfway through cooking.
4. Stir in chickpeas and raisins. Cover and microwave until chicken is cooked through, about 2 minutes longer. Discard cinnamon stick.

PER SERVING (1 chicken breast and about 1 cup vegetables): 365 Cal, 9 g Total Fat, 2 g Sat Fat, 0 g Trans Fat, 86 mg Chol, 985 mg Sod, 36 g Total Carb, 7 g Fib, 38 g Prot, 124 mg Calc.

PointsPlus value: ***9.***

Cook's Note

Couscous is the traditional accompaniment to this Moroccan meal (½ cup cooked whole wheat couscous per serving will increase the ***PointsPlus*** value by ***3***).

Chicken and Vegetables with Fettuccine

SERVES 6

12 ounces whole wheat fettuccine

½ pound asparagus, trimmed and cut into 2-inch pieces

1 pound skinless boneless chicken thighs, cut into 1-inch pieces

½ teaspoon salt

¼ teaspoon black pepper

4 teaspoons olive oil

1 fennel bulb, sliced

1 small red bell pepper, sliced

1 small yellow bell pepper, sliced

1 red onion, sliced

¼ pound cremini mushrooms, sliced

2 garlic cloves, minced

½ cup reduced-sodium chicken broth

½ cup fresh basil leaves, thinly sliced

1. Cook fettuccine according to package directions omitting salt if desired. Four minutes before pasta is done, add asparagus and cook until pasta and asparagus are tender. Drain and keep warm.
2. Meanwhile, sprinkle chicken with ¼ teaspoon of salt and ⅛ teaspoon of black pepper. Heat 2 teaspoons of oil in large skillet over medium-high heat. Add chicken and cook, turning occasionally, until browned and cooked through, about 5 minutes. Transfer chicken to plate and cover to keep warm.
3. Add remaining 2 teaspoons oil to same skillet. Add fennel, bell peppers, onion, mushrooms, remaining ¼ teaspoon salt, and remaining ⅛ teaspoon black pepper and cook, stirring occasionally, until vegetables are lightly browned and crisp-tender, about 5 minutes. Add garlic to skillet and cook, stirring constantly, until fragrant, 30 seconds. Return chicken to skillet; add fettuccini mixture and broth, and cook, stirring constantly until heated through, 2 minutes. Stir in basil.

PER SERVING (2 cups): 368 Cal, 10 g Total Fat, 2 g Sat Fat, 0 g Trans Fat, 50 mg Chol, 312 mg Sod, 49 g Total Carb, 10 g Fib, 25 g Prot, 71 mg Calc.

PointsPlus value: ***9.***

30 minute meals

Lemony Chicken Kebabs with Couscous

1. Combine chicken, lemon zest and juice, oil, garlic, cumin, salt, and cayenne in large bowl; toss to coat.
2. Spray ridged grill pan with nonstick spray and set over medium-high heat. Alternately thread chicken and onion onto 8 metal skewers. Place skewers in pan and cook, turning occasionally, until chicken is cooked through, about 12 minutes.
3. Meanwhile, prepare couscous according to package directions, omitting salt if desired. Add cilantro and sesame seeds to couscous and stir to combine. Serve with chicken.

PER SERVING (2 skewers and ¾ cup couscous): 289 Cal, 8 g Total Fat, 2 g Sat Fat, 0 g Trans Fat, 68 mg Chol, 835 mg Sod, 26 g Total Carb, 5 g Fib, 30 g Prot, 48 mg Calc.

PointsPlus value: *7.*

Do it Faster

To quickly toast sesame seeds, put them in a small dry skillet and set over medium heat. Toast seeds, stirring frequently, until fragrant and lightly browned, about 2 minutes. Transfer to a plate to cool.

SERVES 4

1 pound skinless boneless chicken breasts, cut into 1-inch pieces

2 teaspoons grated lemon zest

1 tablespoon fresh lemon juice

2 teaspoons olive oil

2 garlic cloves, minced

1 teaspoon ground cumin

¾ teaspoon salt

⅛ teaspoon cayenne pepper

1 red onion, quartered and separated into layers

1 cup whole wheat couscous

3 tablespoons chopped fresh cilantro

2 teaspoons sesame seeds, toasted

30 minute meals

Teriyaki Chicken and Snow Pea Stir-Fry

SERVES 4

2 teaspoons Asian (dark) sesame oil

1 pound skinless boneless chicken breasts, cut into thin strips

2 garlic cloves, minced

1 (½-inch) piece fresh ginger, peeled and minced

1 red bell pepper, thinly sliced

4 scallions, thinly sliced

1 (5-ounce) can sliced water chestnuts, drained

6 ounces snow peas, trimmed

¼ cup reduced-sodium chicken broth

¼ cup teriyaki sauce

Pinch red pepper flakes

2 cups hot cooked brown rice

1. Heat large skillet or wok over medium-high heat until drop of water sizzles in pan. Add oil and swirl to coat skillet.
2. Add chicken to skillet and stir-fry until browned and cooked through, about 5 minutes. Using slotted spoon, transfer chicken to plate.
3. Add garlic and ginger to skillet and stir-fry until fragrant, about 30 seconds. Add bell pepper, scallions, and water chestnuts; stir-fry 2 minutes. Add snow peas and stir-fry until bright green. Add broth, teriyaki sauce, and red pepper flakes; stir-fry until sauce is slightly reduced, about 1 minute longer.
4. Return chicken to skillet and stir-fry until heated through, about 1 minute. Serve with rice.

PER SERVING (1½ cups chicken mixture and ½ cup rice): 325 Cal, 8 g Total Fat, 2 g Sat Fat, 0 g Trans Fat, 70 mg Chol, 805 mg Sod, 33 g Total Carb, 4 g Fib, 32 g Prot, 65 mg Calc.

PointsPlus value: **8.**

Cook's Note

Stir-fries are one of the quickest meals you can make, but once you start cooking, there's little time to do anything but stir! Prep all your ingredients and arrange them near the stove before you begin for stress-free stir-frying.

Quick Chicken Satay with Asparagus

Quick Chicken Satay with Asparagus

SERVES 2

2 (5-ounce) skinless boneless chicken breasts, each cut into 6 long strips

5 teaspoons reduced-sodium teriyaki sauce

16 asparagus spears, trimmed

2 teaspoons reduced-sodium soy sauce

2 teaspoons canola oil

Lemon wedges

1. Preheat oven to 375°F. Line baking sheet with foil and spray with nonstick spray.
2. Toss together chicken and teriyaki sauce in medium bowl.
3. Thread 2 pieces of chicken on each of 6 (12-inch) metal skewers and arrange on baking sheet. Place asparagus next to chicken in one layer. Brush asparagus with soy sauce and oil. Roast until chicken is cooked through and asparagus is tender, about 15 minutes. Serve with lemon wedges.

PER SERVING (3 skewers and 8 asparagus spears): 256 Cal, 9 g Total Fat, 2 g Sat Fat, 0 g Trans Fat, 86 mg Chol, 700 mg Sod, 7 g Total Carb, 3 g Fib, 35 g Prot, 49 mg Calc.

PointsPlus value: **6.**

Cook's Note

If using wooden skewers, soak them in water for 30 minutes to prevent them from burning.

Chicken Picadillo

SERVES 4

2 teaspoons olive oil

1 onion, chopped

2 garlic cloves, minced

1 pound ground skinless chicken breast

1 (14½-ounce) can diced tomatoes

¼ cup dark raisins

¼ cup pimiento-stuffed olives, coarsely chopped

1 teaspoon ground cumin

½ teaspoon salt

¼ teaspoon black pepper

¼ cup slivered almonds

1. Heat oil in large skillet over medium heat. Add onion and garlic and cook, stirring, until softened, about 5 minutes.
2. Add chicken to skillet. Cook, breaking up chicken with wooden spoon, until browned, about 8 minutes.
3. Stir in tomatoes, raisins, olives, cumin, salt, and pepper, and bring to boil over medium-high heat. Reduce heat and simmer until slightly thickened, about 5 minutes. Stir in almonds.

PER SERVING (generous 1 cup): 278 Cal, 12 g Total Fat, 2 g Sat Fat, 0 g Trans Fat, 68 mg Chol, 652 mg Sod, 17 g Total Carb, 3 g Fib, 28 g Prot, 84 mg Calc.

PointsPlus value: *7.*

Cook's Note

You can make the picadillo using ground skinless turkey breast instead of chicken breast if you wish.

Warm Lentil Salad with Baked Salmon

SERVES 4

4 cups water

1 cup green (French) lentils, picked over and rinsed

1 (1-pound) piece center-cut salmon fillet, skinned

½ teaspoon salt

¼ teaspoon black pepper

½ cup roasted red bell pepper, chopped (not packed in oil)

¼ cup reduced-sodium chicken broth

2 teaspoons olive oil

1¼ teaspoons white-wine vinegar

½ teaspoon salt

2 cups torn frisée lettuce

½ small red onion, finely chopped

1. Bring water to boil in medium saucepan. Add lentils and cook until just tender, about 15 minutes; drain.
2. Meanwhile, preheat oven to 300°F. Line baking sheet with foil.
3. Put salmon, skinned side down, on prepared baking sheet. Sprinkle with salt and black pepper. Bake until just opaque in center, about 15 minutes.
4. Meanwhile, puree bell pepper, broth, oil, vinegar, and salt in blender. Transfer mixture to large bowl. Add lentils, lettuce, and onion and toss to combine.
5. Cut salmon into 4 portions and put 1 piece of salmon on each of 4 plates. Spoon lentil salad alongside.

PER SERVING (1 piece salmon and 1¼ cups salad): 347 Cal, 9 g Total Fat, 2 g Sat Fat, 0 Trans Fat, 75 mg Chol, 709 mg Sod, 24 g Total Carb, 9 g Fib, 37 g Prot, 65 mg Calc.

PointsPlus value: ***8.***

Do it Faster

To quickly and neatly pick over lentils or beans, pour them into one side of a jelly-roll or other large rimmed pan. Slide the lentils to the other side of the pan using your hand and looking for stones or other debris as you go. Always rinse them before cooking.

30 minute meals

Roasted Salmon with Caramelized Onions and Carrots

1. Arrange oven rack in middle of oven; preheat oven to 450°F. Spray baking sheet with nonstick spray.
2. Heat oil in medium nonstick skillet over medium heat. Add onions and thyme; cook, stirring occasionally, until onions start to brown, about 12 minutes. Add carrot, garlic, ¼ teaspoon of salt, and ⅛ teaspoon of pepper; continue cooking until onions are golden, 3–4 minutes longer. Stir in vinegar and cook 1 minute; remove from heat and keep warm.
3. Meanwhile, sprinkle salmon with remaining ½ teaspoon salt and ⅛ teaspoon pepper and place on baking sheet. Brush top of each fillet with 1 teaspoon of mustard. Roast until fish is opaque in center, 8–10 minutes.
4. Top each fillet with ¼ cup of onion mixture.

SERVES 4

1 teaspoon olive oil

2 red onions, thinly sliced

¼ teaspoon dried thyme

1 carrot, cut into thin 2-inch-long strips

2 garlic cloves, minced

¾ teaspoon salt

¼ teaspoon black pepper

1 teaspoon white-wine vinegar

4 (6-ounce) skinless salmon fillets

4 teaspoons Dijon mustard

PER SERVING (1 fillet and ¼ cup onion mixture): 299 Cal, 11 g Total Fat, 3 g Sat Fat, 0 g Trans Fat, 112 mg Chol, 683 mg Sod, 10 g Total Carb, 2 g Fib, 37 g Prot, 50 mg Calc.

PointsPlus value: *7.*

Cook's Note

Salmon fillets often have small bones—known as pinbones—in their flesh. Before cooking, run your fingertips along the flesh to feel for them. If you find any, use needle-nose pliers or tweezers to pull them out.

Tilapia with Tomato and Feta

1. Preheat oven to 350°F. Spray 7 × 11-inch baking dish with nonstick spray.
2. Stir together tomatoes, ¼ teaspoon of salt, oregano, and ⅛ teaspoon of pepper in small bowl.
3. Spread half of tomato mixture in prepared baking dish. Arrange tilapia on top of sauce in one layer. Sprinkle fish with remaining ¼ teaspoon salt and ⅛ teaspoon pepper. Spoon remaining tomato sauce evenly over fish and sprinkle with feta. Cover dish tightly with foil. Bake until fish is just opaque in center, about 20 minutes.
4. Meanwhile, prepare couscous according to package directions, omitting fat and salt if desired. Serve with fish.

SERVES 4

1 (15-ounce) can crushed tomatoes

½ teaspoon salt

½ teaspoon dried oregano

¼ teaspoon black pepper

2 (½-pound) tilapia fillets, cut crosswise in half

¼ cup crumbled reduced-fat feta cheese

1 cup whole wheat couscous

PER SERVING (½ tilapia fillet, about 3 tablespoons sauce, and about ⅔ cup couscous): 305 Cal, 4 g Total Fat, 2 g Sat Fat, 0 g Trans Fat, 55 mg Chol, 894 mg Sod, 35 g Total Carb, 6 g Fib, 32 g Prot, 82 mg Calc.

PointsPlus value: *7.*

Cook's Note

Quickly dress up the couscous by stirring 2 thinly sliced scallions and a minced garlic clove into the cooking water when you add the couscous.

30 minute meals

Salmon Patties with Chunky Tomato Relish

SERVES 4

- 2 large tomatoes, seeded and diced
- ¼ cup chopped fresh basil
- 2 shallots, finely chopped plus 1 shallot, halved
- 2 teaspoons fresh lemon juice
- 2 teaspoons olive oil
- ¾ teaspoon salt
- ½ teaspoon black pepper
- 1 pound salmon fillet, skinned and cut into small pieces
- 2 tablespoons chopped fresh parsley
- 1 teaspoon grated lemon zest

1. To make relish, toss together tomatoes, basil, chopped shallots, lemon juice, oil, ¼ teaspoon of salt, and ¼ teaspoon of pepper in serving bowl.
2. To make salmon patties, combine salmon, parsley, halved shallot, lemon zest, and remaining ½ teaspoon salt and ¼ teaspoon pepper in food processor; pulse until finely chopped. With damp hands, form salmon mixture into 4 (½-inch-thick) patties.
3. Spray large skillet with olive oil nonstick spray and set over medium heat. Add patties and cook until browned and cooked through, about 5 minutes on each side. Serve with relish.

PER SERVING (1 patty and ½ cup relish): 214 Cal, 9 g Total Fat, 2 g Sat Fat, 0 g Trans Fat, 75 mg Chol, 518 mg Sod, 7 g Total Carb, 2 g Fib, 26 g Prot, 38 mg Calc.

PointsPlus value: **5.**

Cook's Note

The tomato relish is delicious with grilled chicken or shrimp, too.

Salmon Patties with
Chunky Tomato Relish

7 superfast sides

All recipes serve 4.

Kale and Apple Salad

Whisk together **1 tablespoon olive oil, 1 tablespoon apple-cider vinegar, 2 teaspoons honey, ¼ teaspoon salt,** and **¼ teaspoon black pepper** in large bowl. Toss in **½ pound kale, stems removed and leaves thinly sliced, 1 Gala apple, cut into thin strips,** and **2 tablespoons grated Parmesan cheese**. ***PointsPlus*** value: ***3.***

Lemony Spinach and Avocado Salad

Whisk together **1 teaspoon grated lemon zest, 2 tablespoons fresh** lemon juice, 1 tablespoon olive oil, **½ teaspoon Dijon mustard, ¼ teaspoon salt,** and **⅛ teaspoon black pepper** in large bowl. Toss in **4 cups baby spinach, ½ avocado, pitted, peeled, and chopped,** and **¼ cup thinly sliced red onion**. ***PointsPlus*** value: ***2.***

Minted Green Beans with Pine Nuts

Cook **1 pound trimmed green beans** in boiling water until crisp-tender; drain. Transfer to serving bowl; toss in **2 tablespoons chopped fresh mint, 2 tablespoons toasted pine nuts, 2 teaspoons olive oil, grated zest and juice of 1 lemon, ¼ teaspoon salt,** and **⅛ teaspoon black pepper.** ***PointsPlus*** value: ***2.***

Buttered Broccoli with Cilantro and Lime

Place **4 cups broccoli florets** in microwave-safe dish; cover with wax paper and microwave on High until crisp-tender, about 3 minutes. Drain and transfer to serving bowl. Toss in **2 teaspoons unsalted butter, 1 tablespoon chopped fresh cilantro, grated zest and juice of 1 lime,** and **¼ teaspoon salt**. ***PointsPlus*** value: ***1.***

Rosemary-Parmesan Oven Fries

Cut **1 pound baking potatoes** into ½-inch sticks; place in baking pan. **Add 2 teaspoons olive oil, ¼ teaspoon salt,** and **⅛ teaspoon black pepper** and toss to coat. Bake at 425°F, turning once, until potatoes are tender, 30 minutes. Transfer to platter; sprinkle with **2 tablespoons grated Parmesan cheese, 1 garlic clove, minced,** and **1 teaspoon minced fresh rosemary** and toss to coat. ***PointsPlus*** value: ***3.***

Polenta with Goat Cheese and Chives

Bring **2 cups reduced-sodium chicken broth** to boil in medium saucepan. Slowly pour in **½ cup instant polenta** in thin, steady stream, whisking constantly. Cook, whisking constantly, until thick and creamy, 5 minutes. Remove from heat and stir in **2 ounces crumbled goat cheese, 1 tablespoon minced fresh chives, ¼ teaspoon salt,** and **⅛ teaspoon black pepper.** ***PointsPlus*** value: ***3.***

Herbed Parmesan-Garlic Pasta

Cook **6 ounces whole wheat linguine** according to package directions. Heat **2 teaspoons olive oil** in large nonstick skillet. Add **2 cloves minced garlic** and cook, stirring constantly, just until garlic begins to brown. Add pasta and toss to coat. Remove from heat and stir in **3 tablespoons minced fresh parsley, basil, or dill, or a combination, ¼ cup grated Parmesan, ¼ teaspoon salt,** and **⅛ teaspoon black pepper**. ***PointsPlus*** value: ***5.***

Creole-Style Cod Fillets

SERVES 4

2 cups spicy vegetable juice or tomato juice

2 green bell peppers, thinly sliced

1 onion, thinly sliced

2 celery stalks, thinly sliced

4 (6-ounce) cod fillets

2 tablespoons chopped fresh parsley

2 cups hot cooked brown rice

1. Combine vegetable juice, bell peppers, onion, and celery in large skillet; bring to boil over medium-high heat. Reduce heat and simmer until vegetables are just softened, about 4 minutes.
2. Nestle cod into vegetables. Cover and cook until fish is just opaque throughout, about 8 minutes. Sprinkle with parsley and serve with rice.

PER SERVING (1 cod fillet, 1 cup vegetables with sauce, and ½ cup rice): 313 Cal, 3 g Total Fat, 1 g Sat Fat, 0 g Trans Fat, 90 mg Chol, 761 mg Sod, 34 g Total Carb, 6 g Fib, 36 g Prot, 70 mg Calc.

PointsPlus value: *7.*

Cook's Note

If you have leftover vegetable juice from this recipe, consider it for an afternoon pick-me-up. The spicy flavor will wake you up without caffeine—and for only ***1 PointsPlus*** value in a 1-cup serving.

Teriyaki-Glazed Tofu and Vegetable Kebabs

Teriyaki-Glazed Tofu and Vegetable Kebabs

SERVES 4

⅔ cup whole wheat couscous

1 (14-ounce) container firm tofu, drained and cut into 1-inch cubes

½ fresh pineapple, peeled, cored, and cut into 1-inch chunks

2 different colored bell peppers, cut into 1-inch pieces

1 small red onion, quartered and layers separated

16 small white mushrooms

3 tablespoons reduced-sodium teriyaki sauce

3 tablespoons chopped fresh cilantro

1. Prepare couscous according to package directions, omitting fat and salt if desired.
2. Meanwhile, spray ridged grill pan with nonstick spray and set over medium-high heat. Alternately thread tofu, pineapple, bell peppers, onion, and mushrooms onto 8 metal skewers; brush with teriyaki sauce.
3. Place skewers in pan and cook, turning frequently, until tofu is browned and vegetables are softened, about 10 minutes. Serve sprinkled with cilantro.

PER SERVING (2 skewers and ½ cup couscous): 203 Cal, 5 g Total Fat, 1 g Sat Fat, 0 g Trans Fat, 0 mg Chol, 707 mg Sod, 31 g Total Carb, 6 g Fib, 14 g Prot, 232 mg Calc.

PointsPlus value: **5.**

Do it Faster

Save time by buying recipe-ready pineapple for this dish. Most large supermarkets sell fresh peeled and cored pineapples in tall plastic containers in the produce section.

30 minute meals

Chunky Vegetable Paella

SERVES 4

2 teaspoons olive oil

4 celery stalks, thickly sliced

1 onion, chopped

1 large red bell pepper, cut into ¾-inch pieces

1 large zucchini, quartered lengthwise and cut into ¾-inch pieces

2 garlic cloves, minced

½ teaspoon salt

¾ cup quick-cooking brown rice

2¼ cups water

1 (15-ounce) can cannellini (white kidney) beans, rinsed and drained

1 (14½-ounce) can fire-roasted diced tomatoes, drained

1. Heat 1 teaspoon oil in large nonstick skillet over medium heat. Add celery, onion, bell pepper, zucchini, garlic, and salt and cook, stirring, until softened, about 5 minutes. Transfer vegetables to bowl.
2. Wipe out skillet; add remaining 1 teaspoon oil to skillet and set over medium heat. Add rice and cook, stirring, until lightly toasted, about 2 minutes. Stir in water; reduce heat and simmer, covered, until rice is tender and liquid is absorbed, about 10 minutes.
3. Return vegetables to skillet and add beans and tomatoes. Cook, stirring occasionally, until heated through, about 5 minutes.

PER SERVING (about 2 cups): 249 Cal, 4 g Total Fat, 1 g Sat Fat, 0 g Trans Fat, 0 mg Chol, 715 mg Sod, 46 g Total Carb, 11 g Fib, 11 g Prot, 147 mg Calc.

PointsPlus value: ***6.***

Cook's Note

To add more healthful veggies to this dinner, serve the paella with a salad of baby spinach tossed with thinly sliced fresh fennel bulb, grated lemon zest, fresh lemon juice, and salt and pepper to taste.

Linguine with Fontina and Artichokes

SERVES 4

6 ounces whole wheat linguine

4 plum tomatoes, chopped

2 garlic cloves, minced

1 (9-ounce) package frozen quartered artichoke hearts, thawed

⅛ teaspoon black pepper

4 ounces fontina cheese, diced

½ cup thinly sliced fresh basil

1. Cook linguine according to package directions, omitting salt if desired. Drain linguine, reserving ½ cup of cooking water.
2. Add tomatoes and garlic to pasta pot. Cook over medium heat, stirring, until tomatoes begin to soften, about 2 minutes.
3. Return pasta to pot along with artichokes and pepper. Cook, stirring, until heated through, about 4 minutes. (If pasta seems dry, stir in some of reserved cooking water.)
4. Transfer pasta mixture to serving bowl; add fontina and basil and toss to coat.

PER SERVING (1½ cups): 310 Cal, 10 g Total Fat, 6 g Sat Fat, 0 g Trans Fat, 33 mg Chol, 452 mg Sod, 44 g Total Carb, 8 g Fib, 17 g Prot, 221 mg Calc.

PointsPlus value: **8.**

Cook's Note

To safely reserve the cooking water from pasta, use a ladle to spoon out a little of the water into a bowl just before you drain the pasta. The ladle will keep your hands away from the boiling water and you can use it to drizzle as much cooking water as you need into your pasta dish.

30 minute meals

Four-Vegetable Stir-Fry with Tofu

SERVES 4

1 cup quick-cooking brown rice

2 teaspoons canola oil

2 garlic cloves, minced

2 teaspoons minced peeled fresh ginger

12 shiitake mushrooms, stems removed and caps thickly sliced

3 cups broccoli florets

2 carrots, thinly sliced

1 yellow bell pepper, thinly sliced

1 (14-ounce) container firm tofu, drained and cubed

2 tablespoons reduced-sodium soy sauce

1 teaspoon dark (Asian) sesame oil

1. Cook rice according to package directions, omitting salt if desired.
2. Meanwhile, heat large skillet or wok or over high heat until drop of water sizzles in pan. Add canola oil and swirl to coat skillet. Add garlic and ginger and stir-fry until fragrant, about 30 seconds.
3. Add mushrooms, broccoli, carrots, and bell pepper; stir-fry until tender, about 6 minutes. Add tofu, soy sauce, and sesame oil; stir-fry until heated through, about 1 minute longer. Serve with rice.

PER SERVING (1¾ cups stir-fry and ½ cup rice): 267 Cal, 9 g Total Fat, 1 g Sat Fat, 0 g Trans Fat, 0 mg Chol, 754 mg Sod, 38 g Total Carb, 8 g Fib, 14 g Prot, 251 mg Calc.

PointsPlus value: *7.*

Cook's Note

Save the stems of the broccoli when you prepare the broccoli florets. Shred them to make a slaw for serving with sandwiches later in the week.

Four-Vegetable
Stir-Fry with Tofu

Edamame Dip

SERVES 4

- 1 cup frozen shelled edamame
- 4 ounces silken tofu
- 1 scallion, sliced
- 1 garlic clove, chopped
- 1 tablespoon fresh lemon juice
- 1½ teaspoons olive oil
- ½ teaspoon ground cumin
- ¼ teaspoon honey
- ¼ teaspoon salt
- 12 whole wheat crackers
- 12 carrot or other vegetables sticks

1. Cook edamame according to package directions. Drain and rinse under cold running water; drain again.
2. Place edamame, tofu, scallion, garlic, lemon juice, oil, cumin, honey, and salt in food processor; process until smooth, 1–2 minutes. Serve with crackers and vegetable sticks.

PER SERVING (about ¼ cup dip, 3 crackers, and 3 carrot sticks): 169 Cal, 7 g Fat, 1 g Sat Fat, 0 g Trans Fat, 0 mg Chol, 264 mg Sod, 18 g Total Carb, 5 g Fib, 9 g Prot, 78 mg Calc.

PointsPlus value: ***4.***

Cook's Note

Edamame, or green soybeans, are a great source of protein and fiber and they cook in about 5 minutes, making them perfect for quick meals and snacks. Try them in soups, stir-fries, and salads to appreciate their nutty taste, firm texture, and spring-green color.

Smoky Pumpkin Seeds

SERVES 16

2 cups shelled pumpkin seeds (about 10 ounces)

2 teaspoons Worcestershire sauce

1 teaspoon liquid smoke

1 teaspoon ground cumin

1 teaspoon chili powder

½ teaspoon salt

½ teaspoon garlic powder

⅛ teaspoon cayenne pepper

1. Preheat oven to 325°F. Line large baking sheet with parchment paper.
2. Toss together pumpkin seeds, Worcestershire sauce, and liquid smoke in large bowl.
3. Combine remaining ingredients in small bowl. Sprinkle spice mixture over pumpkin seeds and stir vigorously with wooden spoon until evenly coated.
4. Spread pumpkin seeds on prepared baking sheet. Bake, stirring twice, until dried and lightly browned, about 15 minutes. Let cool on baking sheet on rack.

PER SERVING (2 tablespoons): 152 Cal, 12 g Total Fat, 2 g Sat Fat, 0 g Trans Fat, 0 mg Chol, 160 mg Sod, 8 g Total Carb, 2 g Fib, 10 g Prot, 16 mg Calc.

PointsPlus value: ***5.***

Cook's Note

You can store this healthy snack in a zip-close plastic bag or airtight container at room temperature for up to 1 month.

Pizza Margherita

Pizza Margherita

SERVES 6

1 (10-ounce) prebaked thin whole wheat pizza crust

3 plum tomatoes, thinly sliced

2 garlic cloves, minced

2 cups shredded fat-free mozzarella cheese

¼ cup thinly sliced fresh basil

1 teaspoon dried oregano

2 teaspoons olive oil

1. Preheat oven to 450°F. Spray baking sheet with nonstick spray.
2. Place crust on baking sheet. Arrange tomatoes on crust and sprinkle with garlic. Top evenly with mozzarella, basil, and oregano; drizzle with oil. Bake until cheese is melted, about 8 minutes. Cut into 6 wedges.

PER SERVING (⅙ of pizza): 198 Cal, 4 g Total Fat, 1 g Sat Fat, 0 g Trans Fat, 4 mg Chol, 544 mg Sod, 25 g Total Carb, 4 g Fib, 17 g Prot, 609 mg Calc.

PointsPlus value: **5.**

Cook's Note

Turn this quick pizza into dinner by tossing a big green salad to serve alongside while the pizza bakes. For dessert, enjoy a scoop of vanilla fat-free frozen yogurt topped with a teaspoon of raspberry fruit spread (½ cup fat-free frozen yogurt and 1 teaspoon fruit spread will increase the ***PointsPlus*** value by **3**).

30 minute meals

Mushroom, Scallion, and Cheddar Quesadillas

SERVES 8

8 ounces sliced white mushrooms

8 (7-inch) fat-free whole wheat flour tortillas

¾ cup shredded reduced-fat Cheddar cheese

2 scallions, thinly sliced

2 tablespoons sliced pickled jalapeño peppers, drained and finely chopped

1. Spray large skillet with nonstick spray and set over medium heat. Add mushrooms and cook, stirring occasionally, until liquid is evaporated, about 6 minutes. Using slotted spoon, transfer mushrooms to plate and let cool slightly.
2. Lay out 4 tortillas on work surface. Layer each with one-fourth of mushrooms, Cheddar, scallions, and jalapeños. Top with remaining 4 tortillas, pressing down lightly.
3. Wipe skillet clean. Spray with nonstick spray and set over medium heat. Add 1 quesadilla and cook until crisp and cheese begins to melt, about 1½ minutes on each side. Transfer to cutting board and cover loosely with foil to keep warm. Repeat with remaining 3 quesadillas. Cut each quesadilla into 4 wedges, making total of 16 wedges.

PER SERVING (2 wedges): 128 Cal, 1 g Total Fat, 1 g Sat Fat, 0 g Trans Fat, 2 mg Chol, 468 mg Sod, 23 g Total Carb, 4 g Fib, 8 g Prot, 124 mg Calc.

PointsPlus value: ***3.***

Mushroom, Scallion, and Cheddar Quesadillas

30 minute meals

Ricotta, Bacon, and Spinach Pizza

SERVES 6

2 slices bacon, chopped

2 garlic cloves, thinly sliced

1 (5-ounce) package baby spinach

¼ teaspoon red pepper flakes

1 (10-ounce) prebaked whole wheat thin pizza crust

⅔ cup fat-free ricotta cheese

½ cup reduced-fat shredded mozzarella cheese

1. Preheat oven to 450°F. Spray large baking sheet with nonstick spray.
2. Cook bacon in large skillet over medium-high heat, stirring occasionally, until crisp, about 5 minutes. Transfer bacon to plate lined with paper towels. Drain off and discard all but 1 teaspoon drippings.
3. Add garlic to skillet; cook over medium heat, stirring constantly, until golden, about 1 minute. Add spinach to skillet a few handfuls at a time, stirring constantly and adding more spinach as it will fit. Continue cooking until spinach is wilted, about 2 minutes more. Stir in reserved bacon and red pepper flakes.
4. Place crust on baking sheet. Spread ricotta evenly over crust. Top evenly with spinach mixture. Sprinkle with mozzarella. Bake until mozzarella cheese is bubbling, about 8 minutes. Cut into 6 wedges.

PER SERVING (1 wedge): 218 Cal, 6 g Total Fat, 2 g Sat Fat, 0 g Trans Fat, 13 mg Chol, 438 mg Sod, 27 g Total Carb, 5 g Fib, 11 g Prot, 203 mg Calc.

PointsPlus value: ***5.***

Baked Cheesy Nachos

1. Preheat oven to 400°F. Spray 9 × 13-inch baking dish with nonstick spray.
2. Arrange 24 tortilla chips in single layer in baking dish. Top evenly with beans, tomatoes, onion, jalapeño pepper, lime juice, and sour cream.
3. Crush remaining 12 tortilla chips and sprinkle over sour cream. Top evenly with Monterey Jack. Bake until heated through and cheese is melted and bubbling, about 20 minutes. Sprinkle with cilantro.

PER SERVING (¼ of dish): 266 Cal, 2 Fat, 0 g Sat Fat, 0 g Trans Fat, 6 mg Chol, 514 mg Sod, 36 g Total Carb, 6 g Fib, 15 g Prot, 500 mg Calc.

PointsPlus value: **5.**

SERVES 4

36 baked low-fat tortilla chips

1 (15½-ounce) can pinto beans, rinsed and drained

2 tomatoes, chopped

½ small red onion, chopped

1 jalapeño pepper, seeded and minced

1 tablespoon fresh lime juice

½ cup fat-free sour cream

1 cup shredded fat-free Monterey Jack or Cheddar cheese

3 tablespoons chopped fresh cilantro

Blueberries with Whipped Ricotta and Balsamic Syrup

Blueberries with Whipped Ricotta and Balsamic Syrup

SERVES 4

½ cup balsamic vinegar

1 cup fat-free ricotta cheese

2 teaspoons grated orange zest

2 pints blueberries

Orange zest strips

1. Bring vinegar to boil in medium saucepan over medium-high heat; boil until reduced by half, about 4 minutes. Remove saucepan from heat and let cool about 10 minutes.
2. Meanwhile, puree ricotta in food processor. Transfer cheese to small bowl and stir in orange zest.
3. Divide blueberries evenly among 4 dessert dishes; top evenly with ricotta mixture. Drizzle evenly with vinegar and sprinkle with orange zest strips.

PER SERVING (1 cup blueberries and ¼ cup ricotta): 137 Cal, 1 g Total Fat, 0 g Sat Fat, 0 g Trans Fat, 10 mg Chol, 76 mg Sod, 26 g Total Carb, 6 g Fib, 6 g Prot, 133 mg Calc.

PointsPlus value: **3.**

30 minute meals

Oven-Roasted Peaches with Raspberries and Sorbet

SERVES 4

4 ripe peaches halved and pitted

1½ tablespoons sugar

1 pint sorbet, such as lemon or raspberry, slightly softened

1 (6-ounce) container raspberries

1. Preheat oven to 425°F.
2. Arrange peaches on baking sheet, cut side up, and sprinkle evenly with sugar. Roast fruit until softened, about 20 minutes. Set aside until just warm.
3. Place 2 peach halves on each of 4 plates. Place ¼-cup scoop of sorbet in each peach half. Scatter raspberries around peaches.

PER SERVING (1 dessert): 229 Cal, 1 g Total Fat, 0 g Sat Fat, 0 g Trans Fat, 0 mg Chol, 10 mg Sod, 59 g Total Carb, 6 g Fib, 2 g Prot, 24 mg Calc.

PointsPlus value: ***6.***

Do it Faster

Sorbet is a quick cook's secret ingredient for dressing up dessert. Serve it alongside pound cake, angel food cake, or any fresh fruit to instantly elevate the ordinary into something special—and ½ cup sorbet has just ***2 PointsPlus*** value.

Oven-Roasted Peaches with
Raspberries and Sorbet

30 minute meals

Frozen Vanilla Yogurt with Sugared Shredded Wheat

SERVES 4

2 original-size shredded wheat cereal

1 tablespoon unsalted butter, melted

1 tablespoon sugar

1 pint frozen vanilla low-fat yogurt

2 cups mixed berries

1. Preheat oven to 400°F.
2. Break each piece of shredded wheat crosswise into quarters and place in medium bowl. Drizzle with butter and toss to coat. Sprinkle with sugar and toss to coat.
3. Arrange shredded wheat in one layer on baking sheet. Bake until deep golden brown, about 15 minutes. Let cool about 5 minutes on baking sheet.
4. Place ½-cup scoop of yogurt in each of 4 dessert dishes. Divide berries evenly among dishes. Coarsely crumble shredded wheat on top of yogurt.

PER SERVING (1 dish): 242 Cal, 5 g Total Fat, 3 g Sat Fat, 0 g Trans Fat, 15 mg Chol, 78 mg Sod, 44 g Total Carb, 3 g Fib, 7 g Prot, 209 mg Calc.

PointsPlus value: **6.**

Black and White Muffin Bites

SERVES 18

1 cup all-purpose flour

½ cup sugar

⅓ cup unsweetened cocoa

1 teaspoon baking soda

¼ teaspoon salt

½ cup fat-free milk

3 tablespoons canola oil

1 large egg

1 large egg white

1 teaspoon vanilla extract

¾ cup white chocolate chips

1. Preheat oven to 350°F. Line 36 mini muffin cups with paper liners.
2. Whisk together flour, sugar, cocoa, baking soda, and salt in large bowl. Whisk together milk, oil, egg, egg white, and vanilla in small bowl. Add milk mixture and ½ cup of chocolate chips to flour mixture, stirring just until moistened. Spoon batter evenly into prepared muffin cups, filling each about halfway.
3. Sprinkle remaining ¼ cup chocolate chips evenly over tops of muffins. Bake until muffins spring back when lightly pressed, about 10 minutes. Let muffins cool in pans on wire racks 10 minutes. Remove muffins from pans and let cool completely on racks.

PER SERVING (2 mini muffins): 116 Cal, 6 g Total Fat, 2 g Sat Fat, 0 g Trans Fat, 14 mg Chol, 118 mg Sod, 16 g Total Carb, 0 g Fib, 2 g Prot, 28 mg Calc.

PointsPlus value: **3.**

bonus on the weekend

Spend Some Time

Slow Cookers Save Time

Something Sweet

Beef-Vegetable Soup

SERVES 6

1 tablespoon olive oil

¾ pound lean top round steak, trimmed and cut into ½-inch pieces

4 carrots, thinly sliced

4 celery stalks, sliced

3 parsnips, peeled and diced

1 large onion, chopped

5 cups reduced-sodium beef broth

1 (14½-ounce) can petite diced tomatoes

½ teaspoon dried thyme

½ teaspoon salt

¼ teaspoon black pepper

2 cups lightly packed baby spinach

1½ cups hot cooked brown rice

1. Heat oil in Dutch oven over medium heat. Add beef, in batches, and cook, stirring, until browned, about 4 minutes. Using slotted spoon, transfer beef to plate.
2. Add carrots, celery, parsnips, and onion to Dutch oven; cook, stirring, until slightly softened, about 5 minutes. Add beef and any accumulated juices, broth, tomatoes, thyme, salt, and pepper; bring to boil. Reduce heat and simmer until beef is tender, about 20 minutes longer. Stir in baby spinach and rice.

PER SERVING (about 1⅓ cups): 255 Cal, 6 g Total Fat, 1 g Sat Fat, 0 g Trans Fat, 31 mg Chol, 658 mg Sod, 38 g Total Carb, 7 g Fib, 20 g Prot, 95 mg Calc.

PointsPlus value: *7.*

Cook's Note

Finish with a fresh dessert of plain fat-free Greek yogurt topped with sliced strawberries (½ cup of plain fat-free Greek yogurt per serving will increase the ***PointsPlus*** value by ***2***).

Cuban-Style Shredded Beef and Rice

SERVES 4

1 (1-pound) lean flank steak, trimmed

1 (14½-ounce) can reduced-sodium beef broth

3 garlic cloves, peeled plus 2 garlic cloves, minced

1 teaspoon olive oil

1 onion, chopped

1 (14½-ounce) can diced tomatoes

1 jalapeño pepper, seeded and minced

1 teaspoon dried oregano

1 teaspoon ground cumin

¼ cup chopped fresh cilantro

4 cups hot cooked brown rice

Lime wedges

1. Combine steak, broth, and peeled garlic in medium skillet and bring to boil over high heat. Reduce heat and simmer, covered, until steak is very tender, about 1 hour.
2. Remove skillet from heat and let stand 15 minutes. Reserve ½ cup of broth; save remaining broth for another use. Discard garlic. Transfer steak to cutting board; with two forks, shred beef.
3. Wipe out skillet. Add oil and set over medium-high heat. Add onion and minced garlic and cook, stirring occasionally, until onion is slightly softened, about 4 minutes. Stir in tomatoes, jalapeño, oregano, and cumin; cook, stirring, 5 minutes longer. Stir in shredded beef and reserved ½ cup broth. Continue to cook until most of liquid is evaporated, about 3 minutes.
4. Remove skillet from heat and stir in cilantro. Serve with rice and lime wedges.

PER SERVING (¾ cup beef mixture and 1 cup rice): 466 Cal, 8 g Total Fat, 2 g Sat Fat, 0 g Trans Fat, 82 mg Chol, 824 mg Sod, 55 g Total Carb, 9 g Fib, 42 g Prot, 85 mg Calc.

PointsPlus value: ***11.***

Cook's Note

Finish this hearty dinner with a quick fruit dessert made with sliced papaya, mango, and orange segments tossed with grated orange zest.

Beef-Barley Stew with
Roasted Vegetables

Beef-Barley Stew with Roasted Vegetables

SERVES 8

1 celery root, peeled and cut into ¾-inch chunks

4 carrots, cut into ¾-inch chunks

2 parsnips, peeled and cut into ¾-inch chunks

2 onions, chopped

1 tablespoon chopped fresh thyme or 1½ teaspoons dried

1½ pounds lean boneless beef chuck, trimmed and cut into 1-inch chunks

6 cups reduced-sodium beef broth

3 garlic cloves, chopped

½ teaspoon salt

¼ teaspoon black pepper

1 (8-ounce) package sliced cremini mushrooms

1 cup pearl barley, rinsed

1. Preheat oven to 450°F and spray large shallow roasting pan with nonstick spray.
2. Put celery root, carrots, parsnips, onions, and thyme in pan and spray with nonstick spray; toss to coat. Roast, stirring occasionally, until vegetables are browned and crisp-tender, about 30 minutes.
3. Meanwhile, spray Dutch oven with nonstick spray and place over medium-high heat. Cook beef, in batches, until browned on all sides, about 4 minutes. Transfer beef to plate as it is browned.
4. Return beef to pot. Add 5½ cups of broth, garlic, salt, and pepper; bring to boil. Reduce heat and simmer, covered, for 45 minutes.
5. Stir in mushrooms and barley and bring to boil. Reduce heat and simmer, covered, stirring occasionally, 15 minutes. Stir in roasted vegetables and bring to boil. Reduce heat and simmer, covered, until beef is fork-tender and barley is tender, about 15 minutes, adding remaining ½ cup broth if stew seems too thick.

PER SERVING (generous 1 cup): 318 Cal, 11 g Total Fat, 4 g Sat Fat, 0 g Trans Fat, 44 mg Chol, 366 mg Sod, 35 g Total Carb, 7 g Fib, 22 g Prot, 61 mg Calc.

PointsPlus value: ***8.***

Cook's Note

Serve the stew with steamed Swiss chard and a reduced-calorie whole wheat roll (1 reduced-calorie whole wheat roll per serving will increase the ***PointsPlus*** value by ***2***).

Citrus-Marinated Roast Pork

SERVES 8

⅓ cup fresh lime juice

¼ cup finely chopped onion

6 garlic cloves, minced

1 tablespoon olive oil

1 teaspoon dried oregano

1 teaspoon ground cumin

¼ teaspoon red pepper flakes

1 (2-pound) lean boneless center-cut pork loin roast, trimmed

1 teaspoon salt

¼ teaspoon black pepper

12 carrots, cut into 2-inch chunks

1. Combine lime juice, onion, garlic, oil, oregano, cumin, and red pepper flakes in large zip-close plastic bag. Add pork to bag. Squeeze out air and seal bag; turn to coat pork. Refrigerate, turning bag occasionally, for about 3 hours.
2. Preheat oven to 425°F. Place rack in large roasting pan and spray rack with nonstick spray.
3. Remove pork from plastic bag and place on rack. Discard marinade. Sprinkle pork with salt and black pepper. Spray carrots with olive oil nonstick spray and scatter around pork. Roast until an instant-read thermometer inserted into center of pork registers 145°F and carrots are tender, about 35 minutes.
4. Transfer pork to cutting board and let stand 10 minutes. Cut pork into 16 slices and serve with carrots.

PER SERVING (2 slices pork and about ⅔ cup carrots): 252 Cal, 11 g Total Fat, 3 g Sat Fat, 0 g Trans Fat, 72 mg Chol, 404 mg Sod, 0 g Total Carb, 3 g Fib, 26 g Prot, 47 mg Calc.

PointsPlus value: **5.**

Cook's Note

Serve the pork with a flavorful brown rice side dish. Toss cooked brown rice with thinly sliced scallions, chopped fresh cilantro, and lime zest and juice to taste (½ cup cooked brown rice per serving will increase the ***PointsPlus*** value by ***3***).

Pork and Bean Adobo Chili

SERVES 5

1 tablespoon olive oil

1 pound boneless pork loin, trimmed and cut into ½-inch pieces

1 onion, chopped

1 green bell pepper, chopped

1 red bell pepper, chopped

3 garlic cloves, minced

1 (14½-ounce) can fire-roasted diced tomatoes

2 teaspoons chopped canned chipotle en adobo

2 teaspoons chili powder

2 teaspoons ground cumin

¾ teaspoon salt

1 (15½-ounce) can red kidney beans, rinsed and drained

1. Heat 1½ teaspoons of oil in large saucepan over medium-high heat. Add pork and cook, stirring occasionally, until browned, about 4 minutes. Transfer to plate.
2. Add remaining 1½ teaspoons oil to saucepan. Add onion, bell peppers, and garlic; cook, stirring occasionally, until softened, about 5 minutes. Stir in tomatoes, chipotle, chili powder, cumin, and salt; bring to boil. Add beans and pork to saucepan. Reduce heat and simmer, covered, until pork is tender, about 10 minutes.

PER SERVING (about 1¼ cups): 292 Cal, 11 g Total Fat, 3 g Sat Fat, 0 g Trans Fat, 58 mg Chol, 666 mg Sod, 23 g Total Carb, 6 g Fib, 27 g Prot, 74 mg Calc.

PointsPlus value: *7.*

Cook's Note

Serve a refreshing citrus-dressed salad with this hearty chili. Toss together baby greens, halved grape tomatoes, lime zest and juice, and salt and pepper to taste.

Apricot-Mustard Glazed Pork Road

SERVES 4

3 garlic cloves, minced

1 tablespoon chopped fresh rosemary or 1 teaspoon dried

¾ teaspoon salt

¼ teaspoon black pepper

1 (1¼-pound) lean boneless center-cut pork loin roast, trimmed

2 tablespoons apricot jam

2 tablespoons Dijon mustard

1. Preheat oven to 400°F. Spray roasting pan with nonstick spray.
2. Stir together garlic, rosemary, salt, and pepper in small bowl. Rub mixture over pork. Place pork in roasting pan and roast 30 minutes.
3. Stir together jam and mustard in small bowl and brush all over pork. Continue to roast pork until an instant-read thermometer inserted into center registers 145°F, about 5 minutes longer. Transfer to cutting board and let stand 10 minutes. Cut roast into 12 slices.

PER SERVING (3 slices pork): 237 Cal, 10 g Total Fat, 3 g Sat Fat, 0 g Trans Fat, 79 mg Chol, 696 mg Sod, 8 g Total Carb, 0 g Fib, 28 g Prot, 46 mg Calc.

PointsPlus value: ***6.***

Cook's Note

Toss 1 pound of halved baby or fingerling potatoes with minced fresh rosemary, salt, and pepper and lightly spray with nonstick spray. Arrange in the roasting pan with the pork and roast until tender; the per-serving ***PointsPlus*** value will increase by ***2***.

Apricot-Mustard Glazed Pork Roast

Baked Stuffed Potatoes with Ham and Cheese

SERVES 4

4 (8-ounce) baking potatoes

⅓ cup fat-free sour cream

⅛ teaspoon black pepper

1 cup diced lean deli ham

1 cup shredded fat-free Cheddar cheese

Chopped fresh chives

1. Preheat oven to 400°F. Line baking sheet with foil.
2. Using fork, prick potatoes in several places. Place on baking sheet and bake until fork-tender, about 50 minutes.
3. Wearing oven mitts, cut off and discard thin lengthwise slice from each potato. Scoop out potato pulp, leaving ¼-inch wall. Transfer pulp to medium bowl and mash with sour cream, and pepper. Spoon filling evenly back into potato shells. Top potatoes evenly with ham and Cheddar.
4. Meanwhile, preheat broiler. Return potatoes to baking sheet and broil 5 inches from heat until cheese is melted, about 3 minutes. Sprinkle with chives.

PER SERVING (1 filled potato): 292 Cal, 3 g Total Fat, 1 g Sat Fat, 0 g Trans Fat, 26 mg Chol, 732 mg Sod, 47 g Total Carb, 4 g Fib, 21 g Prot, 297 mg Calc.

PointsPlus value: *7.*

Cook's Note

Serve the potatoes with a healthy green vegetable such as steamed broccoli, zucchini, or green beans.

Roasted Leg of Lamb

SERVES 8

3 garlic cloves, minced

1 tablespoon paprika

2 teaspoons poultry seasoning

1½ teaspoons salt

½ teaspoon black pepper

1 (2¼-pound) lean boneless leg of lamb, trimmed

4 onions, sliced

¾ cup dry white wine or dry vermouth

1. Preheat oven to 400°F. Spray roasting pan with nonstick spray.
2. Stir together garlic, paprika, poultry seasoning, salt, and pepper in small bowl. Add enough water to form thick paste and rub all over lamb.
3. Place lamb in roasting pan and top with onions. Pour wine into pan. Roast until an instant-read thermometer inserted into center of lamb registers 145°F for medium, about 1 hour.
4. Transfer lamb to cutting board and let stand 10 minutes. Cut into 24 slices and serve with onions.

PER SERVING (3 slices lamb and about ½ cup onions): 228 Cal, 9 g Total Fat, 3 g Sat Fat, 0 g Trans Fat, 88 mg Chol, 514 mg Sod, 7 g Total Carb, 1 g Fib, 28 g Prot, 31 mg Calc.

PointsPlus value: **6.**

Cook's Note

An instant-read thermometer is a must-have tool for cooking meats and poultry to a safe temperature as well as ensuring that you don't overcook beef, pork, or lamb roasts. It's an inexpensive investment that will make you a better—and safer—cook.

Stuffed Butterflied Leg of Lamb

Stuffed Butterflied Leg of Lamb

SERVES 8

1 tablespoon olive oil

3 garlic cloves, minced

1 tablespoon chopped fresh rosemary

1½ teaspoons salt

¾ teaspoon black pepper

1 (2½-pound) butterflied lean leg of lamb, trimmed

1 cup whole wheat couscous

½ cup finely chopped fresh parsley

½ cup finely chopped red bell pepper

1. Stir together oil, garlic, rosemary, 1¼ teaspoons of salt, and ½ teaspoon of pepper in small bowl; rub all over lamb. Place lamb on plate; cover and refrigerate at least 2 hours or up to 8 hours.
2. Meanwhile, prepare couscous according to package directions, omitting fat and salt if desired. Stir in parsley, bell pepper, and remaining ¼ teaspoon salt and ¼ teaspoon black pepper.
3. Preheat oven to 400°F.
4. Place lamb, boned side up, on work surface. Spread couscous mixture evenly over lamb. Starting from long side, roll up lamb to enclose filling. Tie lamb securely at 2-inch intervals with kitchen string.
5. Place rack in roasting pan and spray rack with nonstick spray. Place lamb on rack and roast until an instant-read thermometer inserted into thickest part of lamb registers 145°F for medium, about 1 hour.
6. Transfer lamb to cutting board and let stand 10 minutes. Remove string and cut lamb into 16 slices.

PER SERVING (2 slices stuffed lamb): 272 Cal, 11 g Total Fat, 4 g Sat Fat, 0 g Trans Fat, 98 mg Chol, 650 mg Sod, 10 g Total Carb, 2 g Fib, 32 g Prot, 25 mg Calc.

PointsPlus value: *7.*

Cook's Note

Here's how to roast asparagus to serve along with the lamb: When the lamb is almost done, place 2 pounds fresh asparagus spears in a shallow baking pan. Lightly spray with olive oil nonstick spray, sprinkle with salt and pepper and toss to coat. Roast at 400°F, tossing once, until the asparagus is crisp-tender, about 15 minutes.

Cacciatore-Style Chicken and Vegetables

SERVES 6

3 pounds bone-in chicken breasts and thighs, skin removed

½ teaspoon salt

¼ teaspoon black pepper

1 tablespoon olive oil

2 red bell peppers, thinly sliced

1 (8-ounce) package sliced cremini mushrooms

1 celery stalk, thinly sliced

1 carrot, thinly sliced

1 red onion, sliced

3 garlic cloves, minced

2 teaspoons chopped fresh rosemary

2 cups fat-free marinara sauce

1. Sprinkle chicken with salt and black pepper.
2. Heat 2 teaspoons of oil in large skillet over medium-high heat. Add chicken and cook until browned, about 4 minutes on each side. Transfer chicken to plate and set aside.
3. Add remaining 1 teaspoon oil to skillet. Add bell peppers, mushrooms, celery, carrot, onion, garlic, and rosemary; cook, stirring, until vegetables are slightly softened, about 3 minutes.
4. Return chicken to skillet. Add marinara sauce and bring to simmer. Reduce heat and simmer, covered, until chicken is cooked through and vegetables are tender, about 20 minutes.

PER SERVING (1 piece chicken and ¾ cup vegetables with sauce): 296 Cal, 11 g Total Fat, 3 g Sat Fat, 0 g Trans Fat, 95 mg Chol, 635 mg Sod, 12 g Total Carb, 3 g Fib, 36 g Prot, 69 mg Calc.

PointsPlus value: *7*.

Cook's Note

Serve the saucy cacciatore with a slice of crusty bread (a 1-ounce slice of Italian bread will increase the ***PointsPlus*** value by ***2***).

Cacciatore-Style Chicken and Vegetables

bonus on the weekend

Easy Chicken Florentine with Spaghetti

SERVES 4

2 teaspoons olive oil

1 small onion, chopped

2 (10-ounce) packages frozen leaf spinach, thawed

¼ teaspoon black pepper

4 (5-ounce) skinless boneless chicken breasts

1 cup shredded fat-free mozzarella cheese

2 tablespoons grated Parmesan cheese

4 ounces whole wheat spaghetti

½ cup fat-free marinara sauce, heated

2 slices bacon, crisp-cooked and crumbled

1. Preheat oven to 350°F and spray 8-inch square baking dish with nonstick spray.
2. Heat 1 teaspoon of oil in large skillet over medium-high heat. Add onion and cook, stirring frequently, until softened, about 5 minutes. Add spinach and pepper to skillet. Cook until most of liquid has evaporated, about 5 minutes longer. Spoon spinach mixture evenly into prepared baking dish.
3. Wipe out skillet. Add remaining 1 teaspoon oil to skillet and set over high heat. Place chicken in skillet and cook just until browned, about 2 minutes on each side.
4. Arrange chicken over spinach mixture in one layer; sprinkle evenly with mozzarella and Parmesan. Bake until cheeses are melted and chicken is cooked through, about 20 minutes.
5. Meanwhile, cook spaghetti according to package directions, omitting salt if desired; drain. Toss together spaghetti and marinara sauce. Sprinkle chicken with bacon and serve with spaghetti.

PER SERVING (¼ of casserole and ½ cup pasta): 432 Cal, 11 g Total Fat, 3 g Sat Fat, 0 g Trans Fat, 97 mg Chol, 870 mg Sod, 35 g Total Carb, 7 g Fib, 51 g Prot, 473 mg Calc.

PointsPlus value: ***11.***

Cook's Note

Skinless boneless chicken breasts are a universal favorite for easy-to-make dinners. If you use them often, save time and money by buying in bulk when they're on sale. Then, portion them into zip-close bags in the quantity you prepare for most recipes (usually 4), and freeze up to 6 months.

Best-Ever Country Captain

SERVES 4

2 teaspoons canola oil

1¼ pounds skinless boneless chicken breasts, cut into 1-inch pieces

1 large onion, chopped

1 Granny Smith apple, peeled, cored, and diced

1 green bell pepper, chopped

1 tablespoon minced garlic

1 tablespoon minced peeled fresh ginger

1 tablespoon Madras curry powder

¼ teaspoon cinnamon

¼ teaspoon salt

1 (14½-ounce) can diced tomatoes

1 cup reduced-sodium chicken broth

¼ cup dark raisins

1 tablespoon sliced or slivered almonds, toasted

1. Heat 1 teaspoon of oil in Dutch oven or large saucepan over medium-high heat. Add chicken and cook, turning occasionally, until browned, about 6 minutes. Transfer to plate.
2. Add remaining 1 teaspoon oil to Dutch oven and reduce heat to medium. Add onion, apple, bell pepper, garlic, and ginger; cook, stirring, until vegetables are softened, about 5 minutes. Stir in curry powder, cinnamon, and salt; cook, stirring, 1 minute longer.
3. Return chicken to Dutch oven along with tomatoes, broth, and raisins; bring to boil. Reduce heat and simmer, covered, until chicken is cooked through, about 15 minutes. Serve sprinkled with almonds.

PER SERVING (about 1½ cups): 309 Cal, 8 g Total Fat, 2 g Sat Fat, 0 g Trans Fat, 86 mg Chol, 516 mg Sod, 24 g Total Carb, 4 g Fib, 35 g Prot, 90 mg Calc.

PointsPlus value: ***8.***

Do it Faster

Toasting almonds enhances their flavor and crisps their texture. To toast sliced or slivered almonds in a hurry, place them in a small heavy skillet over medium heat. Toast, shaking the pan frequently, until the nuts are lightly browned, about 5 minutes. Transfer to a plate to cool.

Chicken with Mushrooms and White Wine

Chicken with Mushrooms and White Wine

SERVES 4

4 (5-ounce) skinless boneless chicken breasts

½ teaspoon salt

¼ teaspoon black pepper

2 teaspoons olive oil

¼ pound mixed mushrooms, halved

1 onion, chopped

1 carrot, chopped

1 celery stalk, chopped

3 garlic cloves, minced

1 teaspoon herbes de Provence

1 tablespoon all-purpose flour

1 cup reduced-sodium chicken broth

¾ cup dry white wine

8 ounces whole wheat fettuccine

Chopped fresh parsley

1. Sprinkle chicken with salt and pepper. Heat 1 teaspoon of oil in large skillet over medium-high heat. Add chicken and cook, turning occasionally, until browned, about 4 minutes. Transfer chicken to plate.
2. Add remaining 1 teaspoon oil and mushrooms to skillet. Cook, stirring frequently, until mushrooms are browned, about 5 minutes. Stir in onion, carrot, celery, garlic, and herbes de Provence. Cook just until onion is softened, about 3 minutes, then sprinkle with flour. Cook, stirring constantly, 1 minute longer. Stir in broth and wine and bring to boil.
3. Return chicken and any accumulated juices to skillet. Reduce heat and simmer, covered, until sauce is thickened and chicken is cooked through, about 10 minutes.
4. Meanwhile, cook fettuccine according to package directions, omitting salt if desired; drain.
5. Divide fettuccine among 4 plates; top with chicken and sauce. Sprinkle with parsley.

PER SERVING (1 chicken breast, ⅔ cup sauce and vegetables, and 1 cup pasta): 466 Cal, 7 g Total Fat, 1 g Sat Fat, 0 g Trans Fat, 84 mg Chol, 528 mg Sod, 51 g Total Carb, 8 g Fib, 42 g Prot, 67 mg Calc.

PointsPlus value: ***12.***

Cook's Note

Herbes de Provence is a blend of dried rosemary, marjoram, thyme, and savory that adds the unique flavor of Southern France to a dish. If you don't have it, you can substitute dried thyme in this dish and it will still be delicious.

bonus on the weekend

Chicken and Vegetable Ragu with Herbed Dumplings

SERVES 4

1 pound skinless boneless chicken breasts, cut into 1-inch pieces

¾ teaspoon salt

¼ teaspoon black pepper

1 onion, chopped

1 tablespoon plus ½ cup all-purpose flour

2 cups reduced-sodium chicken broth

2 (5-ounce) red potatoes, scrubbed and diced

¼ cup whole wheat flour

1½ teaspoons baking powder

½ cup fat-free milk

2 teaspoons unsalted butter, melted

2 tablespoons chopped fresh parsley

2 tablespoons chopped fresh chives

1½ cups frozen mixed peas and carrots, thawed

1 teaspoon dried thyme

1. Spray Dutch oven with nonstick spray and set over medium-high heat. Add chicken and sprinkle with ¼ teaspoon of salt, and pepper. Cook, stirring occasionally, until chicken is lightly browned, about 6 minutes. Add onion and cook until softened, about 4 minutes longer.
2. Stir in 1 tablespoon of flour and cook, stirring constantly, 1 minute. Stir in broth and potatoes and bring to boil. Reduce heat and simmer, covered, until potatoes are tender, about 15 minutes.
3. Meanwhile, to make dumpling dough, whisk together remaining ½ cup all-purpose flour, whole wheat flour, baking powder, and remaining ½ teaspoon salt in medium bowl. Add milk, butter, parsley, and chives; stir just until soft dough forms. Set dumpling dough aside.
4. Stir peas and carrots and thyme into Dutch oven and simmer 2 minutes. Drop 8 rounded tablespoonfuls of dumpling dough onto surface of simmering stew. Cover and simmer 8 minutes. Uncover and simmer until dumplings are doubled in size and cooked through, about 3 minutes longer.

PER SERVING (1 cup stew and 2 dumplings): 390 Cal, 7 g Total Fat, 3 g Sat Fat, 0 g Trans Fat, 74 mg Chol, 920 mg Sod, 47 g Total Carb, 6 g Fib, 35 g Prot, 211 mg Calc.

PointsPlus value: ***10.***

Chicken and Rice with Artichoke Hearts

SERVES 4

2 teaspoons olive oil

4 (5-ounce) skinless bone-in chicken thighs

½ teaspoon dried oregano

½ teaspoon salt

¼ teaspoon black pepper

2 red bell peppers, chopped

1 onion, chopped

3 garlic cloves, minced

1 cup brown rice

1 (14½-ounce) can diced tomatoes

1 cup water

1 cup frozen artichoke hearts, thawed and coarsely chopped

1 tablespoon capers, drained

1. Heat 1 teaspoon of oil in large nonstick skillet over medium heat. Sprinkle chicken with oregano, ¼ teaspoon of salt, and black pepper. Add chicken to skillet and cook until browned, about 3 minutes on each side. Transfer to plate.
2. Add remaining 1 teaspoon oil to skillet. Add bell peppers, onion, and garlic; cook, stirring frequently, until vegetables begin to soften, about 4 minutes. Add rice and cook, stirring, 1 minute longer. Return chicken to skillet. Add tomatoes, water, and remaining ¼ teaspoon salt; bring to boil. Reduce heat and simmer, covered, until rice is tender, liquid is absorbed, and chicken is cooked through, about 40 minutes longer.
3. Uncover pan and scatter artichokes and capers over rice. Cook, covered, just until artichokes are heated through, about 3 minutes.

PER SERVING (1 chicken thigh and 1⅓ cups rice mixture): 422 Cal, 10 g Total Fat, 3 g Sat Fat, 0 g Trans Fat, 57 mg Chol, 602 mg Sod, 56 g Total Carb, 6 g Fib, 27 g Prot, 106 mg Calc.

PointsPlus value: ***11.***

Cook's Note

A peppery watercress salad is the perfect partner for this one-pan meal. Toss together watercress sprigs, plum tomato wedges, balsamic vinegar, and salt and pepper to taste.

Spaghetti with Fresh Tomato Sauce and Meatballs

SERVES 4

8 ounces whole wheat spaghetti

1 pound ground skinless turkey breast

1 large egg white

1 tablespoon cornmeal

1 teaspoon dried oregano

½ teaspoon salt

3 teaspoons olive oil

2 garlic cloves

8 plum tomatoes, chopped

1 teaspoon dried basil

Pinch red pepper flakes

1. Cook spaghetti according to package directions, omitting salt if desired. Drain and keep warm.
2. Meanwhile, mix together turkey, egg white, cornmeal, oregano, and ¼ teaspoon of salt in large bowl. With damp hands, shape mixture into 24 meatballs.
3. Heat 2 teaspoons of oil in large nonstick skillet over medium heat. Cook meatballs, in batches, turning often, until browned, about 4 minutes. Transfer to plate.
4. To make sauce, wipe out skillet and set over medium heat. Add remaining 1 teaspoon oil and garlic. Cook, stirring, until garlic is fragrant, about 30 seconds. Add tomatoes, basil, remaining ¼ teaspoon salt, and red pepper flakes; cook, stirring frequently, until tomatoes are softened, about 5 minutes. Return meatballs to skillet and simmer, covered, until cooked through, about 5 minutes longer.
5. Divide pasta evenly among 4 large bowls and top evenly with meatballs and sauce.

PER SERVING (1 cup spaghetti, 6 meatballs, and 1 cup sauce): 392 Cal, 6 g Total Fat, 1 g Sat Fat, 0 g Trans Fat, 75 mg Chol, 574 mg Sod, 51 g Total Carb, 6 g Fib, 37 g Prot, 60 mg Calc.

PointsPlus value: ***10.***

Cook's Note

You can serve the pasta sprinkled with freshly grated Parmesan cheese (1 tablespoon grated Parmesan cheese per serving will increase the ***PointsPlus*** value by ***1***). If served with Parmesan, this recipe does not work with Simple Start or with the Simply Filling technique.

Spaghetti with Fresh Tomato Sauce and Meatballs

bonus on the weekend

time well spent

Use these kitchen tricks when you have some extra time on the weekends. They take a little effort, but will pay off with big rewards when you're in a weeknight time crunch.

FREEZE YOUR FAVORITE BREAKFAST. Premade muffins, pancakes, and waffles make breakfast a breeze with just a zap in the microwave.

PREP AND FREEZE FRUITS FOR SMOOTHIES. If fruits like mangos, peaches, and berries are prepped and frozen ahead of time, it makes your morning smoothie fuss-free. You're more likely to make nutritious fruit a part of your day if it's easy to do.

DOUBLE UP. Always make two batches of soups, chilis, casseroles, or other dishes that freeze well for instant meals later on. No more starting dinner from scratch on a rushed weeknight. It feels good to come home to something made earlier.

OR, COOK ONCE FOR THE WEEK. Invest some time on the weekend to prepare foods for the entire week. Make a casserole or a stew to reheat for an effortless dinner. Whip up a pesto sauce, marinara sauce, or salad dressing that you can use in several dishes throughout the week. If your weekday schedule is jam-packed, this may be the perfect solution to make sure you have healthy meals.

PREP AHEAD. Chop onions and other vegetables for the week and store them in sealed containers in the refrigerator. Wash three days' worth of lettuce and greens, dry them, and store refrigerated in plastic bags. If you come home feeling too tired to cook, remind yourself that most of the work is already done.

COOK EXTRA WHOLE GRAINS. With cooked barley, farro, or wheat berries on hand, it's easy to add them to pancake batter, soups, or meat loaves to boost flavor and fiber. And, they all make delicious side dishes on their own when seasoned with salt, pepper, and a fresh grating of lemon zest. Store them in clear containers in the refrigerator so you can see exactly what you have on hand at a glance.

MAKE A MENU AND SHOPPING LIST. Mapping out a weekly menu and shopping list will save trips to the supermarket, save time spent shopping, and take away the stress of what to cook for dinner every night.

MAINTAIN A QUICK-MEAL PANTRY. When you shop each week, check for long-lasting pantry staples that are on sale and stock up. Keep your shelves replenished with canned beans, tomatoes, tomato sauce, and broths; dried pasta; and grains such as rice, quinoa, and bulgur. Always have oils and vinegars, soy sauce, and bouillon cubes on hand. Buy red onions, celery, carrots, garlic, and a few fresh herbs such as basil and flat-leaf parsley each week. With these mealtime building blocks, you can make a healthy dinner in minutes.

MASTER A FEW NO-BRAINER DISHES. When you've got to make dinner fast, but don't have the time or energy for anything that requires a recipe, learn to make quesadillas, frittatas, grilled sandwiches, and pasta with sauce. With a well-stocked pantry, you can alter the ingredients in these dishes based on what you have on hand—no recipe required!

LABEL LEFTOVERS. Store leftovers in plastic or glass containers and label them with what is inside (if you don't have clear containers) and the date. You'll save time looking through containers to find what you're looking for.

Rosemary Chicken Thighs with Roast Potatoes

SERVES 4

4 (¼-pound) skinless boneless chicken thighs

2 teaspoons olive oil

2 garlic cloves, minced

1 teaspoon grated lemon zest

1 tablespoon fresh lemon juice

1½ teaspoons dried rosemary

1 teaspoon dried thyme

¾ teaspoon salt

6 small new potatoes, scrubbed and quartered

1. Combine chicken, 1 teaspoon of oil, garlic, lemon zest and juice, rosemary, thyme, and ½ teaspoon of salt in large zip-close plastic bag. Squeeze out air and seal bag; turn to coat chicken. Refrigerate, turning bag occasionally, at least 30 minutes or up to overnight.
2. Toss together potatoes and remaining 1 teaspoon oil and ¼ teaspoon salt in medium bowl. Spray rimmed baking sheet with nonstick spray and spread potatoes on baking sheet. Place potatoes in oven and turn oven on to 425°F. When temperature reaches 425°F, remove potatoes from oven. Toss potatoes, then push them to one side of pan.
3. Remove chicken from marinade and place on baking sheet alongside potatoes. Discard marinade. Roast until chicken is cooked through and potatoes are tender and browned, about 20 minutes.

PER SERVING (1 piece chicken and ½ cup potatoes): 273 Cal, 11 g Total Fat, 3 g Sat Fat, 0 g Trans Fat, 71 mg Chol, 512 mg Sod, 16 g Total Carb, 2 g Fib, 25 g Prot, 57 mg Calc.

PointsPlus value: *7.*

Cook's Note

This herbal lemon marinade is also great to use for pork chops or pork tenderloin.

bonus on the weekend

Lentil and Sausage Soup

SERVES 4

- 2 teaspoons olive oil
- 2 carrots, thinly sliced
- 1 onion, diced
- 2 garlic cloves, minced
- ¼ pound turkey kielbasa, thinly sliced
- 1¼ cups brown lentils, picked over and rinsed
- 5 cups water
- 1 (14½-ounce) can diced tomatoes
- ½ teaspoon salt
- ¼ teaspoon black pepper

1. Heat oil in large saucepan over medium heat. Add carrots, onion, and garlic; cook, stirring frequently, until softened, about 5 minutes.
2. Add kielbasa, lentils, and water; bring to boil. Reduce heat and simmer until lentils are tender, about 30 minutes.
3. Stir in tomatoes, salt, and pepper. Simmer until heated through, about 5 minutes longer.

PER SERVING (1¾ cups): 296 Cal, 6 g Total Fat, 1 g Sat Fat, 0 g Trans Fat, 15 mg Chol, 760 mg Sod, 44 g Total Carb, 12 g Fib, 21 g Prot, 95 mg Calc.

PointsPlus value: *7.*

Cook's Note

Turkey kielbasa is a great ingredient for the shortcut cook to keep on hand. As you'll see in this recipe, just a small amount is so flavorful that you don't need to add other herbs or spices to a dish to make it satisfying and delicious.

Lentil and Sausage Soup

Provençal-Style
Vegetable-Chickpea Stew

Provençal-Style Vegetable-Chickpea Stew

SERVES 4

- **1 eggplant (1 pound), cut into ¾-inch cubes**
- **2 teaspoons olive oil**
- **1 (28-ounce) can fire-roasted diced tomatoes, drained**
- **3 tablespoons tomato paste**
- **2 red bell peppers, cut into ¾-inch pieces**
- **1 large zucchini, cut into ¾-inch pieces**
- **1 large onion, coarsely chopped**
- **2 large garlic cloves, minced**
- **1 teaspoon dried thyme**
- **¾ teaspoon salt**
- **¼ teaspoon black pepper**
- **¼ cup chopped fresh parsley**
- **2½ cups rinsed and drained canned chickpeas**
- **¼ cup grated Parmesan cheese**

1. Stir together eggplant and oil in large microwavable bowl. Cover bowl with wax paper. Microwave on High until eggplant is softened, about 4 minutes.
2. Add all remaining ingredients except chickpeas and Parmesan to eggplant and stir to combine. Cover bowl with wax paper. Microwave on High until vegetables are softened, about 15 minutes, stirring every 5 minutes. Stir in chickpeas and let stand about 5 minutes. Serve warm or at room temperature sprinkled with Parmesan.

PER SERVING (about 1½ cups): 119 Cal, 5 g Total Fat, 1 g Sat Fat, 0 g Trans Fat, 0 mg Chol, 405 mg Sod, 18 g Total Carb, 6 g Fib, 4 g Prot, 55 mg Calc.

PointsPlus value: ***3.***

Cook's Note

Intensely flavored ingredients like fire-roasted tomatoes add fantastic taste to a dish with little effort. These tomatoes are cooked over an open flame, which concentrates their flavor and adds a touch of smokiness.

bonus on the weekend

Baked Ziti with Summer Squash

SERVES 5

2 cups (about 6 ounces) whole wheat ziti or penne

2 teaspoons olive oil

1 yellow summer squash, thinly sliced

1 small zucchini, thinly sliced

2 garlic cloves, minced

2 cups fat-free marinara sauce

2 cups fat-free ricotta cheese

1 cup shredded fat-free mozzarella cheese

1. Cook ziti according to package directions, omitting salt if desired; drain.
2. Preheat oven to 375°F. Spray 8-inch square baking dish with nonstick spray.
3. Heat oil in large nonstick skillet over medium heat. Add squash, zucchini, and garlic; cook, stirring, until softened, about 6 minutes. Stir in cooked ziti and marinara sauce.
4. Transfer mixture to prepared baking dish and top evenly with ricotta and mozzarella. Bake until heated through and bubbling, about 20 minutes.

PER SERVING (generous 1½ cups): 370 Cal, 6 g Total Fat, 1 g Sat Fat, 0 g Trans Fat, 13 mg Chol, 956 mg Sod, 55 g Total Carb, 5 g Fib, 26 g Prot, 409 mg Calc.

PointsPlus value: ***9.***

Cook's Note

To add even more flavor to this dish with just a couple minutes effort, stir a handful of chopped fresh basil into the pasta before baking.

Bountiful Beef Stew

SERVES 4

- 1 tablespoon olive oil
- 1 pound lean boneless beef bottom round, trimmed and cut into 1-inch chunks
- ½ teaspoon salt
- ¼ teaspoon black pepper
- 3 onions, thinly sliced
- 1¼ pounds baby red potatoes, halved
- 1½ cups baby carrots
- 1 (14½-ounce) can reduced-sodium beef broth
- 2 teaspoons finely chopped fresh tarragon
- ⅓ cup water
- 2 tablespoons all-purpose flour

1. Heat oil in large skillet over medium-high heat. Add beef and sprinkle with salt and pepper. Cook, turning frequently, until browned, about 4 minutes. Transfer beef to 5- or 6-quart slow cooker.
2. Add onions to skillet; cook, stirring occasionally, until softened and browned, about 8 minutes. Transfer onions to slow cooker and stir in potatoes, carrots, broth, and tarragon. Push potatoes down into liquid. Cover and cook until beef and vegetables are fork-tender, 4–6 hours on high or 8–10 hours on low.
3. About 20 minutes before cooking time is up, whisk together water and flour in small bowl until smooth. Whisk in ¼ cup of stew liquid until blended; stir flour mixture into stew. Cover and cook on high until mixture simmers and thickens, about 15 minutes longer.

PER SERVING (1¾ cups): 403 Cal, 9 g Total Fat, 2 g Sat Fat, 0 g Trans Fat, 84 mg Chol, 454 mg Sod, 41 g Total Carb, 6 g Fib, 40 g Prot, 74 mg Calc.

PointsPlus **value: *10.***

Beef and Bean Soft Tacos

Beef and Bean Soft Tacos

SERVES 6

1½ cups reduced-sodium beef broth

1 teaspoon chili powder

1 (1-pound) lean flank steak, trimmed

¾ cup chunky tomato salsa plus additional for serving (optional)

½ cup rinsed and drained canned black beans

¼ cup chopped fresh cilantro

2 tablespoons canned chopped mild green chiles, drained

12 (6-inch) flour tortillas, warmed

¼ cup fat-free sour cream

1. Whisk together broth and chili powder in 5- or 6-quart slow cooker. Add steak. Cover and cook until steak is fork-tender, 4–5 hours on high or 8–10 hours on low.
2. Transfer steak to cutting board; discard all but ¼ cup of cooking liquid. Using two forks, finely shred beef. Return beef to slow cooker and stir in reserved cooking liquid, ¾ cup of salsa, beans, cilantro, and chiles. Cook on high until heated through, about 5 minutes.
3. Top each tortilla evenly with beef mixture and sour cream. Fold tortillas in half and serve with additional salsa on side, if using.

PER SERVING (2 tacos without salsa): 274 Cal, 5 g Total Fat, 1 g Sat Fat, 0 g Trans Fat, 56 mg Chol, 373 mg Sod, 30 g Total Carb, 4 g Fib, 28 g Prot, 78 mg Calc.

PointsPlus value: *7.*

Do it Faster

This dish requires just a few minutes prep before going into the slow cooker, making it perfect for rushed mornings when you want to get something cooking for dinner before you leave for work.

Beef Stew Provençal

SERVES 6

- 1 pound lean boneless beef bottom round, trimmed and cut into 1-inch chunks
- 4 leeks, cleaned and sliced, white and light green parts only
- 1 fennel bulb, diced (fronds reserved)
- 6 garlic cloves, minced
- 1 (28-ounce) can diced tomatoes
- 1 cup dry red wine
- 2 teaspoons herbes de Provence or Italian seasoning
- ¾ teaspoon salt
- 2 teaspoons olive oil
- 1½ pounds white mushrooms, halved
- ½ cup pitted black olives
- Grated zest of ½ orange

1. Stir together beef, leeks, diced fennel bulb, garlic, tomatoes, wine, herbes de Provence, and salt in 5- or 6-quart slow cooker. Cover and cook until beef is fork-tender, 4–5 hours on high or 8–10 hours on low.
2. About 20 minutes before cooking time is up, heat oil in large skillet over medium-high heat. Add mushrooms and cook, stirring, until browned and liquid is evaporated, about 5 minutes.
3. Stir mushrooms and olives into slow cooker. Cover and cook on high until mushrooms are very tender, about 10 minutes longer.
4. Meanwhile, chop enough of reserved fennel fronds to equal 3 tablespoons. Combine fennel fronds and orange zest in small bowl.
5. Ladle stew evenly into 6 serving bowls; sprinkle evenly with fennel frond mixture.

PER SERVING (1½ cups): 262 Cal, 7 g Total Fat, 2 g Sat Fat, 0 g Trans Fat, 56 mg Chol, 642 mg Sod, 23 g Total Carb, 5 g Fib, 29 g Prot, 127 mg Calc.

PointsPlus value: *7.*

Beef, Beet, and Cabbage Soup

SERVES 8

2 teaspoons olive oil

1 pound lean boneless beef bottom round, trimmed and cut into ¾-inch pieces

2 onions, thinly sliced

8 cups reduced-sodium beef broth

4 beets, trimmed, peeled, and diced

3 carrots, sliced

1 cup thinly sliced green cabbage

1 (14½-ounce) can petite diced tomatoes

½ teaspoon salt

¼ teaspoon black pepper

1 bay leaf

1. Heat oil in large skillet over medium-high heat Add beef, in batches, and cook, stirring, until browned, about 8 minutes. Transfer beef to 5- or 6-quart slow cooker.
2. Add onions to skillet and cook, stirring, until softened, about 5 minutes. Add onions to slow cooker. Add broth, beets, carrots, cabbage, tomatoes, salt, pepper, and bay leaf to slow cooker; stir to combine. Cover and cook until beef and vegetables are fork-tender, 4–6 hours on high or 8–10 hours on low.
3. Remove and discard bay leaf. Ladle soup evenly into 8 bowls.

PER SERVING (about 1⅓ cups): 197 Cal, 9 g Total Fat, 3 g Sat Fat, 0 g Trans Fat, 29 mg Chol, 474 mg Sod, 14 g Total Carb, 3 g Fib, 16 g Prot, 53 mg Calc.

PointsPlus value: **5.**

Cook's Note

To complete the meal, serve the soup with a 1½-ounce light roll, and finish with fresh strawberries for dessert (a 1½-ounce light roll per serving will increase the ***PointsPlus*** value by ***2***).

Low-and-Slow Sloppy Joes

SERVES 6

1 pound ground lean beef (7% fat or less)

1 (14½-ounce) can diced tomatoes

1 small onion, chopped

1 celery stalk, chopped

3 tablespoons packed dark brown sugar

2 teaspoons Worcestershire sauce

1½ teaspoons ground cumin

1 teaspoon chili powder

½ teaspoon salt

6 whole wheat sandwich rolls, split

1. Spray large skillet with nonstick spray and set over medium-high heat. Add beef and cook, breaking it apart with wooden spoon, until browned, about 5 minutes.
2. Transfer beef to 5- or 6-quart slow cooker. Stir in tomatoes, onion, celery, brown sugar, Worcestershire sauce, cumin, chili powder, and salt. Cover and cook until sauce is slightly thickened, 3–4 hours on high or 6–8 hours on low.
3. Spoon ½ cup of beef mixture into each roll.

PER SERVING (1 sandwich): 239 Cal, 6 g Total Fat, 2 g Sat Fat, 0 g Trans Fat, 43 mg Chol, 526 mg Sod, 26 g Total Carb, 4 g Fib, 20 g Prot, 83 mg Calc.

PointsPlus value: **6.**

Cook's Note

Top the sandwiches with thinly sliced cabbage, and serve kosher dill pickles on the side.

Lamb and Vegetable Stew

SERVES 4

2 teaspoons olive oil

3 red onions, thinly sliced

1 (24-ounce) package frozen stew vegetables, thawed

1 pound lean boneless leg of lamb, trimmed and cut into 1-inch chunks

2 cups reduced-sodium vegetable broth

¾ teaspoon dried thyme

½ teaspoon salt

¼ teaspoon black pepper

1. Heat oil in large nonstick skillet over medium heat. Add onions and cook, stirring, until softened, about 8 minutes.
2. Transfer onions to 5- or 6-quart slow cooker and stir in stew vegetables, lamb, broth, thyme, salt, and pepper. Cover and cook until lamb and vegetables are fork-tender, 4–6 hours on high or 8–10 hours on low.

PER SERVING (2 cups): 340 Cal, 11 g Total Fat, 3 g Sat Fat, 0 g Trans Fat, 78 mg Chol, 534 mg Sod, 32 g Total Carb, 6 g Fib, 30 g Prot, 82 mg Calc.

PointsPlus value: ***9.***

Cook's Note

Serve this saucy stew over creamy polenta (½ cup of cooked polenta per serving will increase the ***PointsPlus*** value by ***3***).

bonus on the weekend

Pork Marrakesh

SERVES 4

2 teaspoons olive oil

4 (¼-pound) boneless pork rib or loin chops, trimmed

¾ teaspoon salt

¼ teaspoon black pepper

3 small red onions, thinly sliced

12 dried apricot halves, sliced

¾ cup unsweetened apple juice

2 teaspoons minced peeled fresh ginger

½ teaspoon dried thyme

1 (3-inch) cinnamon stick

¼ cup chopped fresh cilantro

1. Heat 1 teaspoon of oil in large skillet over medium-high heat. Sprinkle pork chops with ¼ teaspoon of salt and pepper. Add chops to skillet and cook until browned, about 2 minutes on each side. Transfer to plate.
2. Reduce heat to medium and add remaining 1 teaspoon oil. Add onions and remaining ½ teaspoon salt and cook, stirring, until onions are golden, about 10 minutes.
3. Place half of apricots and half of onions in bottom of 5- or 6-quart slow cooker. Top with pork chops and remaining onions and apricots. Add apple juice, ginger, thyme, and cinnamon stick. Cover and cook until pork is fork-tender, 3–4 hours on high or 6–8 hours on low. Remove cinnamon stick and serve pork sprinkled with cilantro.

PER SERVING (1 pork chop and ½ cup onion mixture): 281 Cal, 11 g Total Fat, 3 g Sat Fat, 0 g Trans Fat, 73 mg Chol, 492 mg Sod, 18 g Total Carb, 2 g Fib, 27 g Prot, 32 mg Calc.

PointsPlus value: *7.*

Cook's Note

Serve the chops with whole wheat couscous (½ cup cooked whole wheat couscous per serving will increase the ***PointsPlus*** value by **3**).

Pork Marrakesh

bonus on the weekend

Chicken and Vegetable Curry

SERVES 4

2 teaspoons olive oil

2 large onions, thinly sliced

1 teaspoon garam masala or curry powder

1½ cups reduced-sodium chicken broth

1 pound skinless boneless chicken breasts, cut into 1-inch pieces

3 small sweet potatoes, peeled, halved lengthwise, and cut into ½-inch slices

¼ teaspoon salt

¼–½ teaspoon cayenne pepper

1 cup brown rice, preferably basmati

1 (16-ounce) bag frozen broccoli, cauliflower, and carrots, thawed

1. Heat oil in large nonstick skillet over medium heat. Add onions and cook, stirring, until softened, about 6 minutes. Remove skillet from heat and stir in garam masala.
2. Transfer onions to 5- or 6-quart slow cooker. Add broth, chicken, sweet potatoes, salt, and cayenne to slow cooker; stir to combine. Cover and cook until chicken and potatoes are fork-tender, 4–6 hours on high or 8–10 hours on low.
3. Meanwhile, cook rice according to package directions, omitting salt if desired.
4. About 20 minutes before cooking time is up, add thawed vegetables to slow cooker. Cover and cook on high until vegetables are crisp-tender, about 20 minutes longer.
5. Divide rice among 4 bowls and top evenly with curry.

PER SERVING (1¾ cups curry and ½ cup rice): 353 Cal, 6 g Total Fat, 1 g Sat Fat, 0 g Trans Fat, 55 mg Chol, 690 mg Sod, 47 g Total Carb, 9 g Fib, 27 g Prot, 80 mg Calc.

PointsPlus value: ***8.***

Cook's Note

Finish this Indian-inspired meal with fresh slices of mango tossed with fresh lime juice and grated lime zest.

Braised Chicken in Riesling

SERVES 6

6 skinless chicken thighs, trimmed

½ teaspoon salt

¼ teaspoon black pepper

1 tablespoon olive oil

1½ cups finely shredded green cabbage

1 onion, thinly sliced

1 cup baby carrots

3 garlic cloves, peeled

¾ cup Riesling or other white wine

¾ cup reduced-sodium chicken broth

2 tablespoons tomato paste

⅓ cup water

2 tablespoons all-purpose flour

1. Sprinkle chicken with salt and pepper.
2. Heat oil in large skillet over medium-high heat. Add chicken and cook, turning, until browned, about 8 minutes. Transfer chicken to 5- or 6-quart slow cooker.
3. Add cabbage and onion to skillet. Reduce heat to medium and cook, stirring, until onion is softened, about 5 minutes. Transfer to slow cooker and top with carrots and garlic.
4. Whisk together wine, broth, and tomato paste in bowl, then pour over chicken. Cover and cook until chicken and carrots are fork-tender, 4–6 hours on high or 8–10 hours on low. Using slotted spoon, transfer chicken to deep platter. Keep warm.
5. Whisk together water and flour in small bowl until smooth. Whisk in about ¼ cup of hot stew liquid until blended, then stir flour mixture into slow cooker. Cover and cook on high until mixture simmers and thickens, about 15 minutes. Spoon sauce over chicken.

PER SERVING (1 chicken thigh and ½ cup vegetables with sauce): 177 Cal, 8 g Total Fat, 2 g Sat Fat, 0 g Trans Fat, 43 mg Chol, 367 mg Sod, 9 g Total Carb, 2 g Fib, 16 g Prot, 44 mg Calc.

PointsPlus value: **5.**

Cook's Note

If you prefer not to use wine for this recipe, you can substitute an equal amount of reduced-sodium chicken broth.

Easy Chicken Gumbo

Easy Chicken Gumbo

SERVES 4

1 tablespoon olive oil

2 onions, thinly sliced

4 skinless boneless chicken thighs, trimmed and cut into ½-inch slices

3 cups thawed frozen or fresh okra

1 (14½-ounce) can petite diced tomatoes

5 celery stalks with leaves, sliced

3 garlic cloves, peeled

1½ cups reduced-sodium chicken broth

1 teaspoon dried thyme

¼–½ teaspoon cayenne pepper

2 teaspoons gumbo filé powder

2 cups hot cooked brown or white rice

1. Heat oil in large skillet over medium-high heat. Add onions and cook, stirring, until softened, about 6 minutes.
2. Transfer onions to 5- or 6-quart slow cooker and stir in chicken, okra, tomatoes, celery, and garlic.
3. Whisk together broth, thyme, and cayenne in large glass measure and add to slow cooker. Cover and cook until chicken is fork-tender, 4–6 hours on high or 8–10 hours on low. Discard garlic. Turn off slow cooker and stir in filé powder. Cover and let stand 10 minutes.
4. Divide rice evenly among 4 bowls and top evenly with gumbo.

PER SERVING (1½ cups): 343 Cal, 10 g Total Fat, 2 g Sat Fat, 0 g Trans Fat, 43 mg Chol, 749 mg Sod, 43 g Total Carb, 7 g Fib, 23 g Prot, 243 mg Calc.

PointsPlus value: **9.**

Cook's Note

Filé powder, used to thicken gumbo and other Creole dishes in New Orleans, is made from ground dried leaves of the sassafras tree. It is always stirred into dish after it is removed from the heat, otherwise it becomes stringy.

bonus on the weekend

Chicken and Vegetable Tagine

SERVES 6

3 zucchini, halved lengthwise and cut into ½-inch slices

1 (15½-ounce) can chickpeas, rinsed and drained

1 (14½-ounce) can diced tomatoes

1 cup reduced-sodium chicken broth

2 garlic cloves, minced

1 (3-inch) cinnamon stick

2 teaspoons ground ginger

¾ teaspoon salt

¼ teaspoon cayenne pepper

6 skinless bone-in chicken thighs, trimmed

1 (12-ounce) package whole wheat couscous

1. Combine zucchini, chickpeas, tomatoes, broth, garlic, cinnamon stick, ginger, salt, and cayenne in 5- or 6-quart slow cooker. Add chicken and press it down into liquid. Cover and cook until chicken is fork-tender, 4–6 hours on high or 8–10 hours on low.
2. About 8 minutes before serving, cook couscous according to package directions, omitting fat and salt if desired.
3. Divide couscous evenly among 6 plates and top evenly with chicken. Discard cinnamon stick. Using slotted spoon, spoon vegetable mixture evenly over chicken. Discard liquid.

PER SERVING (¾ cup couscous, 1 chicken thigh, and generous ¾ cup vegetables): 431 Cal, 9 g Total Fat, 2 g Sat Fat, 0 g Trans Fat, 43 mg Chol, 309 mg Sod, 64 g Total Carb, 12 g Fib, 29 g Prot, 119 mg Calc.

PointsPlus value: ***11.***

Garlicky Braised Turkey Breast

SERVES 12

2 tablespoons unsalted butter, softened

3 garlic cloves, minced

2 teaspoons poultry seasoning

1 teaspoon salt

¼ teaspoon black pepper

1 (6-pound) whole bone-in turkey breast

2 onions, sliced

¼ cup reduced-sodium chicken broth

2 tablespoons cornstarch

1. Mash together butter, garlic, poultry seasoning, salt, and pepper in small bowl. With your fingertips, gently loosen skin from breast meat. Rub butter mixture all over meat under skin.
2. Stir together onions, broth, and cornstarch in 5- or 6-quart slow cooker. Place turkey on top of onion mixture. Cover and cook until turkey is fork-tender, 4–5 hours on high or 8–10 hours on low.
3. Transfer turkey to platter and carve breast into 36 slices. Serve with broth and onions. Remove turkey skin before eating.

PER SERVING (3 slices turkey and ¼ cup broth with onions): 215 Cal, 3 g Total Fat, 2 g Sat Fat, 0 g Trans Fat, 123 mg Chol, 281 mg Sod, 2 g Total Carb, 3 g Fib, 43 g Prot, 23 mg Calc.

PointsPlus value: ***5.***

Do it Faster

If you want to save time on cooking during the week, this is a perfect recipe to make on the weekend. You can reheat the leftovers, or make salads and sandwiches using the leftover turkey.

bonus on the weekend

Chuck Wagon–Style Turkey Chili

1. Spray large skillet with nonstick spray and set over medium-high heat. Add turkey and cook, breaking it up with wooden spoon, until no longer pink, about 5 minutes.
2. Transfer turkey and any juices to 5- or 6-quart slow cooker. Add all remaining ingredients except scallions and stir well. Cover and cook until vegetables are softened, 4–5 hours on high or 8–10 hours on low, stirring in little additional water if chili seems dry.
3. Spoon chili evenly into 4 bowls and sprinkle with scallions.

PER SERVING (1⅔ cups): 386 Cal, 3 g Total Fat, 1 g Sat Fat, 0 g Trans Fat, 75 mg Chol, 897 mg Sod, 57 g Total Carb, 13 g Fib, 37 g Prot, 132 mg Calc.

PointsPlus value: ***9.***

SERVES 4

1 pound ground skinless turkey breast

1 large onion, chopped

1 large red bell pepper, diced

1 large green bell pepper, diced

2 carrots, diced

3 garlic cloves, finely chopped

1 (15½-ounce) can pinto beans, undrained

¾ cup hickory-flavored barbecue sauce

⅓ cup tomato paste

⅓ cup water

2–3 tablespoons chili powder

½ teaspoon ground cumin

½ teaspoon dried oregano

3 scallions, thinly sliced

Firecracker Turkey Chili

SERVES 6

1 tablespoon olive oil

1 pound hot Italian-style turkey sausage links, cut into ¾-inch slices

2 onions, coarsely chopped

2 tablespoons chili powder

1 tablespoon ground coriander

3 (14½-ounce) cans diced tomatoes with green chiles

2 (15½-ounce) cans red kidney beans, rinsed and drained

Chopped fresh cilantro

1. Heat oil in large skillet over medium-high heat. Add sausage and cook, stirring, until browned, about 5 minutes. Transfer sausage to 5- or 6-quart slow cooker.
2. Add onions to skillet and cook, stirring, until they begin to soften, about 5 minutes. Remove skillet from heat and stir in chili powder and coriander.
3. Transfer onion mixture to slow cooker and stir in tomatoes and beans. Cover and cook 4–6 hours on high or 8–10 hours on low.
4. Ladle chili evenly into 6 bowls and sprinkle with cilantro.

PER SERVING (scant 2 cups): 198 Cal, 9 g Total Fat, 2 g Sat Fat, 0 g Trans Fat, 34 mg Chol, 844 mg Sod, 17 g Total Carb, 4 g Fib, 13 g Prot, 63 mg Calc.

PointsPlus **value: 5.**

Cook's Note

This chili is great for no-fuss entertaining or for when you want to have leftovers for effortless meals later in the week.

Caribbean Seafood Stew

SERVES 6

1 onion, chopped

3 large Yukon Gold potatoes, peeled and cut into 1-inch chunks

3 garlic cloves, minced

3 (14½-ounce) cans diced tomatoes with green chiles

1 red bell pepper, coarsely chopped

1 (8-ounce) bottle clam juice

¼ teaspoon salt

¼–½ teaspoon cayenne pepper

1 pound halibut or cod fillets, cut into 1-inch pieces

½ pound medium shrimp, peeled and deveined, tails left on, if desired

2 dozen littleneck clams, scrubbed

¼ cup shredded sweetened coconut, toasted

Grated zest of 1 lime

1. Combine onion, potatoes, garlic, tomatoes, bell pepper, and clam juice in 5- or 6-quart slow cooker. Stir in salt and cayenne. Cover and cook until potatoes are fork-tender, 4–5 hours on high or 8–10 hours on low.
2. Add halibut and shrimp to slow cooker. Cover and cook 10 minutes. Add clams. Cover and cook until halibut and shrimp are just opaque throughout and clams open. Discard any clams that do not open.
3. Turn off slow cooker and let stew stand 5 minutes before serving. Ladle stew evenly into 6 soup bowls and sprinkle with coconut and lime zest.

PER SERVING (about 2 cups): 313 Cal, 3 g Total Fat, 2 g Sat Fat, 0 g Trans Fat, 89 mg Chol, 636 mg Sod, 45 g Total Carb, 6 g Fib, 28 g Prot, 125 mg Calc.

PointsPlus value: **8.**

Cook's Note

Any firm white fish fillets will work well in this stew. Tilapia and catfish are widely available and inexpensive options.

Caribbean Seafood Stew

bonus on the weekend

Vegetarian Burritos with Salsa Verde

SERVES 8

1 (14½-ounce) can fire-roasted diced tomatoes

2 (15½-ounce) cans black beans, rinsed and drained

1 (8¾-ounce) can corn kernels, drained

3 tablespoons taco seasoning or Mexican seasoning

2 cups lightly packed sliced Swiss chard

8 (7-inch) whole wheat tortillas, warmed

1 cup reduced-fat pepper Jack cheese

½ cup fat-free sour cream

½ cup salsa verde

1. Drain tomatoes and reserve all but ½ cup of liquid. Put tomatoes and reserved liquid in 5- or 6-quart slow cooker. Add beans, corn, and taco seasoning. Cover and cook until flavors are blended, 3–4 hours on high or 6–8 hours on low.
2. About 20 minutes before cooking time is up, stir in Swiss chard. Coarsely mash bean mixture with potato masher or wooden spoon.
3. Spoon ½ cup of bean mixture onto each tortilla. Top evenly with pepper Jack, sour cream, and salsa verde. Roll up tortillas to enclose filling.

PER SERVING (1 burrito): 271 Cal, 5 g Total Fat, 2 g Sat Fat, 0 g Trans Fat, 11 mg Chol, 948 mg Sod, 45 g Total Carb, 12 g Fib, 14 g Prot, 210 mg Calc.

PointsPlus value: **6.**

Shrimp Chowder with Dill

SERVES 6

1 pound medium shrimp, peeled and deveined, shells reserved

2 teaspoons canola oil

1 large onion, chopped

1 tablespoon all-purpose flour

1 (14½-ounce) can no-salt-added diced tomatoes

4 small Yukon Gold potatoes, peeled and diced

2 celery stalks with leaves, chopped

4 cups reduced-sodium chicken broth

4 cups water

¼ teaspoon black pepper

½ cup fat-free half-and-half

3 slices turkey bacon, crisp-cooked and crumbled

2 tablespoons chopped fresh dill

1. Put shrimp shells on square of cheesecloth. Gather ends of cloth and tie them together with length of kitchen twine. Refrigerate shrimp and set shells aside.
2. Heat oil in large nonstick skillet over medium heat. Add onion and cook, stirring occasionally, until softened, about 6 minutes. Sprinkle flour over onion and cook, stirring constantly, 2 minutes longer.
3. Transfer onion to 5- or 6-quart slow cooker. Add package of shrimp shells, tomatoes, potatoes, celery, broth, water, and pepper. Cover and cook until vegetables are fork-tender, 4–5 hours on high or 8–10 hours on low.
4. About 20 minutes before cooking time is up, remove and discard shrimp shell package and stir in shrimp. Cover and cook on high until shrimp are just opaque in center, about 15 minutes. Stir in half-and-half and cook 5 minutes longer.
5. Ladle chowder evenly into 6 bowls; sprinkle evenly with turkey bacon and dill.

PER SERVING (about 2 cups): 217 Cal, 5 g Total Fat, 1 g Sat Fat, 0 g Trans Fat, 85 mg Chol, 928 mg Sod, 27 g Total Carb, 3 g Fib, 16 g Prot, 106 mg Calc.

PointsPlus value: **5.**

Vegetable Minestrone with Pasta

Vegetable Minestrone with Pasta

SERVES 6

1 (15½-ounce) can chickpeas, rinsed and drained

1 (14½-ounce) can petite diced tomatoes

2 carrots, diced

2 onions, diced

2 small zucchini, halved lengthwise and sliced

1 small yellow squash, halved lengthwise and sliced

2 celery stalks with leaves, sliced

½ pound green beans, trimmed and cut into 1-inch pieces

2 garlic cloves, minced

½ teaspoon salt

¼ teaspoon black pepper

7 cups water

1½ cups whole wheat rigatoni or other short pasta

¼ cup chopped fresh basil or parsley

1. Combine all ingredients except rigatoni and basil in 5- or 6-quart slow cooker. Cover and cook until vegetables are fork-tender, 4–5 hours on high or 8–10 hours on low.
2. About 30 minutes before cooking time is up, cook rigatoni according to package directions, omitting salt if desired. Stir pasta and basil into soup.

PER SERVING (about 2 cups): 247 Cal, 2 g Total Fat, 0 g Sat Fat, 0 g Trans Fat, 0 mg Chol, 408 mg Sod, 50 g Total Carb, 9 g Fib, 12 g Prot, 111 mg Calc.

PointsPlus value: **6.**

Cook's Note

Carry out the Italian theme with a fresh green salad to serve with the soup. Toss together romaine lettuce, halved cherry tomatoes, thinly sliced zucchini, red-wine vinegar, and dried oregano, salt, and pepper to taste. Top each salad with 1 tablespoon shredded fat-free mozzarella cheese.

bonus on the weekend

Onion Soup with Herbed Cheese Toasts

SERVES 6

1 tablespoon olive oil

6 large onions (about 3 pounds), sliced

½ teaspoon salt

1 tablespoon all-purpose flour

8 cups reduced-sodium beef broth

½ teaspoon black pepper

½ cup light cream cheese (Neufchâtel)

6 (½-inch) slices French or Italian whole wheat bread, toasted

1 teaspoon chopped fresh thyme

1. Heat oil in large Dutch oven over medium heat. Add onions and salt and cook, stirring occasionally, until deep golden brown and very soft, about 35 minutes. Sprinkle flour over onions and cook, stirring constantly, until flour is lightly browned, about 2 minutes longer.
2. Combine onions, broth, and ¼ teaspoon of pepper in 5- or 6-quart slow cooker. Cover and cook until flavors are blended, 4–5 hours on high or 8–10 hours on low.
3. Spread cream cheese evenly over slices of toast. Sprinkle evenly with thyme and remaining ¼ teaspoon pepper.
4. Ladle soup evenly into 6 bowls and float slice of toast in each bowl.

PER SERVING (1⅔ cups soup and 1 cheese toast): 258 Cal, 10 g Total Fat, 4 g Sat Fat, 0 g Trans Fat, 15 mg Chol, 652 mg Sod, 31 g Total Carb, 5 g Fib, 14 g Prot, 94 mg Calc.

PointsPlus value: *7.*

Carrot-Apple Cupcakes with Cream Cheese Frosting

SERVES 12

1¼ cups all-purpose flour

⅔ cup granulated sugar

2 carrots, shredded

1 apple, peeled, cored, and shredded

⅓ cup golden raisins

¼ cup sweetened flaked coconut

1 teaspoon grated orange zest

1 teaspoon cinnamon

1 teaspoon baking soda

¼ teaspoon salt

2 large eggs, lightly beaten

¼ cup canola oil

6 ounces fat-free cream cheese, at room temperature

¼ cup confectioners' sugar, sifted

1 tablespoon milk

1 teaspoon vanilla extract

1. Preheat oven to 350°F. Spray 12-cup muffin pan with nonstick spray.
2. Stir together flour, granulated sugar, carrots, apple, raisins, coconut, orange zest, cinnamon, baking soda, and salt in large bowl. Beat eggs and oil together in another bowl. Stir egg mixture into flour mixture just until combined. Spoon batter evenly into muffin cups and bake until toothpick inserted into center of each cupcake comes out clean, 20–25 minutes. Cool in pan on rack 5 minutes; remove cupcakes from pan and cool completely on rack.
3. To make frosting, combine cream cheese, confectioners' sugar, milk, and vanilla in bowl of electric mixer and beat just until creamy. Spread frosting over cooled cupcakes.

PER SERVING (1 frosted cupcake): 202 Cal, 6 g Total Fat, 1 g Sat Fat, 0 g Trans Fat, 38 mg Chol, 262 mg Sod, 32 g Total Carb, 1 g Fib, 5 g Prot, 81 mg Calc.

PointsPlus value: **5.**

Spice-Glazed Cherry Bundt Cake

Spice-Glazed Cherry Bundt Cake

SERVES 20

3 cups all-purpose flour

1¾ cups granulated sugar

4 teaspoons baking powder

½ teaspoon ground nutmeg

½ teaspoon salt

½ teaspoon cinnamon

1 cup plus 4½ teaspoons fat-free milk

1 cup dried cherries

6 tablespoons canola oil

4 large egg whites, lightly beaten

1 tablespoon grated orange zest

½ teaspoon almond extract

1 cup confectioners' sugar

1. Arrange oven rack in middle of oven; preheat oven to 350°F. Spray 10-inch Bundt pan with nonstick spray.
2. Whisk together flour, granulated sugar, baking powder, nutmeg, salt, and ¼ teaspoon of cinnamon in large bowl. Stir together 1 cup of milk, cherries, oil, egg whites, zest, and almond extract in separate bowl. Add milk mixture to flour mixture and stir until well combined. Pour batter into prepared pan.
3. Bake until toothpick inserted into center of cake comes out clean, 40–45 minutes. Cool in pan on rack 15 minutes. Remove cake from pan and let cool completely on rack.
4. To make glaze, stir together confectioners' sugar and remaining ¼ teaspoon cinnamon in bowl. Slowly stir in remaining 4½ teaspoons milk until thick glaze forms. Drizzle glaze over top of cooled cake. Let cake stand until glaze sets, about 20 minutes; cut into 20 slices.

PER SERVING (1 slice): 226 Cal, 4 g Total Fat, 0 g Sat Fat, 0 g Trans Fat, 0 mg Chol, 174 mg Sod, 44 g Total Carb, 1 g Fib, 3 g Prot, 80 mg Calc.

PointsPlus value: **6.**

Cook's Note

Bundt pans make it easy to make an attractive dessert because of the pretty pattern they create in a cake. However, the crevices in the pan that make the decorative look sometimes result in the cake sticking to the pan. Be sure to thoroughly spray a Bundt pan with nonstick spray, taking care to coat the entire pan.

life's too short to make . . .

Though you may think homemade is always best, many foods are not worth your precious time to prepare. These store-bought versions will save you hours of time and taste just as good.

BEEF, CHICKEN, AND VEGETABLE BROTHS. Good-quality prepared broths are available everywhere and easy to keep on your pantry shelf in cans or resealable cartons. Besides, so many recipes use broths, you could never make enough!

DRIED BEANS. Cooking your own beans is a big time commitment and since canned varieties are delicious, inexpensive, and recipe-ready, why bother?

GRAHAM CRACKERS. This crunchy, low-fat, lightly sweetened snack is tough to replicate. Leave it to the manufacturers.

GREEK YOGURT. Even the fat-free version of this strained yogurt tastes rich and thick. It's a healthy staple for adding tangy flavor to meals and snacks, but leave the straining to someone else.

HOMEMADE PASTA. Unless you're an Italian "nonna" with time on your hands, fresh or dried pasta from the supermarket is almost as good.

ICE CREAM AND FROZEN YOGURT. These might be nostalgic and fun to make for a summer get-together (see Raspberry-Orange Sorbet, page 336 and Frozen Strawberry-Maple Yogurt, page 335), but the rest of the year, pick them up on your cruise through the frozen foods aisle.

KETCHUP, MUSTARD, AND MAYONNAISE. Foodies may extol the delights of homemade recipes, but leave it to food company chefs to create new-fangled versions of your favorite sandwich spreads.

MARSHMALLOWS. No need to spend hours whipping up this delicate confection; your supermarket baking aisle will accommodate all your needs.

PEELED AND DEVEINED SHRIMP. Buy shrimp that's ready to use in your favorite pasta or soup recipe and save yourself the time and tedium of peeling and deveining. It's definitely worth the extra price per pound for someone else to do this kitchen chore.

PHYLLO DOUGH. Making this flaky pastry from translucent sheets of dough will take many more hours than it's worth. Instead, use good-quality frozen phyllo for all your recipes.

PRESERVES, JELLY, AND MARMALADE. Even if you grew up canning your own with grandma, with your busy life, you don't have time. Stock up on jars of fruity, low-sugar options.

PUMPKIN PUREE. There's no discernible difference in flavor or quality of canned pumpkin puree and the homemade version. Save yourself hours of prep and use convenient, silky-textured cooked canned pumpkin.

ROASTED RED PEPPERS. No time to roast your own? Not to worry! The jarred varieties are just as good as homemade and they add fabulous flavor to salads, soups, pasta dishes, meat loaf, and stews. Just make sure to buy varieties that are not packed in oil.

SUSHI. Don't try this messy, time-consuming dish at home. Get your sushi fix at a restaurant or a fish counter.

WHOLE-GRAIN BREAD. Kneading your own loaves may make you feel self-sufficient, but bread making can take up an entire afternoon. Local bakery and supermarket versions are almost as delicious and much more convenient.

Pumpkin Pie Muffins

SERVES 12

1 cup all-purpose flour

¾ cup whole wheat pastry flour

1¼ cups Sucanat or granulated sugar

1¼ teaspoons baking soda

1 teaspoon cinnamon

½ teaspoon salt

½ teaspoon ground nutmeg

½ teaspoon ground cloves

½ cup raisins

2 large eggs, lightly beaten

1 cup canned pumpkin puree

⅓ cup canola oil

⅓ cup water

2 tablespoons raw pumpkin seeds

1. Preheat oven to 350°F. Spray 12-cup muffin pan with nonstick spray.
2. Whisk together all-purpose flour, pastry flour, Sucanat, baking soda, cinnamon, salt, nutmeg, and cloves in large bowl; stir in raisins. Beat eggs, pumpkin puree, oil, and water together in another bowl. Add pumpkin mixture to flour mixture and stir just until blended.
3. Spoon batter into muffin cups, filling each about two-thirds full. Sprinkle with pumpkin seeds. Bake until toothpick inserted into muffin comes out clean, about 20 minutes. Cool in pan on rack for 10 minutes; remove muffins from pan and serve warm or cool completely on rack.

PER SERVING (1 muffin): 235 Cal, 8 g Total Fat, 1 g Sat Fat, 0 g Trans Fat, 35 mg Chol, 241 mg Sod, 40 g Total Carb, 2 g Fib, 4 g Prot, 20 mg Calc.

PointsPlus value: *7.*

Cook's Note

Sucanat is short for "sugar cane natural." It's made from evaporated sugar cane juice, giving it a light brown color and a natural molasses flavor.

Apricot and Toasted
Almond Galette

Apricot and Toasted Almond Galette

SERVES 8

1⅓ cups all-purpose flour

½ cup, plus 2 tablespoons sugar

1 tablespoon baking powder

Pinch salt

⅓ cup part-skim ricotta cheese

2 tablespoons cold unsalted butter, cut into pieces

2 large egg whites

2 teaspoons water

2 pounds ripe apricots, halved, pitted, and cut into ½-inch wedges

2 tablespoons slivered almonds

1. To make dough, combine flour, ½ cup of sugar, baking powder, and salt in food processor and pulse to mix. Add ricotta, butter, 1 egg white, and water to food processor; pulse just until dough begins to come together. Shape dough into disk and wrap in plastic wrap; refrigerate at least 1 hour or up to overnight.
2. Preheat oven to 350°F. Lightly spray large baking sheet with nonstick spray.
3. Roll out dough between 2 sheets of wax paper to form 10-inch round. Place dough on prepared baking sheet. Fold edge of dough over to form ½-inch rim. Bake for 10 minutes, then let cool on rack, about 5 minutes.
4. Lightly beat remaining egg white and brush it over crust. Arrange apricots on crust in concentric circles and sprinkle with remaining 2 tablespoons sugar and almonds. Bake until crust is golden and apricots are softened, about 10 minutes. Let cool slightly on rack.
5. Cut into 8 wedges. Serve warm or at room temperature.

PER SERVING (1 wedge): 241 Cal, 5 g Total Fat, 2 g Sat Fat, 0 g Trans Fat, 11 mg Chol, 246 mg Sod, 45 g Total Carb, 2 g Fib, 5 g Prot, 145 mg Calc.

PointsPlus value: **6.**

Peach-Blueberry Crostatas

SERVES 8

½ cup whole wheat pastry flour

½ cup all-purpose flour

½ teaspoon salt

2 tablespoons cold unsalted butter, cut into pieces

2 tablespoons canola oil

2–4 tablespoons ice water

2 ripe peaches, peeled, halved, pitted, and cut into ½-inch wedges

1 cup fresh blueberries

3 tablespoons granulated sugar

½ teaspoon fresh lemon juice

1 tablespoon fat-free milk

2 teaspoons turbinado or granulated sugar

1. Whisk together whole wheat flour, all-purpose flour, and salt in medium bowl. Using pastry blender or two knives used scissor-fashion, cut in butter and oil until mixture resembles coarse crumbs. Gradually add water to flour mixture, tossing lightly until pastry is just moist enough to hold together. Shape dough into 4 equal-size disks. Wrap each disk in plastic wrap and refrigerate until chilled, at least 30 minutes or up to overnight.
2. Preheat oven to 425°F. Line large baking sheet with foil; spray with nonstick spray.
3. Toss together peaches, blueberries, granulated sugar, and lemon juice in medium bowl.
4. Using floured rolling pin, roll out each disk of dough on sheet of floured wax paper to form 6-inch round. Flip dough onto baking sheet and peel away wax paper. (If dough tears, patch it together with your fingers.) Mound one-quarter of fruit filling on each round, leaving 1-inch border. Fold rim of dough over filling, pleating it as you go around. Brush crusts with milk and sprinkle evenly with turbinado sugar. Bake until peaches are tender and crust is browned, about 25 minutes. Let cool slightly on rack.
5. Cut each crostata in half and serve warm or at room temperature.

PER SERVING (½ crostata): 158 Cal, 7 g Total Fat, 2 g Sat Fat, 0 g Trans Fat, 8 mg Chol, 150 mg Sod, 27 g Total Carb, 2 g Fib, 2 g Prot, 12 mg Calc.

PointsPlus value: **5.**

Peach-Blueberry Crostatas

Banana-Walnut Bread

SERVES 18

¾ cup sugar

5 tablespoons unsalted butter, softened

2 large eggs

3 ripe bananas, mashed

½ cup fat-free milk

1½ teaspoons vanilla extract

1¾ cups all-purpose flour

1 tablespoon baking powder

¾ teaspoon salt

½ cup walnuts, coarsely chopped

1. Arrange oven rack in middle of oven; preheat oven to 350°F. Spray 5 × 9-inch loaf pan with nonstick spray.
2. Combine sugar and butter in medium bowl; beat with an electric mixer on medium speed until light and fluffy, about 3 minutes. Beat in eggs, beating well after each addition. Beat in bananas, milk, and vanilla. In separate bowl, whisk together flour, baking powder, and salt. Add flour mixture to banana mixture and mix on low speed until just combined. Stir in walnuts.
3. Pour batter into pan and bake until toothpick inserted into center of loaf comes out clean, 50–55 minutes. Cool in pan 10 minutes. Remove bread from pan and cool completely on rack. Cut into 18 slices.

PER SERVING (1 slice): 153 Cal, 6 g Total Fat, 2 g Sat Fat, 0 g Trans Fat, 29 mg Chol, 190 mg Sod, 23 g Total Carb, 1 g Fib, 3 g Prot, 63 mg Calc.

PointsPlus value: ***4.***

Cook's Note

Banana bread is always a welcome gift and it freezes beautifully. When you have extra bananas on hand, make a loaf and freeze it for up to 3 months to have on hand when you need to give a special handmade gift, but have no time.

Brown Rice–Banana Pudding

SERVES 2

1 cup cooked brown rice

1 cup fat-free milk

Pinch salt

1 ripe banana, mashed

1 teaspoon vanilla extract

½ teaspoon cinnamon

1. Combine rice, milk, and salt in medium saucepan and bring to boil over medium-high heat. Reduce heat and simmer, stirring occasionally, until slightly thickened, about 15 minutes. Transfer rice mixture to medium bowl and let cool.
2. Stir in banana, vanilla, and cinnamon. Spoon pudding evenly into 2 dessert dishes.

PER SERVING (⅔ cup pudding): 212 Cal, 2 g Total Fat, 0 g Sat Fat, 0 g Trans Fat, 2 mg Chol, 138 mg Sod, 44 g Total Carb, 4 g Fib, 8 g Prot, 164 mg Calc.

PointsPlus value: **6.**

Lemon Soufflés

Lemon Soufflés

SERVES 4

2 teaspoons plus ⅓ cup granulated sugar

⅓ cup fat-free milk

2 large eggs, separated

1½ tablespoons all-purpose flour

3 tablespoons fresh lemon juice

2 teaspoons grated lemon zest

1 large egg white

⅛ teaspoon salt

2 teaspoons confectioners' sugar

1. Preheat oven to 400°F. Spray 4 (6-ounce) ramekins or custard cups with nonstick spray and coat them with 2 teaspoons granulated sugar.
2. Combine milk, egg yolks, flour, lemon juice, and remaining ⅓ cup granulated sugar in small saucepan over medium-low heat. Cook, whisking constantly, until mixture becomes thick and creamy, 6–7 minutes; do not allow mixture to boil or yolks will scramble. Immediately transfer to bowl and stir in zest; let cool to room temperature.
3. Beat 3 egg whites with salt in bowl with an electric mixer on medium speed for 20 seconds. Increase speed to high and beat just until soft peaks form, 1–2 minutes. Stir one-fourth of egg whites into cooled yolk mixture to lighten. Gently fold in remaining whites in two additions until just mixed.
4. Spoon mixture into ramekins; use paper towel to wipe off edge of each. Place on small baking sheet and bake until soufflés have risen above rims of ramekins and edges are set (the centers will still be slightly loose), about 12 minutes. Sprinkle top of each with confectioners' sugar and serve at once.

PER SERVING (1 soufflé): 140 Cal, 3 g Total Fat, 1 g Sat Fat, 0 g Trans Fat, 106 mg Chol, 127 mg Sod, 24 g Total Carb, 0 g Fib, 5 g Prot, 42 mg Calc.

PointsPlus value: ***4.***

Cook's Note

While it's true that soufflés need to be eaten immediately out of the oven, you can make the batter partially ahead. Prepare the recipe through step 2, cover the cooled mixture with plastic wrap, and refrigerate for up to 24 hours. Return the mixture to room temperature before folding in the egg whites. Bake as directed.

bonus on the weekend

Pumpkin-Cranberry Bread Puddings

SERVES 12

3 cups fat-free half-and-half

1 cup fat-free egg substitute

½ cup packed dark brown sugar

¼ teaspoon ground allspice

1 teaspoon cinnamon

¼ teaspoon ground nutmeg

¼ teaspoon salt

1 cup canned pumpkin puree

2 teaspoons vanilla extract

1 (1-pound) loaf day-old whole wheat bread, cut into 1½-inch pieces

½ cup dried cranberries

½ cup chopped pecans

1. Bring half-and-half to boil in medium saucepan over medium-high heat; remove saucepan from heat.
2. Whisk together egg substitute, brown sugar, allspice, cinnamon, nutmeg, and salt in medium bowl. Slowly add ½ cup of hot half-and-half to brown sugar mixture, whisking constantly.
3. Add egg substitute mixture to saucepan and set over medium-low heat. Cook, whisking constantly, until custard thickens and coats back of spoon, about 5 minutes. Immediately pour custard through sieve set over medium bowl. Whisk in pumpkin and vanilla. Add bread and cranberries to bowl, gently stirring until moistened. Let stand about 20 minutes.
4. Meanwhile, preheat oven to 325°F. Spray 12 (6-ounce) ramekins or 10-cup baking dish or casserole with nonstick spray.
5. Pour pudding mixture into prepared ramekins and sprinkle evenly with pecans. Place ramekins in roasting pan. Add enough boiling water to roasting pan to come halfway up sides of ramekins. Cover tightly with foil. Bake individual puddings 20 minutes and large pudding 1 hour. Uncover and bake until knife inserted into center comes out clean, 5–15 minutes longer. Serve warm or at room temperature.

PER SERVING (1 pudding): 239 Cal, 5 g Total Fat, 1 g Sat Fat, 0 g Trans Fat, 3 mg Chol, 438 mg Sod, 41 g Total Carb, 2 g Fib, 8 g Prot, 143 mg Calc.

PointsPlus value: ***6.***

Pumpkin-Cranberry Bread Puddings

Orange Flan with Macerated Oranges

Orange Flan with Macerated Oranges

SERVES 12

1 cup plus 1 tablespoon sugar

½ cup water

6 large eggs, lightly beaten

1¼ cups fresh orange juice

1 cup low-fat (1%) milk

¾ cup fat-free sweetened condensed milk

2 teaspoons grated orange zest

3 navel oranges

2 tablespoons fresh lemon juice

1. Preheat oven to 350°F.
2. Combine 1 cup of sugar and water in heavy-bottomed medium saucepan over medium-high heat; bring to boil and cook, shaking pan occasionally, until sugar turns into golden caramel, about 12 minutes. Immediately pour caramel into 9-inch deep-dish glass pie plate. Carefully tilt pan to coat bottom evenly with caramel; set aside until hardened, about 10 minutes.
3. Whisk together eggs, orange juice, low-fat milk, sweetened condensed milk, and zest in bowl. Pour mixture into pie plate.
4. Place pie plate in large roasting pan. Pour enough hot water into roasting pan to come halfway up side of pie plate. Bake until custard is set and jiggles just in center when shaken, 45–50 minutes. Remove pie plate from roasting pan and cool completely on rack. Cover with plastic wrap and refrigerate at least 3 hours or up to 2 days.
5. Meanwhile, with sharp knife, peel oranges, removing all white pith. Working over bowl, cut between membranes to release segments. Stir in remaining 1 tablespoon sugar and lemon juice; cover and refrigerate.
6. To serve, run tip of knife around edge of flan. Place large plate upside down over top of pie plate and quickly invert; lift off pie plate. Cut flan into 12 wedges; spoon caramel sauce that collects on plate over wedges and garnish with orange segments.

PER SERVING (1 wedge and 2 tablespoons orange segments): 202 Cal, 3 g Total Fat, 1 g Sat Fat, 0 g Trans Fat, 107 mg Chol, 60 mg Sod, 39 g Total Carb, 1 g Fib, 6 g Prot, 113 mg Calc.

PointsPlus value: **5.**

Triple Berry Summer Pudding

SERVES 6

2 pints blueberries

⅓ cup sugar

2 tablespoons water

Grated zest and juice of ½ lemon

1 (6-ounce) container raspberries

1 (6-ounce) container blackberries, halved if large

10 slices firm-textured white bread, crusts removed

1 cup thawed frozen fat-free whipped topping (optional)

1. Combine blueberries, sugar, water, and lemon zest and juice in large saucepan and set over medium heat. Cook, stirring, until berries begin to release their liquid, about 3 minutes. Bring to boil over medium-high heat. Cook, stirring occasionally, until slightly thickened, about 5 minutes. Remove saucepan from heat and stir in raspberries and blackberries.
2. Line 2-quart bowl with 2 sheets of overlapping plastic wrap, allowing excess to extend over rim of bowl by 4 inches. Line bottom and side of bowl with bread, cutting to fit as needed. Spoon berry mixture into bowl. Cover with layer of bread. Fold plastic wrap over top of pudding. Place plate, slightly smaller than bowl, on top of pudding and weigh it down with two heavy cans of food. Refrigerate at least 8 hours or up to 2 days.
3. Fold back plastic wrap and invert pudding onto serving plate. Lift off bowl and remove plastic wrap. Cut pudding into 6 wedges. Serve with whipped topping, if using.

PER SERVING (1 wedge without whipped topping): 205 Cal, 2 g Total Fat, 0 g Sat Fat, 0 g Trans Fat, 0 mg Chol, 229 mg Sod, 46 g Total Carb, 4 g Fib, 4 g Prot, 65 mg Calc.

PointsPlus value: **6.**

Cook's Note

Serve each portion of the pudding with a sprinkle of fresh berries and a sprig of mint if desired.

Frozen Strawberry-Maple Yogurt

SERVES 8

1 (1-pound) container strawberries, hulled and chopped

1 cup sugar

2 tablespoons fresh lemon juice

1 cup maple or vanilla low-fat yogurt

1 cup fat-free half-and-half

½ teaspoon maple extract

1. Stir together strawberries, sugar, and lemon juice in medium bowl; let stand 30 minutes.
2. Whisk together yogurt, half-and-half, and maple extract in large bowl. Stir in strawberry mixture. Cover and refrigerate until chilled, at least 2 hours or up to overnight.
3. Pour strawberry mixture into an ice-cream maker and freeze according to manufacturer's instructions.
4. Transfer yogurt to freezer container and freeze until firm, at least 2 hours or up to 6 hours.

PER SERVING (½ cup): 159 Cal, 1 g Total Fat, 1 g Sat Fat, 0 g Trans Fat, 3 mg Chol, 100 mg Sod, 37 g Total Carb, 1 g Fib, 3 g Prot, 91 mg Calc.

PointsPlus value: ***4.***

bonus on the weekend

Raspberry-Orange Sorbet

SERVES 8

2 cups water

½ cup sugar

2 (3-inch) strips orange zest, removed with vegetable peeler

3 tablespoons fresh orange juice

3½ cups fresh or thawed frozen unsweetened raspberries

1. To make sugar syrup, combine water, sugar, and orange zest in medium saucepan and set over high heat. Bring to boil, stirring until sugar is dissolved. Reduce heat and simmer 5 minutes. Remove saucepan from heat and let cool about 5 minutes. Discard orange zest; stir in orange juice.
2. Puree 1 cup of sugar syrup with raspberries in food processor or blender. Stir raspberry mixture into sugar syrup in saucepan. Pour raspberry mixture through sieve set over medium bowl, pressing on solids to extract as much liquid as possible. Discard solids. Cover berry mixture and refrigerate until chilled, at least 2 hours or up to overnight.
3. Transfer raspberry mixture to an ice-cream maker and freeze according to manufacturer's instructions.
4. Transfer sorbet to freezer container and freeze until firm, at least 2 hours or up to 6 hours.

PER SERVING (about ½ cup): 90 Cal, 0 g Total Fat, 0 g Sat Fat, 0 g Trans Fat, 0 mg Chol, 44 mg Sod, 22 g Total Carb, 1 g Fib, 43 g Prot, 17 mg Calc.

PointsPlus value: **6.**

Warm Spice-Baked Apples

SERVES 4

4 baking apples, cored and halved

2 tablespoons packed brown sugar

1 teaspoon pumpkin pie spice

3 tablespoons water

¼ cup chopped walnuts or pecans, toasted

1. Preheat oven to 400°F.
2. Place apples, cut side up, in 9 × 13-inch baking dish. Sprinkle evenly with brown sugar and pumpkin pie spice.
3. Sprinkle water in bottom of baking dish. Cover baking dish with foil. Bake apples until tender when pierced with tip of knife, about 25 minutes. Sprinkle apples evenly with walnuts.

PER SERVING (2 apple halves): 144 Cal, 4 g Total Fat, 0 g Sat Fat, 0 g Trans Fat, 0 mg Chol, 3 mg Sod, 30 g Total Carb, 5 g Fib, 2 g Prot, 38 mg Calc.

PointsPlus value: ***4.***

Cook's Note

If you don't have an apple corer, cut each apple in half, then use a melon baller or a small paring knife to remove the core.

bonus on the weekend

White Wine-Poached Pears

SERVES 8

4 cups water

1 cup dry white wine

1 cup sugar

Zest of 1 lemon, removed with vegetable peeler

1 tablespoon fresh lemon juice

4 large firm-ripe Bartlett or Bosc pears, peeled, halved, and cored

1. Combine all ingredients except pears in large saucepan and bring to boil over high heat; boil 10 minutes. Remove saucepan from heat.
2. Add pears to saucepan. Reduce heat and gently simmer, covered, until pears are tender when pierced with fork, about 15 minutes. Using slotted spoon, carefully transfer pears to large shallow bowl.
3. Bring poaching liquid to boil over high heat; boil until reduced to about 2 cups, about 15 minutes. Pour poaching liquid over pears and refrigerate until cool before serving.

PER SERVING (½ pear and ¼ cup syrup): 172 Cal, 0 g Total Fat, 0 g Sat Fat, 0 g Trans Fat, 0 mg Chol, 8 mg Sod, 44 g Total Carb, 4 g Fib, 0 g Prot, 17 mg Calc.

PointsPlus value: **5.**

Do it Faster

Peeling and coring pears is quick and simple to do. Use a vegetable peeler to cut away the skins, then cut the pears in half lengthwise. To scoop out the core, use a teaspoon or a melon baller.

White Wine–Poached Pears

bonus on the weekend

Chunky Pink Apple-Raspberry Sauce

SERVES 4

2 pounds red apples, cored and coarsely chopped

¼ cup water

2 tablespoons packed light brown sugar

¼ teaspoon grated lemon zest

1 tablespoon fresh lemon juice

1 (6-ounce) container raspberries

1. Combine all ingredients except raspberries in large heavy saucepan and bring to boil over high heat. Reduce heat to medium and cook, stirring occasionally, until apples are softened, about 20 minutes.

2. Remove pan from heat and let stand, covered, until apples are completely tender, about 10 minutes longer. Mash apples, then gently stir in raspberries. Divide apple-raspberry sauce among 4 dessert dishes.

PER SERVING (¾ cup): 157 Cal, 1 g Total Fat, 0 g Sat Fat, 0 g Trans Fat, 0 mg Chol, 6 mg Sod, 41 g Total Carb, 8 g Fib, 1 g Prot, 30 mg Calc.

PointsPlus value: ***4.***

Roasted Pears with Balsamic Glaze

SERVES 4

2 teaspoons unsalted butter, melted

2 teaspoons fresh lemon juice

4 ripe pears, halved and cored

¼ cup packed brown sugar

1 tablespoon balsamic vinegar

4 (½-ounce) slices soft (mild) goat cheese

1. Preheat oven to 425°F.
2. Stir together butter and lemon juice in small bowl.
3. Place pears, cut side up, on large baking sheet. Brush cut side of pear halves with butter mixture. Roast until softened when pierced with fork, about 30 minutes.
4. Meanwhile, combine brown sugar and vinegar in small saucepan and cook over low heat, whisking until dissolved. Increase heat to high and boil until thickened, about 30 seconds. Transfer to cup.
5. Arrange 2 pear halves on each of 4 plates and place slice of goat cheese next to each pear. Using teaspoon, drizzle balsamic glaze over pears. Serve warm.

PER SERVING (2 pear halves and 1 slice goat cheese): 202 Cal, 5 g Total Fat, 3 g Sat Fat, 0 g Trans Fat, 12 mg Chol, 61 mg Sod, 39 g Total Carb, 5 g Fib, 3 g Prot, 48 mg Calc.

PointsPlus value: ***5.***

Mixed Berry Shortcakes

Mixed Berry Shortcakes

SERVES 8

1 (16-ounce) bag frozen unsweetened mixed berries, thawed

2 teaspoons fresh lemon juice

½ cup sugar

1¾ cups all-purpose flour

2 teaspoons baking powder

½ teaspoon ground ginger

¼ teaspoon salt

4 tablespoons cold unsalted butter, diced

⅔ cup fat-free milk

¾ cup thawed frozen fat-free whipped topping

1. Preheat oven to 425°F. Spray baking sheet with nonstick spray.
2. Combine berries, lemon juice, and ¼ cup of sugar in medium bowl.
3. Combine remaining ¼ cup sugar, flour, baking powder, ginger, and salt in large bowl. Using pastry blender or two knives, cut butter into flour mixture until mixture resembles coarse crumbs. Using rubber spatula, stir in milk until mixture is just moistened. With your hands, gather dough into ball and knead once or twice until it just holds together.
4. Turn dough out onto lightly floured surface. Press dough out until it is about ½ inch thick. Cut 8 shortcakes with 2½-inch biscuit cutter; press dough scraps together to cut more biscuits if necessary. Transfer shortcakes to baking sheet and bake until they are golden brown, 12–15 minutes. Remove from oven and cool on rack at least 5 minutes. (Biscuits can be cooled completely and stored in an airtight container up to 24 hours.)
5. To serve, cut shortcakes in half horizontally and fill each with ¼ cup of berries and 1½ tablespoons of whipped topping.

PER SERVING (1 filled shortcake): 241 Cal, 6 g Total Fat, 4 g Sat Fat, 0 g Trans Fat, 16 mg Chol, 209 mg Sod, 43 g Total Carb, 2 g Fib, 4 g Prot, 107 mg Calc.

PointsPlus value: ***6.***

Whole Grain and Fruit Oatmeal Cookies

MAKES 36

1½ cups rolled (old-fashioned) oats

½ cup whole wheat flour

½ cup toasted wheat germ

½ cup low-fat granola

¼ cup golden raisins

¼ cup mini semisweet chocolate chips

2 tablespoons unsalted sunflower seeds

2 tablespoons finely chopped dried apricots

1 teaspoon baking powder

½ teaspoon salt

½ cup (1 stick) unsalted butter, softened

½ cup packed brown sugar

¼ cup water

1 large egg

1 teaspoon vanilla extract

1. Preheat oven to 375°F. Spray 2 large baking sheets with nonstick spray.
2. Toss together oats, whole wheat flour, wheat germ, granola, raisins, chocolate chips, sunflower seeds, apricots, baking powder, and salt in large bowl.
3. Using electric mixer on medium speed, beat butter and brown sugar until light and fluffy. Beat in water, egg, and vanilla just until smooth. Using rubber spatula, stir in flour mixture until combined.
4. Drop dough by level measuring tablespoons, about 1 inch apart, onto baking sheets and flatten until 1½ inches in diameter. Bake until cookies are golden brown and edges are deep brown, 10–12 minutes.
5. Let cookies cool slightly on baking sheet on wire rack. Using metal spatula, transfer cookies to rack to cool completely. Repeat with remaining dough.

PER SERVING (1 cookie): 79 Cal, 4 g Total Fat, 2 g Sat Fat, 0 g Trans Fat, 13 mg Chol, 54 mg Sod, 10 g Total Carb, 1 g Fib, 2 g Prot, 17 mg Calc.

PointsPlus value: ***2.***

Cook's Note

These forgiving cookies will save you a trip to the grocery store, since you can use almost any dried fruits or nuts to make them. Substitute chopped almonds or walnuts for the sunflower seeds and dried cranberries or raisins for the apricots.

Chocolate-Cherry Brownies

SERVES 16

¾ cup all-purpose flour

½ cup unsweetened cocoa powder

1 teaspoon baking powder

¼ teaspoon baking soda

⅛ teaspoon salt

2 large eggs, lightly beaten

1 cup granulated sugar

2 teaspoons vanilla extract

5 tablespoons unsalted butter

1 ounce semisweet chocolate, chopped

⅔ cup dried cherries

1 tablespoon confectioners' sugar (optional)

1. Preheat oven to 350°F. Spray 8-inch square baking pan with nonstick spray.
2. Whisk together flour, cocoa powder, baking powder, baking soda, and salt in large bowl. Combine eggs, granulated sugar, and vanilla in separate bowl.
3. Combine butter and chocolate in top of double boiler or a bowl set over saucepan of simmering water and stir until melted, about 3 minutes. Let cool about 1 minute; stir into egg mixture. Stir chocolate mixture into flour mixture, stirring until just combined. Fold in cherries. Pour batter into pan and even top.
4. Bake brownies until toothpick inserted into center comes out with few moist crumbs clinging to it, about 20 minutes. Cool in pan on rack about 15 minutes. Remove brownies from pan, cut into 16 squares, and sprinkle with confectioners' sugar, if using.

PER SERVING (1 brownie): 145 Cal, 5 g Total Fat, 3 g Sat Fat, 0 g Trans Fat, 36 mg Chol, 77 mg Sod, 24 g Total Carb, 2 g Fib, 2 g Prot, 30 mg Calc.

PointsPlus value: ***4.***

Cook's Note

For the moistest brownies, take care not to overbake them. The toothpick should not come out with batter clinging to it, but don't bake the brownies so long that the toothpick comes out clean.

Recipes by **PointsPlus** *value*

6 *PointsPlus* value

7 *PointsPlus* value

8 *PointsPlus* value

9 *PointsPlus* value

10 *PointsPlus* value

11 *PointsPlus* value

12 *PointsPlus* value

Index

C

D

O

P

Q

R

S

T

U

V

weightwatchers

Thank you **for your *Weight Watchers® Cook it Fast* cookbook purchase**

U.S. and Canadian residents (excluding Quebec), your purchase entitles you to a one-year (6-issue) subscription to *Weight Watchers Magazine*—see details below. *Weight Watchers Magazine* gives readers the tools they need to look and feel their best and to make instant, positive changes in their lives. Each issue is packed with dozens of easy, mouthwatering recipes; smart tips on cooking and eating out; the latest news on fitness, weight loss, and nutrition; and an inspirational dose of success stories.

Offer valid through July 31, 2015.

To claim your subscription, please provide your original receipt, fill out this form and return by July 31, 2015, to Weight Watchers Magazine, Cook it Fast sub offer, PO Box 6245, Harlan, IA 51593-1745.

Name ________________________________

Address ________________________________

City/State/Zip ________________________________

E-mail Address ________________________________

Offer valid through July 31, 2015, for U.S. and Canada (excluding Quebec) addresses only. Mailed offer redemption, including receipt as described below, must be received by July 31, 2015, to be eligible to receive the one-year (6-issue) *Weight Watchers Magazine* subscription only, or while supplies last. Information must be typed or legibly printed, and be accompanied by either your original in-store receipt, with purchase price circled, OR a copy of your e-mail confirmation of your online order showing your name and address, telephone number, order number, vendor name, and date of order. Limit one subscription per person or household. No refunds, exchanges, or substitutions. You must purchase a copy of the *Weight Watchers Cook it Fast* cookbook to be eligible for this offer. Offer void if obtained through non-authorized channels, including, without limitation, free-offer or "freebie" directories. Theft, diversion, reproduction, transfer, sale or purchase of proofs-of-purchase or receipts is prohibited and may constitute fraud. Please allow 4–6 weeks for delivery of your first issue of *Weight Watchers Magazine*. Neither St. Martin's Press nor Weight Watchers will be responsible for late, lost, or misdirected mail.

S14SMP1